Gender and Informal Institutions

Feminist Institutionalist Perspectives

Why do institutions and international organisations continue to affect the daily lives of women and men (and different groups of women and men) differently? Why do institutions often reproduce or exacerbate patterns of disadvantage and discrimination, even when formally espousing ideals of equality? As well as seeking to expose the rules, norms and practices through which institutions produce gendered outcomes, feminist institutionalism is also concerned – through detailed examples from across the globe – with the potential for, and limits of, institutional innovation and reform in pursuit of gender equality and gender justice.

Published in partnership with the Feminism and Institutionalism International Network (FIIN network) this series represents the 'next stage' of development of feminist institutionalism (FI), a novel approach to the study of politics, which combines insights from gendered analysis and institutionalist theory to expose, understand and explain the dynamics of gendered power inequalities in public and political life and their gendered effects. It aims to create a 'home' for FI scholars as an emerging intellectual community, while encouraging dialogue between FI and wider academic communities and engaged practitioner communities.

Animated by questions that impact the lives of multiple political actors globally, the series draws together cutting-edge work from across disciplines and around the world. An important part of its agenda will be to explore the interplay between the local and the global; the domestic and the international. It will include contributions from a wide range of feminist institutionalism approaches, ranging from rational choice to discursive paradigms, as well as those that combine elements from across the variants. The series welcomes *proposals* for monographs and carefully curated edited collections that cover single and comparative cases from the global North and global South, as well as the international system (such as the United Nations and International Criminal Court). While the primary focus of the series is upon gendered institutional analysis, the series actively encourages submissions which take an intersectional approach.

Series Editors

Fiona Mackay, Professor of Politics, Dean and Head of the School of Social and Political Science at the University of Edinburgh

Elin Bjarnegård, Associate Professor and Senior Lecturer in Development Studies at Uppsala University in Sweden

Meryl Kenny, Lecturer in Gender and Politics at the University of Edinburgh

Titles in the Series

Criminalizing the Client: Institutional Change, Gendered Ideas, and Feminist Strategies, by Josefina Erikson

Towards Gendering Institutionalism: Equality in Europe, edited by Heather MacRae and Elaine Weiner

Gender and Informal Institutions, edited by Georgina Waylen

Gender, Power and Institutions in Sweden, by Lenita Freidenvall (forthcoming)

Gender and Informal Institutions

Edited by
Georgina Waylen

ROWMAN & LITTLEFIELD
London • New York

Published by Rowman & Littlefield International Ltd
Unit A, Whitacre Mews, 26–34 Stannary Street, London SE11 4AB
www.rowmaninternational.com

Rowman & Littlefield International Ltd. is an affiliate of Rowman & Littlefield

4501 Forbes Boulevard, Suite 200, Lanham, Maryland 20706, USA
With additional offices in Boulder, New York, Toronto (Canada), and Plymouth (UK)
www.rowman.com

British Library Cataloguing in Publication Data

A catalogue record for this book is available from the British Library

ISBN: HB 978-1-7866-0002-8
PB 978-1-7866-0003-5

Library of Congress Cataloging-in-Publication Data Is Available

ISBN 978-1-78660-002-8 (cloth : alk. paper)
ISBN 978-1-78660-003-5 (pbk. : alk. paper)
ISBN 978-1-78660-004-2 (electronic)

∞™ The paper used in this publication meets the minimum requirements of American National Standard for Information Sciences – Permanence of Paper for Printed Library Materials, ANSI/NISO Z39.48–1992.

Printed in the United States of America

Contents

Acknowledgements

A large number of people and organizations have made this volume possible. I would like to thank European Research Council for funding the Advanced Grant 'Understanding Institutional Change: A Gender Perspective (UIC-295576)' which not only funded some of the research reported in this volume but also the workshop on 'Understanding Informal Institutions' held in Manchester in September 2015 and at which early versions of most of the chapters in this edited collection were discussed. We would not have been able to publish this volume without the generous support from the European Research Council which allowed us to bring together a number of excellent scholars and which has over the last few years played such a key role in promoting research in the UK.

I would also like to thank all the participants at the Understanding Informal Institutions workshop whose work and comments have greatly influenced the chapters that are included here, including Claire Annesley, Faith Armitage, Karen Beckwith, Rosie Campbell, Sarah Childs, Emma Crewe, Francesca Gains, Vivien Lowndes and Shirin Rai.

Louise Chappell and Fiona Mackay also deserve special thanks for all their help with the shape and content of the volume.

Finally, I would like to thank Lisa Jenkins for the invaluable role she played pulling the final manuscript together as well as Leah Culhane for her sterling efforts on the bibliography.

Figures and Tables

FIGURES

TABLES

Chapter 1

Analysing Gender in Informal Institutions: An Introduction

Georgina Waylen

The rationale underpinning this book is that there is now widespread agreement that informal institutions are important, but that we still do not know enough about them, theoretically, empirically or methodologically. Bringing together leading scholars and new research in gender and politics, this volume addresses some of these theoretical, empirical and methodological challenges. It interrogates what informal institutions are, how they are gendered, how they interact with formal institutions and what role they can play in efforts to promote gender equality.

The book comes out of the wider endeavour of developing a feminist institutionalism (FI). A number of gender scholars (including many in this volume) have been participating in this project for more than a decade. To date, FI has, according to Mackay, Kenny and Chappell (2010), engaged with both the strengths and limits of existing institutionalisms. It has recognised the considerable analytical strengths of new institutionalism and shown the potential of many new institutionalist concepts and tools to help feminist political scientists answer questions of concern to them. However, it also highlights the gender-blindness of these existing institutionalisms, arguing that they need to ensure that women are included as actors in political processes, to 'gender' institutionalism and to ensure that the research agendas of institutionalists also include questions that consider how gender and operation and effects of political institutions interact (Mackay et al. 2010, 574).

As a result of this work, FI has already increased our understanding of the gender dynamics of institutions, building on both the research of institutionalist scholars, particularly historical institutionalism (HI), and the existing gender scholarship that has shown us how gender is deeply implicated in institutions both nominally and substantively (Mackay et al. 2010; Krook and Mackay 2011; Chappell and Waylen 2013). In keeping with other recent

1

institutionalisms, FI sees institutions as gendered rules, norms and processes that have both formal and informal guises, and examines how these shape actors' strategies and preferences. The formal 'rules of the game' and their enforcement are crucial, but the informal aspects of institutions – that are often less visible or taken for granted by actors inside and outside institutions – are also central. Recent work by FI scholars has shown, for example, that even when formal barriers have been removed, informal norms, such as around the 'ideal candidate', can remain, ensuring that male bias in political recruitment continues (Bjarnegård 2013; Kenny 2013). Such informal rules and norms are not always perceived, as explicit sanctions for non-compliance do not always have to be invoked.

Alongside other institutionalist scholars, FI has also recognised the importance of the interaction between formal and informal institutions, not only the capacity for pre-existing or new informal institutions to subvert and compete with formal institutions, but also their potentially complementary, completing and adaptive roles (Helmke and Levitsky 2004; Tsai 2006; Grzymala-Busse 2010; Azari and Smith 2012). As a result, when FI scholars try to uncover the 'hidden life' of institutions such as the executive, they look at all their gendered rules and norms (Chappell and Waylen 2013; Waylen 2016). The key aims of this book are therefore to analyse and further develop some of the core concepts that comprise FI relevant to the analysis of informal institutions, and to lay out some of the key debates around what these core concepts are.

How far there is, or there needs to be, unanimity about the core concepts that underpin FI is not yet resolved in this fast-growing field. Much like other forms of institutionalism, there is a degree of variation in the positions that FI scholars take. As this volume demonstrates, there is agreement that informal institutions matter but at the moment not all FI scholars would agree about the characteristics attributed to informal institutions. Similarly, all FI scholars agree that understanding the relationship between actors and institutions (structure versus agency) is absolutely central to any FI, but as we will see in this volume, again they may have differing conceptualisations of the nature of that relationship.

To reflect this very exciting phase in the development of FI, this book has deliberately brought together a range of contributors – those who have been centrally involved in studying institutions and developing FI for more than a decade as well as younger scholars, and also some 'critical friends' to give some slightly different perspectives. Earlier versions of the chapters were delivered at a workshop on informal institutions held as part of the European Research Council (ERC) Advanced Grant on 'Understanding Institutional Change: A Gender Perspective' held in Manchester in September 2015. The workshop started off by assessing the current state of our knowledge – both in theoretical and in empirical terms – and then outlining the remaining gaps.

It also focused on the practical and methodological challenges of undertaking research on informal institutions from the participants' own experience. The empirically focused panels examined areas of central importance for gender and politics scholars: political recruitment, the executive, and policy and practice. But the workshop also engaged with key themes in the study of informal institutions which are elaborated in more depth in this volume. It ended with critical reflections from both 'insiders' and 'outsiders', as well as thoughts about future research agenda and in particular the potential to design and alter informal institutions as well as the different approaches and methods, debates which are all reflected in this volume.

The book is therefore premised on an assumption that underpins FI: if we are trying to get inside black box of institutions, that is uncover their 'hidden life' and understand how they are gendered, we have to go beyond just the inputs and outputs of institutions – we also need to get to grips with informal as well as formal institutions (Chappell and Waylen 2013). To do this, we face three core questions concerned with both conduct of the research and its broader theoretical and political implications. The first section of this chapter examines these core questions. First, it asks how FI scholars should recognise, define and classify informal institutions. This takes up most of the section, broadening out to consider the bigger category of the informal and the role of networks within it, as well as the interaction between formal and informal institutions. Second, the chapter considers what methods FI scholars can use to undertake this research. Finally, it asks what are the implications for feminists – namely how can this research inform gender equality strategies? Understanding how we can change informal institutions is an important research goal for feminist scholars. The contributors to this volume take up some or all of these questions but without necessarily coming to the same conclusions. The second part of this chapter outlines the structure of the volume and how the individual chapters fit into and elaborate the key debates and themes at the core of the book.

DEFINING AND CLASSIFYING
INFORMAL INSTITUTIONS

A large number of scholars using a range of different approaches now agree that informal institutions are important – whether they are described as institutions by self-professed institutionalists or talked of more generally as informal norms and practices by scholars using somewhat different theoretical frameworks. The rather negative view of informal institutions as a primordial hangover undermining good governance through particularism, clientelism, patronage and nepotism, and often involving illegal practices, has been reappraised, as it is clear that informal institutions are durable, and not just the result of weak formal institutions or a hangover of tradition (Lauth 2000; Radnitz 2011).

New institutionalism (NI) has influenced the emergence of a more nuanced view of informal institutions and their interaction with the formal to counter this predominantly negative one (Helmke and Levitsky 2004, 2006). For NI scholars, rules, norms and practices are centrally important. They distinguish between formally codified rules and more informally understood conventions and norms, and understanding this distinction has become an increasingly important recent focus for them (Peters 1999). Helmke and Levitsky (2004, 727) define institutions as 'rules and procedures (both formal and informal) that structure social interaction by constraining and enabling actors' behavior'. In their now-classic definition, they see informal institutions as 'socially shared rules, usually unwritten, that are created, communicated and enforced outside of officially sanctioned channels' in contradistinction to formal institutions which are 'rules and procedures, that are created, communicated and enforced through channels widely accepted as official' (Helmke and Levitsky 2004, 727).

However, informal institutions can often be difficult to perceive – somewhat like dark matter – but we know they are there because of their effects on other things. One important task of this chapter is therefore to clarify what FI scholars mean by informal institutions. Most of the FI scholars investigating informal institutions to date have used Helmke and Levitsky's broad definition of informal institutions as a starting point for their research (Chappell and Waylen 2013; Waylen 2014a). But beyond this, there is less agreement about what informal institutions are.

For FI scholars, one necessary first step in researching institutions is therefore to identify the formal and informal rules. Formal rules, for example about gender, are relatively easy to identify. Ones that treat men and women differently in official and legal terms, such as prohibitions on voting or the roles that women can play in the military, are usually widely publicised, if not universally supported. However, although many institutional rules (but not all everywhere) are now formally gender neutral, for example for employment, political participation and education, a huge array of informal rules about gender, such as dress codes and the sexual division of labour, remain. But to analyse how the informal as well as the formal is gendered, scholars need to delve beneath the often gender-neutral appearances of institutions to uncover the myriad ways in which gender plays out. This is not an easy task as both gender norms and informal institutions can be difficult to uncover. Gendered informal rules interacting and coexisting with formal rules often pass unnoticed as they run parallel to, complement or complete formal rules. So, for example, although formal rules enforcing gender norms do not usually forbid men from wearing skirts to work or school in most of Europe/North America, infringements of informal rules about dress are enforced using informal mechanisms of ridicule and social opprobrium. Consequently, these informal rules are not always perceived, as explicit sanctions are rarely invoked (Waylen 2014a). Gender norms and informal institutions often remain unperceived or unremarked as they are naturalised as part of the status quo.

However, some scholars such as Lowndes (2014) argue that both formal and informal rules need to be recognised by participants in order for them to count as an institutional rule. This stricture can bring difficulties when considering how institutions are gendered. As a result, many FI scholars, including Waylen (2014a) and Chappell and Mackay (this volume), argue that although informal rules around gender are not always widely perceived, this does not invalidate the claim that they are informal institutions. The invisibility of some informal institutions also does not contradict the widely held view that all institutions – whether formal or informal – are governed and enforced by sanctions, both positive and negative, but that these vary considerably (Azari and Smith 2012, 40). As we have seen, the enforcement of informal institutions often takes the form of shunning, social ostracism and even violence rather than legal recognition or the power of the state and the other mechanisms used to enforce formal institutions (Grzymala-Busse 2010, 313). Azari and Smith (2012, 41) suggest that if informal institutions are unwritten rules, we must assess their content and scope, the nature of deviance and by whom it is rewarded or punished, but again they too recognise the difficulty of researching informal institutions because the informal is harder to uncover than the formal. In addition the often taken-for-granted nature of informal institutions of gender makes this task doubly difficult.

Therefore, defining and categorising informal institutions is complex. But, as Chappell and Mackay point out in the next chapter, FI scholars need to be clear about what an institution is – whether formal or informal – and what it is not. For example, one organisation may contain within it both formal and informal institutions interacting together. Posing these questions raises a further series of questions about informal institutions, which are in many ways long-standing ones, but also those that we do not yet have the answers to. How do we understand the differences/relationship between organisations, formal institutions, informal institutions and formal and informal rules and norms? Are some of these the same things/do they overlap/are they interchangeable/and do they shade into each other? Most institutionalist scholarships, including FI scholarship, assumes implicitly, if not explicitly, that there is a distinction to be made between formal and informal institutions, with formal rules predominant in a formal institution, and informal norms and practices dominant in an informal institution. These are crucial distinctions to resolve, if we fear a danger that informal institutions could become a residual category and everything not clearly a formal institution is put into the informal category, so, as a result, it loses explanatory power.

However, some argue that there is more of a *continuum* from formal to informal institutions rather than a dichotomy between them (see Verge and Claveria's chapter in this volume for an example of this position). From this perspective, formal rules, informal rules and informal norms are all institutions that simply differ in their levels of formality/informality. Extending this notion of a continuum, we need to examine two further questions that demonstrate the complexity of this terrain. First, how do networks fit into our schema – what are they – actors, institutions or an intermediary between the two, and what roles do they play? And second, is there a broader category of informality that informal institutions, networks, informal norms and practices can be subsumed into?

Recent FI analyses of informal institutions have increasingly looked at the role of informal networks. For example, the important role of both male and female informal networks has been identified in instances of the creation of new institutions, such as the design of the new South African constitution (Waylen 2014b). Elin Bjarnegård (2013) has identified how homosocial bonding renders networks around political recruitment in political parties in Thailand as predominantly male. Interest in networks and network analysis has also increased among institutional scholars and political scientists as a means 'of addressing one of the holy grails of the social sciences: effectively analysing the interdependence and flows of influence among individuals, groups, and institutions' (Ward, Stovel and Sacks 2011, 245).

Of course, networks have long been recognised by many gender scholars as an important mechanism, both for gender activists organising around equality concerns and also as a way of excluding women. Much of the long-standing feminist scholarship that has looked at women's networks at national, regional and transnational levels advocating around women's rights, such as gender-based violence and reproductive rights, has focused on networks operating primarily on the outside of state and global institutions trying to pressure them for change (Friedman 1994; Meyer and Prugl 1999; Liebowitz 2008). More recently, FI scholars have begun to look at informal women's networks that have operated *within* and *across* different formal institutional arenas rather than operating primarily outside of those arenas. The consideration of networks in many chapters of this volume also reflects this growing realisation among FI scholars that it is important to investigate their roles and theorise them if we are to improve our understanding of informal institutions and their relationship to formal institutions.

As yet, few FI scholars – in common with many other political scientists and also institutional scholars – have engaged much with the vast quantity of research and writing on networks in a range of other disciplines. In addition to the emphasis on homophily (a bond to those similar to you), FI scholars could draw more extensively on all this work whether it focuses on policy and governance networks or social movements and other forms of networks less prominent within political science. However, this is now beginning. For example, in their chapter in this volume Chappell and Mackay draw on institutionalist scholars who want to bring the analysis of networks together with institutionalist analysis.

To date, the implicit assumption has been that there is a shared but unstated understanding of what networks are. But, as yet there are no fixed definitions of networks among FI scholars, or of how they operate and their relationship to formal and informal institutions. Indeed, there is no consensus on whether they are institutions or actors in their own right, or whether they are simply bearers of institutions. As many of the chapters in this volume demonstrate, FI scholars need to move beyond agreeing that networks are important to systematically investigating the various roles that networks can play and how they might act to protect, challenge and change formal and informal rules.

The first key question to be answered about networks is therefore definitional: what are they? Hafner-Burton, Kahler and Montgomery (2009) in their analysis of the usefulness of network analysis for International Relations argue for a definition of a network as any collection of actors that pursue repeated enduring exchange relations with one another and at the same time lack a legitimate organisational authority to arbitrate and resolve disputes. Many scholars, including most of the contributors to this volume, agree that networks are not institutions, but there is no consensus as yet as to whether they are actors or some intermediary between actors and institutions. For example, FI scholars Bjarnegård, Kenny and Verge (2016) argue that networks are not institutions because they do not comprise a set of rules in the same way as an institution, but that they do often bolster and sustain informal institutions. For some FI scholars, networks are an intermediate variable. For example, Chappell and Mackay argue in this volume that networks can be carriers of informal institutions. And for others, often focused primarily on political recruitment, they are a middle ground between individual actors that make up the network and the institution that they operate for (Bjarnegård et al. 2016). At the same time, some scholars see networks as actors (see Piscopo this volume). However, some blurring of categories remains – Bjarnegård et al. (2016) use the term networking interchangeably with networks even though networking is an action undertaken by actors, whereas networks are more clearly an entity or even an organisation in their own right.

But again, the difficulties with the concept of networks may reflect bigger, long-standing and unresolved tensions regarding the relationship between actors and institutions (structure and agency), hinted at by Ward et al. (2011) earlier, namely what is the relative importance of each and how do they relate to each other? Questions about the relative importance of structure and agency are also not new to gender and politics scholarship. Some gender scholars have tended to see agency, often collective, as key – whether of men as oppressors or of women's movements as change agents – while others have focused more on the determining effects of big overarching structures such as patriarchy.

Some FI scholars, like Chappell and Mackay who take up this question in their chapter in this volume, give primacy to institutions. But others ally themselves more with the position of early HI theorists, Steinmo and Thelen (1992, 10), who argue that it is the *interaction* of structure and agency, and of actors and institutions, that is key because institutions can shape and constrain actors' political strategies 'but they themselves are also the outcome (conscious or unintended) of deliberate political strategies of political conflict and change' (Steinmo and Thelen 1992, 10; Waylen 2009, 2014a,b).

One way to resolve this tension with regard to networks, in keeping with the HI view of the interrelationship of structure and agency, is to adhere to Keck and Sikkink's (1999) claim in their classic analysis of transnational advocacy networks that 'part of what is elusive about networks is how they seem to embody elements of agent and structure simultaneously. Our approach must therefore be both structural and actor centred'. For them, networks are not in a gap in the middle of two separate things – institutions and actors – but span both and impact on both.

However networks are defined, the question of how they operate and what they do remains open. To date, most gender scholars' research on networks has considered male and female networks separately, attributing different characteristics to them. So far, there has been a tendency within the FI literature to see male networks as implicitly bad for women and gender equality, as they preserve male power and the status quo while acting to exclude women. This has been particularly marked in work on political recruitment which has focused on male networks within political parties. Wider gender research, often influenced by a social movement or transnational advocacy framework, has also tended to see female networks as more benign, compensating for a lack of power and challenging the status quo.

Although many predominantly male and female networks have had these characteristics, it is not inevitable. We now need a broader sense that not just male networks can exist to preserve the status quo, and that more generally all networks attempt to convey advantages to their members – often through informal mechanisms – and promote shared interests, for example, via reciprocity. The informal male networks in the South African constitutional negotiations were not protecting an existing institution or necessarily protecting male privilege (indeed some gender positive measures such as LGBT rights were promoted through the male lawyers network) (Waylen 2014b).

Networks and how they operate are therefore context-dependent. Networks are not necessarily good or bad for women, men or gender equality, as this too is context-dependent (see Nazneen, Piscopo and Culhane in this volume for differing examples). FI scholars need to explore whether and how networks of individuals (and sometimes organisations) can be used as a way to shortcut any formal channels to get what they want and whether this is more effective (or speedier) than using formal mechanisms; or whether they are used as a way of side-stepping formal mechanisms or compensating for or utilising gaps in those formal mechanisms (which ties in with discussions about incomplete institutions).

Finally, we need to address our second question: whether broadening our focus to consider things like networks also gives us a bigger category of *informality* or the informal in general. What does informality mean in different contexts? The term is used in different ways by several authors in this volume. Is it, as Susan Franceschet claims in her chapter in this volume, the absence of rules both formal and informal, an understanding of informality which many FI scholars would take issue with? On the other hand, Piscopo (this volume) sees informality as particular relationships and practices that link actors in certain contexts. But again, if we broaden the notion of informality to encompass all informal institutions, norms, practices and networks does the term risk becoming too vague and overarching to be of any use?

Having discussed some key aspects of informal institutions – including the nature of rules, sanctions and the relationship of informal institutions with networks and informality – we can now consider the relationship between informal and formal institutions in more depth. For more than a decade now, premised on the assumption that a distinction can be made between formal and informal institutions even if the boundaries can sometimes be indistinct, institutionalist scholars have been exploring the interaction between the formal and the informal more systematically. Several typologies distinguishing the different roles played by informal institutions in relation to formal ones have emerged. All recognise that informal institutions can have positive and negative effects on the strength and functioning of formal institutions. Helmke and Levitsky (2004) see informal institutions as either: complementary, accommodating, substitutive or competing with formal institutions. Azari and Smith (2012) argue in their study of established democracies that informal institutions can complete, exist in parallel to or coordinate formal institutions, while Grzymala-Busse (2010) claims that in transitional regimes in East Central Europe, they can replace, undermine, support or strengthen (by promoting competition between elites) formal institutions irrespective of strength of the formal institutions that they are interacting with. Levitsky and Slater (2011) argue that informal institutions can trump, compete with and be congruent with formal institutions or something in between. Although this literature on informal institutions is still underdeveloped and the ideas under-conceptualised, these typologies share common ground, reinforcing the need for us to explore the different ways in which the formal and informal interact together (Waylen 2014a).

Instead of seeing informal institutions as pre-existing or even as a residual category, scholars are investigating the emergence and adaptation of different informal institutions. This new emphasis on the potential dynamism and mutability of informal institutions makes a significant contribution to the burgeoning discussions of the interaction of formal and informal institutions in institutional change. Interest is focusing on the factors affecting the relationship between them in institutional change – looking at the reasons for change, varying interactions and outcomes in different contexts.

Grzymala-Busse (2010) focuses on the interaction of existing informal institutions with new formal institutions in transitions in East Central Europe, arguing that this influences the types of formal institutions that can emerge and the kinds of informal institutions that are perpetuated. Getting away from notions of informal institutions as primordial, Kellee Tsai (2006) argues that new informal institutions can develop as a response to formal institutions and play a key part in endogenous institutional change. She sees the emergence of certain 'adaptive' informal institutions in China as a creative response, reconciling the demands of different, sometimes incompatible, formal institutions (similar to Azari and Smith's notion of coordinating informal institutions). Other scholars highlight how, as a result of an interactive process, formal institutions can change because of violations of or dissatisfaction with informal institutions as actors mobilise to press for changes to formal rules to alleviate the problems (Azari and Smith 2012). Azari and Smith (2012, 43) argue that the processes that give rise to change at the formal/informal interface will play out differently depending on whether those informal rules are completing, in parallel or coordinating formal institutions. Formal rule change can, for example, fail because completing informal institutions to fill gaps and resolve ambiguities in those formal rules are absent. The direction of causality therefore runs both ways. Both formal and informal institutions impact on each other.

Levitsky and Slater (2011) argue that several factors determine whether formal rule change will take root or be distorted or subverted by informal institutions. They claim that it is important to analyse why formal rule change occurs – is it internally or externally driven or as a result of a crisis? Both state capacity and the actors involved are significant. It is necessary to ascertain which actors make changes and whether the rule makers are different to rule enforcers, as this too can diminish the likelihood of formal institutional change taking root. Levitsky and Slater (2011) speculate that outsiders may have more success in changing formal rules than the existing old guard. The durability of the institutional designers can also matter as do perceptions about their durability – do other actors think they (and also their institutions) will last?

Informal institutions can therefore both hinder and enhance the implementation of formal rule changes. But the nature of the interaction is complex, and the multiple factors discussed earlier have to be investigated – simple conclusions are not possible (Waylen 2014a).

To date, none of these scholars have systematically tried to integrate gender into their analyses, but despite this, when we focus on the interaction between the formal and informal, and the different roles the informal plays in either upholding or subverting the formal in different contexts, we need a hybrid model of the relationship between formal and informal developed using the analysis outlined earlier. Until recently, many gender scholars have often assumed that informal institutions play a primarily reinforcing role – maintaining the gender status quo – and therefore can play a subverting role when positive gender change is attempted. For example, despite formal rules forbidding sexual abuse, the extent to which informal norms and practices facilitated many men and particularly 'celebrities' and other authority figures blatantly abusing victims – often women and girls – without fear of sanction in the 1960s, 1970s and 1980s when victims were ignored or disbelieved, is now being revealed in the UK and more widely (*Huffington Post*, 20 March 2013). But many assumptions about informal institutions as subverting change derive from a rather static notion of informal institutions as preserving the status quo. More dynamic models that accommodate scenarios, ranging from the emergence of new informal institutions to contexts where informal institutions can undermine existing gender-unequal formal institutions, among others, are needed. Analyses that distinguish between reinforcing and subverting informal institutions are still at an early stage (Waylen 2014a).

FI scholars therefore could use more nuanced frameworks that delineate different reinforcing roles: such as coordinating or completing informal institutions, substituting informal institutions, as well as parallel formal institutions. We can envisage scenarios where gendered informal institutions reinforce formal institutions by filling in gaps, and play a completing role when formal rules are vaguely specified. The two are therefore in sync when informal institutions reinforce rather than undermine formal ones. This fits the pattern described earlier where informal rules about masculinity and femininity reinforce supplementary and caring roles for women and decision-making roles for men within institutions, and have served to uphold the male domination of those institutions. But we also need to identify the informal institutions that play a replacement role when formal institutions are too weak or have been abolished or diminished in power or influence.

Furthermore, in addition to analysing informal institutions that subvert or compete with new formal institutions when attempts are made to implement positive gender change, we can also explore other scenarios where new informal institutions are created. First, as we have seen causality can run both ways, so it follows that change in informal rules about gender can lead to change in formal rules. Formal rules, around marriage, illegitimacy, contraception and abortion, are sometimes altered in gender positive ways – granting rights to illegitimate children, legalising civil partnerships and gay marriage – because the informal rules (like the widespread acceptability of unmarried heterosexual couples having children) have become increasingly at odds with formal ones. The Catholic Church stands out as an exception here. Although its formal rules about contraception remain unchanged, informal rules subvert the formal ones as in many countries priests informally sanction contraceptive use. But the two sets of rules remain out of sync as efforts to change formal rules have failed (or it may be that informal rules have sometimes replaced the formal ones). And in the UK, 'historic' sexual abuse cases have now been prosecuted as changed informal rules about acceptable behaviour mean that past violations of formal rules are now treated differently (*Huffington Post*, 20 March 2013). The new informal rules do not subvert the formal ones but now complete them.

This brings us to consider the second core question of the chapter – how can we research informal institutions, as methodological questions are inextricably linked to the kinds of conceptual and definitional questions we have just been considering? As we have seen, scholars recognise the challenges of researching informal institutions (Radnitz 2011). Implicit in much work is an assumption that in-depth qualitative methods – particularly participant observation and ethnography – may be most appropriate. As we see in Chappell and Galea's discussion of 'rapid ethnography' in this volume, this can require a variant of methods more frequently associated with anthropology than political science and sometimes frowned upon by political scientists as not sufficiently rigorous and unscientific (Radnitz 2011).

There are a number of difficulties that researchers face in attempting to collect qualitative data on informal institutions. First, if informal rules do not have to be recognised by participants themselves, or perhaps not until infractions invoke sanctions, for example around dress codes (as we saw at the Cannes Film Festival in 2015 when women were turned away for not wearing high heels), how does the researcher identify them? Interviews alone will not necessarily yield this information unless the researcher is prepared to reinterpret answers to questions like 'how are things done around here' (Lowndes 2014). Observation and interpretation may therefore be one important way forward. Second, where informality shades into something else such as clientelism or corruption, actors are not always going to be open about how the informal rules and norms operate, and sustained observation may be difficult to do. Third, in-depth qualitative and often ethnographic research of this kind often has implications for the positionality of the researcher. Feminist scholars researching women's networks that they may sometimes have connections with, for example, may then find themselves in a difficult position (see Nazneen, this volume).

The potential hazards of qualitative research lead us to ask how far informal institutions may also be suitable for mixed methods research, as it is important to consider the whole range available to social scientists when choosing the appropriate methods to research informal institutions. Some FI scholars are utilising quantitative methods to uncover the 'hidden life', which perhaps appears inappropriate to some, but can expose broader gendered patterns relevant to the analysis of informal institutions (Weldon 2014). When Waylen and Southern (2016) investigated how the informal institution of the pre-2009 UK parliamentary expenses regime was gendered, they examined overall expenses claims to see whether male and female MPs had different claim patterns. This method revealed gender differences that it would not be possible to discern simply through interviews with actors such as MPs and parliamentary officials. However, although it is possible to use quantitative techniques to research informal institutions as Verge and Claveria demonstrate very effectively in their chapter in this volume, most of the contributors to this collection use predominantly qualitative methods, as do the majority of FI scholars.

The final core question to consider here is how this research on informal institutions can help practice, particularly for gender equality activists hoping to change institutions. Existing work has shown that the formal is relatively easier to identify and target than the informal but that gender-friendly institutional change requires changing informal rules and norms too. Given that institutional change cannot be achieved just by passing a law or creating a new formal rule, how can we change the informal? First, identifying hitherto unrecognised informal rules is an important first step to challenging and undermining them. Second, understanding the complex interrelationship between the formal and informal is also a very important part of any efforts to bring about change. We need, for example, to enhance our understanding of how to prevent pre-existing informal norms that can subvert attempts to bring positive gender change such as new equality rules. Cases of 'nested newness' where new institutional rules are undermined by pre-existing norms such as in the Scottish parliament or the ICC are already well known (Mackay 2014; Chappell 2015).

Third, it would be useful to know more about how new informal norms can emerge to bolster/ uphold/fill-in gaps or undermine formal rules. For example, in her chapter in this volume, Magda Hinojosa details how a new informal practice emerged to undermine a gender equality strategy. It is also important to understand how changes in informal norms can lead to changes in formal rules, such as same-sex marriage which is now widely formalised in many countries. How has change in these norms come about, and how can it be replicated in other contexts or for other issues? There appear to be some areas or issues that are more susceptible to change – for example, the introduction of same-sex marriage versus abortion rights seen in both Chile and Ireland recently. The introduction of civil partnerships in Chile has been relatively much easier to achieve than the legalisation of even therapeutic abortion, yet both are doctrinal issues in Htun and Weldon's (2010) schema (Waylen 2016). Fourth, it is important to ascertain how far changes in formal rules, if they are effective and enforced, can lead to changes in informal norms and under what circumstances this can happen. A final and un-researched area to date is to consider the potential of 'nudges' and behaviour change strategies to bring about change in informal rules and norms around gender (Bohnet 2016). More research in all these areas would help gender equality activists to develop more effective strategies to change informal rules and norms.

THE STRUCTURE OF THE VOLUME

All the chapters in this volume address some or all of the issues raised in the previous discussion and further our understanding of informal institutions. Although this book is not divided into sections, the chapters in the volume do cover some distinct areas and are organised to reflect this. The first two chapters – this introduction and the overview chapter by Louise Chappell and Fiona Mackay that follows it – survey the intellectual terrain and set up the analytical framework for the rest of the book by elaborating the key questions and debates relevant to the study of informal institutions and gender. While there are some differences between these two chapters in their understanding of questions like the relationship of institutions and actors, together they outline a core of a feminist institutionalist approach to informal institutions.

The next four chapters (Culhane; Chappell and Galea; Verge and Claveria; Franceschet) – taking up a number of the key themes elaborated in the previous two chapters – are concerned primarily with identifying the informal. They focus on institutions, but in most of the chapters on informal networks as well, examining their interaction with the formal. Each chapter analyses informal institutions in a different context, examining how they are gendered and investigating key aspects such as the role of sanctions and of male networks. First, Leah Culhane examines how certain informal institutions and networks have contributed to male dominance in political recruitment in Ireland. Then Louise Chappell and Natalie Galea, using rapid ethnography, identify informal institutions in the construction industry focusing particularly on mechanisms of sanction and reward, and how these operate in gendered ways. Next, Tánia Verge and Sílvia Claveria examine formal and informal mechanisms of patronage and networks, and how these can act to bolster male privilege in political parties. And last in this grouping of four chapters, Susan Franceschet analyses how informal rules of executive recruitment and the informality of cabinet operation are gendered.

The next three chapters (Piscopo, Nazneen, Hinojosa) change the focus to examine the relationship between instances of gender positive formal rule change and the informal, looking particularly at the roles played by informal norms, practices and networks in either promoting or blocking gender positive change. Jennifer M. Piscopo examines a case of gender positive rule change achieved by an informal feminist network set up to prevent circumventing of formal gender parity rules. Next, Sohela Nazneen analyses a case of gender positive formal rule change – around violence against women – which was achieved by an informal female network but she also shows how subsequently there have also been issues with implementation because of informal constraints. Magda Hinojosa then examines how new informal practices were used to undermine a gender positive formal rule change in the electoral arena. All three chapters therefore examine different instances of gender positive formal rule change and differing forms of relationship with the informal – both how informal women's networks contributed to the formal rule change and how informal practices were used to undermine a formal rule change. All the chapters highlight the centrality and variability of the relationship between the formal and informal. The final substantive chapter (Bjarnegård and Kenny) and the conclusion (Waylen) both sum up some key themes of the volume and highlight ways forward. Elin Bjarnegård and Meryl Kenny look at how work on informal institutions has informed research in one important area for gender and politics scholars: political recruitment, and they outline a future research agenda for gender scholars. The conclusion then draws together the lessons from the more empirically based material together with the key themes and questions outlined in the first two chapters.

We can now see how the overall themes of the volume emerge in different ways in each of the chapters in more detail. To further develop the analytical terrain outlined in this chapter, Chappell and Mackay contribute to the crucial efforts to incorporate formal and informal institutional analysis into feminist political science in their overview chapter. After laying out some of the foundational concepts and approaches regarding informal institutions in particular, and identifying the contours of key research developments in the area, they argue that, in order to extend the range and analytical leverage of FI in particular, and feminist political science in general, the necessary next stage is to develop a common vocabulary of gendered institutionalist analysis, and to more systematically specify and operationalise key concepts, including the notion of an informal institution itself. But they accept that this is no easy task, acknowledging that the wider institutionalist literature is already fraught with definitional disputes. In working towards greater clarity about informal institutions and their relationship to gender politics, they set out their answers to four core questions: What are informal institutions, and how do they differ and interact with formal institutions? What is the relationship between gender and informal institutions? How do institutions, actors and networks differ? (or, in other words, what is not an institution?); and how do we research informal institutions to capture their gendered nature and effects? Ultimately, in addressing these questions their aim is to strengthen FI's ability to build and test theory, and to consolidate the empirical findings and theoretical insights emerging from investigations into the interactions between formal and informal institutions. They also seek to draw some boundaries around FI and clarify its distinguishing features vis-à-vis other feminist approaches. For Chappell and Mackay, this means making a distinction between the roles of institutions and actors in shaping political and policy outcomes. Their assumption is that institutions are likely to *matter as much if not more* than anything else in explaining the determinants of political life, but as we have already seen this is an assumption that not all FI scholars may be wholly in agreement with.

In the first of the more empirically focused chapters, Leah Culhane analyses the role of informal institutions in political parties, and particularly in party candidate recruitment and selection processes, in maintaining and reproducing these gendered patterns of male over-representation. Using the Republic of Ireland as its case study, this chapter speaks to the growing body of work that seeks to gender the informal 'rules of the game' that govern candidate recruitment and selection. It asks how localism, understood as an informal institution, shapes intra-party processes and why this has bestowed disproportional privilege to male aspirants. The key argument of the chapter is that central to localism is the need for aspirants to have pre-existing personal networks, both within the electorate and the party, which has enabled the maintenance of male political dominance. With regards to recruitment criteria, the desire for aspirants with pre-existing local connections and networks is gendered insofar as it privileges those who already have political experience at the local level, the majority of whom are men. However, the analysis also suggests that, due to a masculinised perception of politics, men are more likely to be seen as potential political brokers, as both local heroes and 'cute hoors' and are therefore more likely to be encouraged to put themselves forward. Second, the need for pre-existing networks at the selection stage rewards longevity and thus bestows disproportionate preference and privilege to incumbents, reproducing the masculine nature of Irish politics.

In their chapter, Louise Chappell and Natalie Galea look at another male-dominated arena to highlight a key aspect of informal institutions that has been relatively neglected to date. Despite the growing awareness of the centrality of informal institutions to (gendered) political outcomes, they argue that little attention has been paid to the mechanisms through which sets of rules and practices are *enforced* and *sanctioned*, primarily through penalties and rewards. Chappell and Galea want to bring a fresh perspective to the notion of enforcement of informal political institutions by drawing on experiences of actors – professionals in the Australian construction sector – in another highly masculinised environment and using an innovative method, 'rapid' ethnography. They pursue two core questions: what are the key enforcement mechanisms of informal institutions, and how do they operate 'on the ground' in the context of the Australian construction sector? And, what are the best methods for 'seeing' gendered institutions and mechanisms that operate 'under the surface' in male-dominated environments? This chapter highlights the value of paying closer attention to institutional enforcement mechanisms, and discusses the advantages and limitations of using rapid ethnography for studying these processes in other male-dominated political sites including parliaments, state bureaucracies, and institutions of global governance.

In the next chapter, Tánia Verge and Sílvia Claveria investigate whether holding a position within the ranks of a party organisation has gendered implications for political advancement. They argue that the identification of the gendered effects of holding party office in the last stages of the ladder of political recruitment – including parliamentary candidacy as well as ministerial and post-ministerial appointments – allows us to pinpoint how formal and informal institutions form a continuum. In their view, party patronage is a formal institution but is distributed in informal ways to party members and officers. They argue that the informal norms and practices upon which patronage is distributed build on the gendered composition and operation of (typically male) informal networks within the party organisation, which constitute themselves a bearer of informal institutions underpinned by (male) homosocial capital. While based on the formal positional power derived from holding party office, this political resource is riddled with informality and most crucially is overridden by gender: party office is not only more accessible to men but is also more valued in men, all else being equal, thereby rendering women party officers outsiders on the inside.

To conclude this grouping of four chapters on the role of informal institutions, Susan Franceschet aims to show the importance of distinguishing informal rules from informality, defined by her as the absence of both formal and informal rules. Using the case study of cabinet formation and the organisation and functioning of the executive branch in Chile, Franceschet demonstrates how strong informal rules about ministerial recruitment are gendered in ways that advantage men and are difficult to change. Franceschet's chapter shows that the absence of formal or informal rules about how the executive branch is organised and does its work also disadvantages women to the extent that power has become ever more concentrated among a small group of individuals close to the president. However, she also claims, somewhat controversially, that because this trend is not rule-governed at all, there are greater possibilities for change, although change is only likely to come about as a result of agency and political will.

The next three chapters move the focus to consider gender positive formal rule change and the informal. Jennifer M. Piscopo explores how formal parity laws – requiring 50/50 gender balance in public office – have been strengthened through informal mechanisms such as networks. Whereas gender quota laws were typically pushed by legislative actors in Latin America, parity laws have been driven by informally constituted networks of feminist party activists, electoral regulators and high court judges. Piscopo argues that although FI scholars have demonstrated convincingly that informal practices often work to leave male political dominance intact, Latin America's pro-parity networks show that informality – defined by Piscopo as the relationships and practices that sustain "back channel" avenues of negotiation and contestation – in fact benefits women's political inclusion. In her chapter, Piscopo conceptualises networks as actors, arguing that they are not institutions, but they can leverage informality to change the formal rules that govern women's access to power. The chapter examines how feminist party women and electoral officials (state regulators and electoral judges) collaborated to adopt and then enforce parity in Mexico's 2015 elections. Piscopo concludes that the Mexican case illustrates how actors working in consort behind the scenes can transform formal rules.

In the following chapter, Sohela Nazneen asks how pro-women policy actors can influence political actors to promote gender equity policies in clientelist contexts where promotion of such policies rarely generates immediate material or political gains. She uses Bangladesh as her case study and investigates how informal institutions operate, particularly through the use of personal relationships and informal networking, and can advance or block the way pro-women policy coalitions promote gender equity concerns, in this case around the successful legal reform on violence against women in 2010. Nazneen examines how informal institutions manifest themselves through women's informal networks, and draws attention to women's informal agency in clientelist political contexts. By investigating the role of informal practices, norms and networking, the chapter illustrates how the subversion of the formal rules may work to advance women's rights in policy spaces but may not facilitate change during implementation. It also raises uncomfortable questions about whether 'going with the grain' furthers women's rights in the long run and highlights the difficulties that may arise for women's rights actors from being embedded within such informal practices.

Continuing the theme of the subversion of new formal gender-friendly rules by informal practices, Magda Hinojosa asks whether informal institutions that misuse political alternate positions in order to sabotage gender quotas have emerged across Latin America in her chapter 'An "Alternate" Story of Formal Rules and Informal Institutions: Quota Laws and Candidate Selection in Latin America'. In many electoral systems, parties nominate political alternates alongside titleholders. If the titleholders cannot serve (i.e. due to illness, travel, taking an ambassadorial post), the alternates step in. Despite its potential importance, little is known about the gender dimensions of this practice. In this study, Hinojosa looks at Latin America as a whole but focuses primarily on the Uruguayan case. Uruguay first applied a gender quota in 2014 and informal practices emerged at the same time to undermine the quota: parties nominated individual women to both the upper and lower house; so women elected to both positions would need to cede one of those seats to an alternate who need not be a woman. This informal practice has not yet been routinised in the Uruguayan case, but provides gender and politics scholars an opportunity to examine how a subverting informal institution can emerge.

In the last substantive chapter of the volume, Elin Bjarnegård and Meryl Kenny outline an important FI research agenda in one area that has been central to gender and politics scholarship to date: political recruitment. They build on previous research that has pointed to the multitude of ways in which women are disadvantaged at the different stages of political recruitment to chart a research agenda using the theoretical tools of feminist institutionalism as they argue there are still important gaps to be filled in this field. Their chapter therefore takes stock of existing research in political recruitment and makes the case for shifting the terms of the debate on political recruitment and informal institutions to focus on three key questions: who, where and how? Based on these three questions, Bjarnegård and Kenny outline a more holistic analytical framework that leaves open the question as to 'what matters' in candidate recruitment – specifically *who* the key actors are, *where* certain identified dynamics are valid and where they are not, and *how* informal institutions help maintain (or break) hegemonic male dominance in the political recruitment process. For Bjarnegård and Kenny, the advantage of this framework is that it allows for a more problem-driven approach to researching political recruitment and informal institutions – broadening the scope of institutional analysis to focus on a wider set of actors, sites and outcomes. The volume ends with a short conclusion by Georgina Waylen in which she discusses how the chapters take up the key themes of the book and the implications for a future FI research agenda.

REFERENCES

Azari, Julia R. and Jennifer K. Smith. 2012. 'Unwritten Rules: Informal Institutions in Established Democracies', *Perspectives on Politics* 10(1): 37–55.

Bjarnegård, Elin. 2013. *Gender, Informal Institutions and Political Recruitment: Explaining Male Dominance in Parliamentary Representation*. Houndmills, Basingstoke: Palgrave Macmillan.

Bjarnegård, Elin, Meryl Kenny and Tánia Verge. 2016. 'Conceptualizing Informal Networks within Feminist Institutionalism', Paper prepared for the 24th World Congress of Political Science, IPSA, Poznan, 23–28 July 2016.

Bohnet, Iris. 2016. *What Works: Gender Equality by Design*. Cambridge, Massachusetts: Harvard University Press.

Chappell, Louise. 2015. *The Politics of Gender Justice at the International Criminal Court: Legacies and Legitimacy*. New York: Oxford University Press.

Chappell, Louise and Georgina Waylen. 2013. 'Gender and the Hidden Life of Institutions', *Public Administration* 91(3): 599–615.

Friedman, Elisabeth. 1995. Women's Human Rights: The Emergence of a Movement. In Julie Peters and Andrea Wolper (eds.). *Women's Rights, Human Rights: International Feminist Perspectives*. New York; London: Routledge, 18–35.

Grzymala-Busse, Ana. 2010. 'The Best Laid Plans: The Impact of Informal Rules on Formal Institutions in Transitional Regimes', *Studies in Comparative International Development* 45(3): 311–33.

Hafner-Burton, Emilie, Miles Kahler and Alexander H. Montgomery. 2009. 'Network Analysis for International Relations', *International Organization* 63(3): 559–52.

Helmke, Gretchen and Steven Levitsky. 2004. 'Informal Institutions and Comparative Politics: A Research Agenda', *Perspectives on Politics* 2(4): 725–40.

Helmke, Gretchen and Steven Levitsky (eds.). 2006. *Informal Institutions and Democracy: Lessons from Latin America*. Baltimore: Johns Hopkins University Press.

Htun, Mala, and Laurel S. Weldon. 2010. 'When Do Governments Promote Women's Rights? A Framework for the Analysis of Sex Equality Policy', *Perspectives on Politics* 8(1): 207–16.

Huffington Post. 2013. 'Child Abuse May Have Been "Ignored" because of Old Values, Says Lord Chief Justice', 20 March 2013.

Keck, Margaret E., and Katherine Sikkink. 1999. 'Transnational Advocacy Networks in International and Regional Politics', *International Social Science Journal* 51(159): 89–101.

Kenny, Meryl. 2013. *Gender and Political Recruitment: Theorizing Institutional Change*. Basingstoke: Palgrave Macmillan.

Krook, Mona Lena and Fiona Mackay (eds.). 2011. *Gender, Politics, and Institutions: Toward a Feminist Institutionalism*. Basingstoke: Palgrave.

Lauth, Hans-Joachim. 2000. 'Informal Institutions and Democracy', *Democratization* 7(4): 21–50.

Levitsky, Steven, and Dan Slater. 2011. 'Ruling Politics: The Formal and Informal Foundations of Institutional Reform', Paper presented at Workshop on Informal Institutions, Harvard University.

Liebowitz, Deborah. 2008. Governing Globalization: Feminist Engagements with International Trade Policy. In Shirin Rai and Georgina Waylen (eds.). *Global Governance: Feminist Perspectives*. Basingstoke; New York: Palgrave Macmillan, 207–34.

Lowndes, Vivien. 2014. 'How Are Things Done around Here? Uncovering Institutional Rules and Their Gendered Effects', *Politics & Gender* 10(04): 685–91.

Mackay, Fiona. 2014. 'Nested Newness, Institutional Innovation, and the Gendered Limits of Change', *Politics & Gender* 10(04): 549–71.

Mackay, Fiona, Meryl Kenny and Louise Chappell. 2010. 'New Institutionalism through a Gender Lens: Towards a Feminist Institutionalism?' *International Political Science Review* 31(5): 573–88.

Meyer, Mary K. and Elisabeth Prügl (eds.). 1999. *Gender Politics in Global Governance*. Lanham, MD: Rowman & Littlefield Publishers.

Peters, Guy B. 1999. *Institutional Theory in Political Science: The New Institutionalism*. London: Continuum.

Radnitz, Scott. 2011. 'Informal Politics and the State', *Comparative Politics* 43(3): 351–71.

Steinmo, Sven, and Kathleen Thelen. 1992. Historical Institutionalism in Comparative Politics. In Sven Steinmo and Kathleen Thelen (eds.). *Structuring Politics: Historical Institutionalism in Comparative Analysis*. New York: Cambridge University Press, 1–33.

Tsai, Kellee. 2006. 'Adaptive Informal Institutions and Endogenous Institutional Change in China', *World Politics* 59(1): 116–41.

Ward, Michael D., Katherine Stovel and Audrey Sacks. 2011. 'Network Analysis and Political Science', *Annual Review of Political Science* 14: 245–64.

Waylen, Georgina. 2009. 'What Can Historical Institutionalism Offer Feminist Institutionalists?' *Politics & Gender* 5(2): 245–53.

Waylen, Georgina. 2014a. 'Informal Institutions, Institutional Change, and Gender Equality', *Political Research Quarterly* 67(1): 212–23.

Waylen, Georgina. 2014b. 'A Seat at the Table – Is It Enough? Gender, Multiparty Negotiations, and Institutional Design in South Africa and Northern Ireland', *Politics & Gender* 10(04): 495–523.

Waylen, Georgina. 2016. Gendering Politics, Institutions, and the Executive: Bachelet in Context. In Georgina Waylen (ed.). *Gender, Institutions, and Change in Bachelet's Chile*. New York: Palgrave Macmillan, 13–38.

Waylen, Georgina and Ros Southern. 2016. 'Gender, Informal Institutions and Corruption: The UK Parliamentary Expenses Scandal', Paper presented at Gothenburg Conference on Gender and Corruption, 23–24 May.

Weldon, Laurel S. 2014. 'Using Statistical Methods to Study Institutions', *Politics & Gender* 10(4): 661–72.

Chapter 2

What's in a Name? Mapping the Terrain of Informal Institutions and Gender Politics

Louise Chappell and Fiona Mackay

Institutionalist scholars of most hues – including feminist institutionalists (FI) – increasingly confer equal status on informal and formal institutions as factors explaining political outcomes. However, as Georgina Waylen outlines in Chapter 1 of this volume, to date the specific nature and influence of informal rules, norms and practices – and the effect of interactions between the formal and informal – have been under-theorised and underplayed in empirical studies in both gendered and non-gendered institutionalist analyses in political science. These trends are slowly changing as scholars – including FI researchers – turn their attention to informal institutions for explaining differences in political life and political outcomes, including comparative analyses of the global North and South (Helmke and Levitsky 2004; Bjarnegård 2013; Piscopo 2016). This chapter seeks to support these crucial efforts to incorporate formal and informal institutional analyses into feminist political science (FPS) generally, and feminist institutionalism specifically, by laying out some of the foundational concepts and approaches regarding informal institutions in particular, and identifying the contours of key research developments in the area.

Whether implicitly or explicitly, feminist scholars in particular have been unable to ignore the informal in their examination of political life. A central insight of FPS is that the 'dynamics of institutional power relations, resistance, reproduction, continuity and change need to be filtered through a gendered lens' (Mackay 2004, 113; see also Chappell 2006; Kenny 2007). Informal gender institutions – including masculine and feminine norms, and daily gendered practices that maintain hierarchies of status and domination, and reproduce expectations about 'appropriate' men's and women's capacities, behaviour and duties – are central to shaping political processes and outcomes, including who has access to political power and to material and symbolic resources. The challenge for researchers is that these rules are often taken for granted – usually submerged and barely visible – and are therefore difficult to study. Finding the right methods to 'see' informal institutions is essential, especially as it is through these rules, norms and practices that wider particular arrangements and power asymmetries are naturalised and institutionalised, and sometimes resisted and discarded, across institutional arenas.

In this chapter we argue that in order to extend the range and analytical leverage of FI in particular, and FPS in general, the necessary next stage of our work is to develop a common vocabulary of gendered institutionalist analysis, and to more systematically specify and operationalise key concepts, including the notion of an informal institution itself. We accept that this is no easy task: the wider institutionalist literature is fraught with definitional disputes and, 'the operationalization of institutionalist concepts is frustratingly vague or surprisingly flexible' (Lowndes 2014, 685). Indeed, we acknowledge our own struggles over time to clarify these slippery concepts and accept that our position may provoke disagreement. We concur with Vivien Lowndes that FI should seize the opportunity – and take up the challenge – to produce greater conceptual clarity and more careful operationalisation of key concepts (Peters 2012, 53; Lowndes 2014, 685). However, in attempting to contribute to this task here, we nonetheless retain our commitment to empirical complexity and the need to capture the 'messiness' of real-world scenarios, and do so in the knowledge that parsimonious models often obscure rather than illuminate gender.

In working towards greater clarity about informal institutions and their relationship to gender politics, this chapter sets out to answer four core questions:

1. What are informal institutions and how do they differ from, and interact with, formal institutions?
2. What is the relationship between gender and informal institutions?
3. How do institutions, actors and networks differ? (Or, in other words, what is and is not an institution?)
4. How do we research informal institutions in order to capture their gendered nature and effects?

Ultimately, in addressing these questions, we hope to be able to contribute to strengthening FI's ability to build and test theory, and to consolidate the rich empirical findings and theoretical insights emerging from feminist scholarship investigating the interactions between formal and informal institutions in a variety of arenas. We also seek to draw some boundaries around FI and be clear about what its distinguishing features are vis-à-vis other feminist approaches. This includes, first, making a distinction between the roles of institutions and actors in shaping political and policy outcomes, starting with the assumption that institutions are likely to *matter as much if not more* than anything else in explaining the determinants of political life, and second, suggesting that contests over the political rules of the game are fundamentally about power, and that power is gendered.

WHAT IS AN INFORMAL INSTITUTION, AND HOW DO THEY DIFFER AND INTERACT WITH FORMAL INSTITUTIONS?

Institutions, it is generally agreed, are 'relatively enduring features of political and social life (rules, norms and procedures) that structure behavior and cannot be changed easily or instantaneously' (Mahoney and Thelen 2010, 4). They are, at a minimum, 'systems of rules that work together to coordinate social [and political] behavior' (Raymond et al. 2014, 198). While accepting these broad definitions, institutionalists take different positions on the specific features, operations and effects of institutions, including on the key definitional questions of what constitutes formal and informal institutions. Some perceive formal and informal as existing on a continuum, and measured in gradations (see Raymond et al. 2014, 198). In this view, the formal is an outgrowth or crystallisation of the informal, existing on a spectrum from taboos and customs through to written constitutions (North 1990, 46). For Olsen, 'evolving behavioural patterns are "frozen" into habits and traditions, and formally codified' (Olsen 2009, 6). Others see the relationship more dichotomously, conceiving the two as mirrors of each other (Helmke and Levitsky 2004). Whichever view is adopted, as Waylen (2014a, 213) suggests, 'informal institutions cannot be looked at in isolation or as separate – they must be analyzed alongside any formal institutions that they are linked to and with which they interact'.

Institutionalist scholar Vivien Lowndes is one who argues against a 'strict separation between informal and formal rules or prejudging their relative significance' (2014, 687–8) preferring to use Ostrom's term 'rules-in-use'. Rules-in-use are defined as the distinctive ensemble of 'dos and don'ts that one learns on the ground' (Ostrom 2005, 38; Lowndes 2014, 688), which are a mix of the formal and informal, and which express 'institutional linkages across political and nonpolitical domains' (Lowndes 2014, 688). But we suggest, before one can understand what are the rules-in-use, there is a prior task which is to excavate and identify the nature of formal and informal institutions in order to specify which informal elements comprise the gendered rules-in-use. Only then can we analyse how the informal and formal institutions interact; how actors deploy the mix; and, what the gendered outcomes are of these arrangements.

Formal institutions are generally understood as being consciously designed and clearly specified (Lowndes and Wilson 2003), and disseminated and enforced through official channels (Helmke and Levitsky 2004). Formal rules are identifiable through codes of conduct, contracts, procedures, policies and laws, for example. Although this seems relatively settled, there is a surprising uncertainty around what is (not) a formal institution among political scientists. While there is not space in this chapter for a full discussion, we think this fuzziness arises from the dissonance between common sense and holistic understandings of *political* institutions (as bureaucracies, executives, legislatures, political parties etc.) and the commitment to disaggregated and differentiated conceptions of institutions within institutional analysis as: 'sets of rules that exist "within" and "between organisations", "as well as under, over and around them"' (Fox and Miller 1995, 92; Lowndes 2010, 67). This second conceptualisation can be counter-intuitive; indeed highly disaggregated understandings of political institutions can also reduce our ability to speak with comparative scholars. For the most part, we think the use of 'institutional arenas' – for example, the Westminster parliament as an institutional arena – works well as a means to bridge understandings of political institutions across conventional and institutionalist accounts. We do not suggest that either conceptualisation is right or wrong, but we do think there will always be a need to clearly specify how we are conceptualising and using political institutions in any given context.

Whatever the definition of formal institutions is used, we can accept that they are distinguished by being official, visible and codified. They are also distinguished by their enforcement mechanisms, including through legal recognition and regulation, by the power of the state or other official sources. In contrast, informal institutional rules are often 'hidden from view', tacit and undocumented (Lauth 2000; Helmke and Levitsky 2004) and enforced through unofficial sanctions, including shunning, social ostracism and violence (Grzymala-Busse 2010, 313; Waylen 2014a, 214), or indeed through positive rewards (see Chappell and Galea, this volume). Informal institutions usually operate through more opaque means – especially norms, practices and narratives (Helmke and Levitsky 2004; Lowndes and Roberts 2013). For political scientists Julia Azari and Jennifer Smith (2012, 39), informal institutions exist 'when shared expectations outside the official rules of the game structure political behaviour'.

While it is important to differentiate between formal and informal rules, it is also necessary to distinguish between informal rules and other patterns of behaviour lest informal institutions become a 'catch all', and analytically powerless. They need to be distinguished from those norms that are more cultural in nature, such as raising an umbrella when it rains (Azari and Smith 2012) or removing a coat in a restaurant (Helmke and Levitsky 2004, 727). For Lowndes (2014, 686), informal political institutional rules are distinct from such personal habits or 'rules of thumb' in that they are specific to a particular political or governmental setting; recognised by actors (if not always adhered to); collective (rather than personal) in their effect; subject to some sort of third-party enforcement (formal or informal); and able to be described and explained to the researcher. Not all institutionalists would agree with every element of Lowndes's definition – again highlighting the challenge of pinning down these concepts. For instance, we would argue that the recognition/description element may not always be evident. Gendered institutions in particular – such as the timing of political meetings which make it impossible for carers to participate, or careers built on the presumption of a 'stay at home wife' – are often not recognised, especially by those institutional actors who are advantaged by them, at least until they are called out.

Refining current definitions, we would argue that informal institutions are distinguished by the following traits:

- *Enduring* rules, norms and practices that shape *collective behaviour* that *may or may not be recognised by institutional actors*;
- Have a *collective effect;*
- Are usually *not codified;*
- Are *enforced* through sanctions and rewards from *within or outwith* an institutional arena.

As with formal institutions, informal institutions perform a variety of functions. The informal can work to 'weaken, substitute for, or work in parallel with' formal institutions (Radnitz 2011, 352). Actors can employ informal rules to *undermine* formal rules to bring about change (see Hinojosa this volume) or to *maintain* the status quo against attempts at reform (Helmke and Levitsky 2004). Informal institutions can also distort and stymie formal institutions (Levitsky and Slater 2011). Informal institutions can fill in the gaps where formal institutions are incomplete, operate as 'a second best strategy' when it is difficult to change formal institutions or allow actors to pursue goals not publicly acceptable including unpopular or illegal activities (Helmke and Levitsky 2004, 730; Azari and Smith 2012, 41). As Helmke and Levistky (2006, 3) note, the interaction between formal and informal institutions leads to 'myriad, complex and often unexpected effects: whereas some informal rules compete with and subvert democratic institutions, others complement and even help sustain them'.

A general point of agreement about informal institutions is that because of their submerged nature, their gradual evolution and embeddedness in organisational operations makes them very 'sticky' and difficult to shift (Lauth 2000); they have, as North notes, a 'tenacious survival ability' (1990, 45). But this is not to argue that institutions are impervious to change. Working through the 'constructive' gaps that emerge between formal and informal rules, actors can shift existing informal institutions (Mahoney and Thelen 2010, Sheingate 2010; Waylen 2014a; Chappell 2016), or indeed create new ones through layering, conversation and other methods (Mahoney and Thelen 2010). As Raymond et al. (2014, 198) discuss, informal institutions, operating via norms, can bring about change and transformation of existing institutional arrangements, due to their 'ambiguity and malleability'. While much of this change is understood to occur incrementally, sometimes change can occur rapidly, for instance informal rules can shift abruptly when changes in formal rules 'create incentives for actors to modify or abandon the informal rule' (Helmke and Levitsky 2004, 732).

FI also agrees that formal and informal 'rules of the game' exist, that each has defining features, as well as interaction effects which shape political and policy outcomes.

WHAT IS THE RELATIONSHIP BETWEEN GENDER AND INFORMAL INSTITUTIONS?

A key contribution of feminist institutionalism (FI) to institutional analysis is to bring a gendered perspective to the field. Its first important intervention has been to show that formal and informal political institutions *are gendered* – in that they are normatively organised around stereotypes about men's and women's attributes, experiences and abilities, and symbolically valorise masculine traits, especially hegemonic ones, over feminine ones. As such, they embody and reproduce particular patterns of status and domination. The second intervention is to reveal the *gender effects* of rules, norms and practices, including on access to and distribution of political power and resources, on political and policy outcomes and on political change. Here we unpack the relationship between gender and (informal) institutions along three axes: gendered institutional logics, particularly logics of appropriateness; gender and power; and gender and change including the significance of the gendered environment.

Gendered Institutional Logics

Institutional logics provide the organising principles, vocabularies of motivation and action and the overall framework of sense-making in a particular institutional arena (Thornton and Ocasio 2008). While rational choice institutionalists have typically focused upon instrumental logics – based upon calculus and the weighing up of consequences – following the groundbreaking work of March and Olsen (1989, 161), new institutionalism has placed great emphasis on informal institutions as creating institutional 'logics of appropriateness'. In a manner analogous with Ostrom's rules-in-use, institutional logics comprise the combination of formal and informal rules and practices which comprise the 'world view' of actors in a particular institutional arena, and which constrain some forms of agency while encouraging others: 'institutional logics are embodied in practices, sustained and reproduced by cultural assumptions, and political struggles' (Thornton and Ocasio 2008, 101). Although this logic is not impermeable, it is difficult to unsettle as it is perpetuated by institutional actors who 'embody and reflect existing norms and beliefs' (McAdam and Scott 2005, 15) and who seek to maintain the rules.

FI has drawn on this concept of institutional logics of appropriateness to explore how institutional rules, norms and practices operate to create a specific 'gendered logic of appropriateness' (see Stivers 2002; Chappell 2006). Their work points to the way political arenas such as parliaments and executives are structured by gender-biased assumptions and 'dispositions' that underpin their operation (Mackay and Waylen 2009; Annesley and Gains 2010; Mackay, Kenny and Chappell 2010; Krook and Mackay 2011; Bjarnegård 2013; Kenny 2013). Formal rules can contribute to a logic of appropriateness – for instance, through instantiating overtly discriminatory rules that ban women from participating in certain professions – such as frontline soldiers – or by disallowing their engagement in political activities – such as denying female enfranchisement. However, more commonly, and working more subtly, are informal rules and norms which influence this logic, especially the masculine and feminine codes of appropriate behaviour that undergird institutional processes. These gender norms are present in all institutional settings, but the balance between them can shift according to the context. In political, bureaucratic and legal settings, a hegemonic masculine ideal – representing rationality, strength and toughness – tends to be 'culturally exalted' (Connell 2000, 84): these are the symbolic codes that shape institutional 'ways of valuing things, ways of behaving, and ways of being' (Duerst-Lahti and Kelly 1995, 20). The antithesis is femininity – represented by traits of passivity, nature, care, emotion and irrationality – which tends to be devalued in political life.

Gendered institutional logics have two key effects. First, they prescribe (as well as proscribe) 'acceptable' masculine and feminine forms of behaviour within institutional arenas. At the heart of gendered logics of appropriateness in political life is the coding of public authority, and political presence and agency as culturally masculine. Because men tend to be associated with masculine codes and women with feminine ones, the gendered logic of appropriateness maintains dominant categories of men in powerful positions and keeps women (and men from marginalised categories) in the role of the 'other', viewed as 'space invaders' (Puwar 2004) in the political realm. Elin Bjarnegård's work on homosocial capital demonstrates this point, showing how masculine privilege accrues capital and pays political dividends, through political networks founded on 'sameness' or homosociality (2013). Second, these logics influence political outcomes. The policies, legislation and rulings that are the outcome of political institutional processes are imbued with gender norms through exposure to the logic of appropriateness: these in turn help to (re)produce broader social and political gender expectations, including for instance the contours of the welfare state (O'Connor, Orloff and Shaver 1999), and women's political participation (Hern 2016). These are what Gains and Lowndes (2014) call 'rules with gender effects', as opposed to 'rules about gender' such as parental leave, equal pay or anti-gender discrimination policies.

Feminists interested in exploring these gendered logics have been careful to point out that they do not present in the same way in all institutional settings. As Lovenduski's important foundational work in this area argues, institutions have distinctively gendered cultures and are involved in processes of producing and reproducing gender in different ways (1998, 348). What we know from comparative work on gender and various institutional settings – including parliaments (Childs 2004; Mackay 2014a), electoral systems (Krook et al. 2006), bureaucracies and women's policy agencies (Stetson and Mazur 1995; Chappell 2002; Stivers 2002), executives (Annesley, Beckwith and Franceschet 2015) and political parties (Kenny 2011, 2013; Bjarngård and Kenny 2015; Kenny and Verge 2016) – is that the gendered logic of appropriateness is complex and plays out differently in similar institutions in different polities and different institutions within the same polity. Taking this area of research forward requires being attentive to these differences and asking questions about how, where and why gendered logics of appropriateness differ across institutional settings, and what difference this makes to gendered political outcomes.

Gender, Informal Institutions and Power

Understanding the gendered nature of political institutions provides tools for understanding how political power is constructed, how it functions and how it might be reconfigured. This insight rests upon the claim of feminist social science – including feminist political scientists – that gender is one of the principal means by which power operates by normalising and naturalising asymmetries. As V. Spike Peterson argues: gender invokes 'a deeply internalised and naturalised binary – the dimorphism of "sex difference" – which is then available to naturalise diverse forms of structural oppression' (2015, 178). Thus gender power naturalises masculine advantage, 'setting the terms of normal, just, and proper arrangements for political and social power' (Duerst-Lahti 2008, 165) and enhancing the legitimacy, status and power of already powerful groups, while doing 'the political work of making the limited options and precarious lives of subordinated groups seem somehow inevitable rather than unconscionable' (Peterson 2015, 178).

This naturalisation has not occurred through a conscious strategy on behalf of all men to dominate all women. As Hooper argues: 'Men gain access to power and privilege not by virtue of their anatomy but through their cultural association with masculinity' (2001, 41). Men's access to power has been reinforced over time through 'constantly repeated processes of exclusion' of women (Lovenduski 2005, 50), and through organisational rules, routines, policies and discourses that have rendered 'women, along with their needs and interests, invisible' (Acker 1992, 567; Hawkesworth 2005, 147). Concepts of gender power thus allow us to expose and explain why seemingly neutral rules can result in outcomes that profoundly disadvantage women (and marginalised groups of men) and also the way in which institutions – as gender regimes (Connell 2002) – reinforce the status quo.

The concept of gender regimes, developed by the Australian sociologist Raewyn Connell (2002), is widely referenced within FI as part of a repertoire of gendered frameworks (see, for example, Lovenduski 2011; Chappell and Waylen 2013). Gender regimes, developed in organisational analysis, provide a framework of interconnecting institutions that comprise the overall pattern of gender arrangements in a formal institutional arena, such as a legislature, a state bureaucracy, a judiciary or a political party. A gender regime involves four dimensions: a gendered division of labour; gendered relations of power (including the way in which control, authority or force is organised along gendered dimensions); gendered patterning of emotions and emotional labour; and gendered culture and symbolism (including cultural scripts about gender difference, prevailing gender norms etc.) (Connell 2002, 53–58). Each dimension is the sum of previous and ongoing gender contestations. The dimensions will include formal elements but predominantly will comprise informal rules, norms and practices.

Paying attention to gender regimes in a specific institutional setting makes visible the asymmetry of institutional power relations (Kenny 2007, 96) and makes us look at how particular combinations of formal rules, informal norms and everyday practices play out, underpinned by specific narratives, and with what effects. For example, local variation in gender patterns may create ambiguities and contradictions that open up spaces for contestation and change, as well as provide rich resources for resistance. Gender regimes are highly influential as concepts, but examples of systematic application are rarer and it will be a key task of FI to systematically apply and develop gender regimes as part of wider theory building processes.

Gender, Informal Institutions and Change

The overtly 'feminist', normative, aspect of feminist institutionalism is most apparent in its concern to better understand how existing formal, but more importantly informal, institutions can be disrupted to bring about greater gender equal political outcomes, in terms of representation, recognition and redistribution (Mackay 2008; Chappell 2016). Theoretically, acknowledging the existence of a gender regime provides insights into the power dimension of political institutions; it also points to a potential mechanism of change. As Karen Beckwith notes, if institutions *are* gendered, they surely can be *regendered*, including in ways that disrupt current patterns of power and inequality (2005). Recent research has shown that the effect of informal institutions in bringing about change is not predictable. They can in some instances play a reinforcing role, maintaining the gender status quo, but they can also be transformative in regendering political processes and outcomes.

The weight of extant FI scholarship on informal institutions points towards informal rules acting to preserve the gender status quo, or gendered logic of appropriateness, in the face of reform efforts, including reform where there has been the creation of new formal rules and policy frameworks. Attention has been paid to the role of the informal in instances where the formal rules have changed, for example to promote gender equality and address gender injustice, but where implementation is patchy and outcomes are negligible in terms of positive change, such as in the area of gender quota subversion (see Piscopo 2015; Verge and Espírito-Santo 2016). Informal mechanisms of resistance and contestation include 'forgetting' new rules and norms and 'remembering' the old, including the reassertion of traditional gender norms (Leach and Lowndes 2007; Mackay 2014a). Research has demonstrated how actors draw upon informal institutions to underpin strategies of partial or non-compliance, for example Chappell's (2016) work on the International Criminal Court, which highlights how judicial interpretations uphold 'gender norms that treat women's rights as less significant than other rights'. Further, work on political recruitment (Kenny 2013) highlights how informally sanctioned rule-breaking, lack of rule enforcement and adoption of alternative conventions has thwarted the implementation of policies aimed at increasing women's entry into politics.

As Azari and Smith note, it is important that informal institutions are characterised not only as 'historic hang-overs' and not always as negative, but also as sometimes positive and creative outcomes of contemporary institutional dilemmas (Azari and Smith 2012, 49) As such, attention in FI research is increasingly being drawn towards identifying how informal institutions can engender change (Waylen 2014a; Chappell 2016) and towards theorising how political arenas may be regendered (in a positive direction) through the mobilisation of informal rules and norms. The work of Beyler and Annesley (2011) on regendering aspects of the welfare state; Jennifer Piscopo (this volume) on using informal rules and norms to strengthen gender quotas in Mexico, and in Sweden and France (Friedenvall and Krook 2011); Leigh Raymond et al. (2014) on shifting norms to develop anti-violence against women policies; and Annesley et al. (2015) on the incorporation of gender equality in Cabinet appointment processes are all cases in point. We agree with Waylen (2014a, 214) that 'this new emphasis on the potential dynamism and mutability of informal institutions can make a significant contribution to the burgeoning discussions of the interaction of formal and informal institutions in institutional change'.

Given the congealed, embedded and often-unrecognised nature of informal gender norms, practices and rules, future researchers are encouraged not (only) to search for major instances of change – the 'punctuated equilibria' many historical institutionalist might look for – but to pay attention to micro-shifts that occur within an institutional arena (see Chappell 2016 as an example). In undertaking an FI analysis, we suggest it is important to pay attention to the 'small wins' that may well add up over time to a significant institutional transformation (see Chappell and Mackay 2015; Chappell 2016, Chapter 7). We also suggest that researchers pay more attention to the 'constructive ambiguities' (Oosterveld 2014; Chappell 2016) embedded in formal rules – which we have found in our work on the Rome Statute of the International Criminal Court (2016) and the operational rules of UN Women (Mackay 2013) – that can provide the gaps through which informal rules can operate. Sometimes these will work to advance progressive gender justice interpretations, although sometimes also in the opposite direction.

WHAT IS *NOT* AN INFORMAL INSTITUTION? ACTORS AND NETWORKS

An area of some ambiguity in both the general and FI literature is the relationship between institutions, actors and networks, and what is *not* an informal institution. This is important because to elide actors or networks and other phenomena with informal institutions muddles analysis and runs the danger of making informal institutions a residual category. In this section, we discuss the distinction we see between these entities in order to provide some greater analytical precision to our understanding of these relationships.

In entering this territory, we are aware that we are travelling towards one of the fundamental debates in the social sciences – the distinction between agency and structure – and the attendant ontological and epistemological considerations this brings (for a detailed discussion on structure and agency see Hay 2002). For the purposes of this discussion, we simply want to point out that as FIs we consider institutions – which sit somewhere on the structural side of the explanatory continuum – as having a primary or more significant role compared to actors and agency, for understanding political life. In adopting this position, we do not suggest that agency and actors are unimportant, to the contrary; rather, our position is that institutional forces will always mediate the influence of actors on political outcomes to a greater or lesser degree, and in some cases the relationship will be co-constitutive. However, even where actors and institutions are conceived as co-constitutive, it is still necessary to be able to distinguish between the characteristics, mechanisms and effects of institutions on political phenomena from the actors who interpret, interact with, shape and are shaped by these institutions.

In some institutionalist literature, including the feminist variant, actors and agencies have an ambiguous presence. Sometimes they are not mentioned at all, with a sense that institutions magically appear and are then monitored, enforced and maintained as if by phantoms. Other times, actors lurk in the background, without a clear sense of the interaction between the rule 'maker' or 'taker' on institutional design or implementation. In other instances, it seems like actors rather than institutions are doing all the work, with no clear sense of what is 'institutionalist' at all about the analysis. We take our position on actors from John Campbell (2004, 72) who suggests that 'institutions enable, empower and constitute actors by providing them with the principles and practices that they can use to modify existing institutional arrangements'. But we also agree with him that actors do not have unimpeded agency because 'institutions also act as constraints by limiting the number of possible innovations that they [actors] can envision and make'. This chimes with Mahoney and Thelen's view (2010, 28) that '[institutional] rules influence the particular type of actors that will emerge and thrive in any context, and the extent of reform possible'. We see actors then as having a critical role in shaping the nature, operations and effects of institutions, but in turn the features and context of institutional settings act to constrain the capacity of actors to design, bend and interpret the rules of the game and ultimately can limit their capacity to influence outcomes.

Institutions constrain actors, but that is not all they do. We also agree, in line with Ostrom, and with Lowndes and Roberts (2013, 94), that institutions can be permissive – more or less so depending on the context – providing spaces for 'rule breaking and shaping' (Lowndes and Roberts 2013, 90). The 'creative agents' able to take advantage of these openings can be the elites who sit at the top of organisational hierarchies, but equally, they can be actors who exist at the base of the pyramid, who can adapt and resist rules, and sometimes force changes in the status quo (Lowndes and Roberts 2013, 105). Identifying those contexts where external and non-elite actors can resist and bend the rules is especially important for those scholars seeking to understand the mechanisms that drive change in gendered institutions where masculine power is entrenched. Feminist scholars including FI scholars have often paid attention not just to political power brokers who may appear to set the rules, but also to those grass-roots actors, social movements and lowly ranked individuals who refuse to play by the rules, whether formal or informal, and through their resistance promote disruption and change. Francesca Gains and Vivien Lowndes (2014, 528) remind us that in identifying the actors who make, interpret, enforce and resist the rules, we also need to pay attention to their gender attributes. As they note: 'Actors occupy male or female (or transexual) bodies, their values and attitudes reflect different positions on a masculine/feminine spectrum, and they hold different perspectives on the gender power balance and possibilities for change (in the context of intersectional identities).'

Another area of uncertainty in institutionalist accounts is the place of networks. Research on institutions and networks has proceeded on largely separate trajectories over the past few decades. The former is more associated with work in organisational and political sociology, and the latter associated with economic sociology (Owen-Smith and Powell 2008). Like informal institutions (Gryzmala-Busse 2010), networks often arise to fill the space of incomplete institutions and to enable collective action in conditions of uncertainty (Schoenman 2014). Some authors argue they are co-constitutive (Owen-Smith and Powell 2008), but even if this is the case, we agree with Azari and Smith (2014, 40), among others, that networks are *not* institutions. It is more useful perhaps to see networks as an intermediate variable: to conceive of them as vehicles for actor engagement, and a key means to transmit and circulate ideas and practices, rather than as institutions themselves. Networks of actors instantiate institutions through daily practices, and through the deployment, contestation and subversion of formal and informal rules and norms. Networks are *groups of actors*, whereas institutions are the rules, norms and practices which set the context within which networks operate. Networks may *deploy* informal institutions; they may be the *carriers* of institutional effects (Owen-Smith and Powell 2008, 595); and network relations may *shape* trajectories of institutional development (Clemens 1993; Schoenman 2014) but they are not institutions in, and of, themselves.

In empirical FI examples, networks (particularly homosocial networks) are often the key carriers of informal institutions, such as clientelism (Bjarnegård 2013); networks also provide actors with the resources to resist and subvert formal rule changes, such as gender quotas (see, for example, Piscopo this volume), although there are also instances of women's networks created for the purposes of promoting gender reforms (see Nazneen this volume). To move FI scholarship forward, we need more work that further unpicks and unpacks the relationships between gendered actors, including networks, and formal and informal institutions. We need analyses that pay close attention to which (gendered) actors get to make the rules, under what conditions are they able to resist the rules and to what ends. We also need closer examination of the work networks do in carrying the demands of collective actors into institutional settings and the resources these networks provide for challenging the old and instituting new formal and informal rules, norms and practices (see Verge and Claveria, and Culhane in this volume as a starting point of these efforts).

HOW DO WE RESEARCH INFORMAL INSTITUTIONS?

Methodologically, it is a challenge for FI to identify 'the complex matrix of rules' (Lowndes 2014, 687), intersecting institutions and causal mechanisms and arrangements that produce gendered effects – particularly the reproduction of masculine dominance – in political life. While not underestimating the methodological challenges of capturing and analysing informal institutions, we concur with Azari and Smith (2012, 49) that 'informal rules can be identified with reasonable precision, observed in the world, and distinguished from other sources of patterned behavior, including strategic self-interest and the operation of formal rules'. For FI, undertaking a gendered analysis of any institutional arena requires three steps: the first step requires an analysis of the mix of the formal and informal 'rules-in-use', the next step is to identify what gendered logic, if any, underpins these rules, and then, finally, to consider their gendered effects and outcomes. Different scholars have experimented with a variety of tools in their efforts to pin down the various formal and informal institutions at play in any context, and to identify their patterns and effects. We outline a few of these here, but do not suggest these are the only techniques that can or should be used.

In line with much historical institutionalist literature, much FI scholarship has adopted a comparative approach, looking across two or more cases to identify similarities and differences in institutional settings and the effect of these on gendered political outcomes. Chappell (2002), Krook (2009) and Waylen (2007, 2014b) are all examples of such an approach. In these comparative studies – and also in single case studies (see, for example, Kenny 2013) – within-case and cross-case analysis is undertaken using qualitative methods such as theory-driven process tracing using documents and interview transcripts (Kenny 2013; Waylen 2014b). Rosemary Grey's (2015) important study of prosecutorial discretion at the International Criminal Court is an interesting legal version of this approach, scrutinising court transcripts and other key documents to excavate gendered path dependencies across time (for a discussion of other legal methods see O'Rouke 2014).

Challenging long-held feminist prejudices about the value of quantitative methods for studying institutions, Laurel Weldon (2014) has recently provided a convincing account of their value, in a mixed-methods framework. For Weldon, quantitative methods can never replace the rich, detailed accounts provided through qualitative methods, but they can help in bringing greater clarity to the 'mushy, amorphous and shifting' (Weldon 2014, 662) contexts in which formal and informal institutions operate. Weldon identifies three core advantages in using statistical techniques:

> (1) the ability to summarize large quantities of information that are difficult to eyeball or summarize using traditional qualitative tools, (2) the ability to estimate the degree to which observed relationships can be attributed to chance, and (3) the ability to parse the degree to which different factors shape outcomes of interest . . . Cross-national comparisons also offer a greater ability to denaturalize local social practices (particularly useful to feminists seeking to critique male dominance).

A good example of the value of a mixed-methods approach to the study of informal institutions is found in Bjarnegård's work (2013, 2015), including her use of statistical techniques alongside interviews and observations to demonstrate how informal party recruitment criteria such as an emphasis on family connections are connected with a higher representation of women in Asian politics. Verge and Claveria (in this volume; see also Claveria and Verge 2015) provide another example of mixed-methods approaches, using a combination of quantitative data and synthetic literature reviews to uncover common patterns and possible causal mechanisms in secondary data.

A third and increasingly common method applied to the study of political institutions and gender is systematic in-depth ethnographies (for a discussion see Radnitz 2011, 365–6; Chappell and Waylen 2013; Smith 2005). Ethnographic studies of parliaments are emerging (see Crewe 2014; also see Childs 2016) alongside political recruitment practices (Bjarnegård 2013), while Mackay's work on UN Women (2013, 2014b) highlights its value for understanding global institutions. In this volume, Chappell and Galea discuss the value of 'rapid' ethnography for identifying and understanding the gendered actors and effects of various enforcement mechanisms in the male-dominated realm of the Australian construction industry. Ethnographic work, while certainly important, can only be one strategy among many. Research findings have to be triangulated with other forms of data, for example with policy documents, rule books and reports, to help maintain a balance between actors and their institutional context.

CONCLUSION

In this chapter we argue that in order to extend the range and analytical leverage of feminist institutionalism, the next essential stage of our work is to develop a common vocabulary of gendered institutionalist analysis, and to more systematically specify and operationalise key concepts. Refining current definitions, we would argue that informal institutions are distinguished by the following traits: *enduring* rules, norms and practices that shape *collective behaviour* that *may or may not be recognised by institutional actors*; have a *collective effect*; are usually *not codified*; and are enforced through sanctions and rewards from *within or outwith* an institutional arena.

Whether implicitly or explicitly, feminist scholars have been unable to ignore the informal in their examination of political life. Informal gender institutions are central to shaping political processes and outcomes, including who has access to political power and to material and symbolic resources. In real-life scenarios, there is a complex admixture of formal and informal, and we need to avoid overly strict separations between informal and formal rules, norms and practices or judging in advance their relative significance. As the emerging stock of FI cases indicate, and as demonstrated in this book, different configurations of formal and informal have different effects: sometimes formal and informal rules work together to maintain the gender status quo; at other times, the informal may compete, undermine or adapt formal rules in both positive and negative ways. How they play out will make a difference to opportunities for changes to the gender status quo and the existing gendered logic of appropriateness. We have argued that there is a prior task of excavating and identifying informal institutions to enable FI scholars to analyse how they interact with formal institutions, and with what gendered outcomes. Where are we now? We have identified a number of important informal institutions that interact with formal.

Not everything is an (gendered) institution. If we are not careful about drawing some definitional boundaries, informal institutions, in particular, run the risk of becoming a residual category. We have argued that it is important to specify what is, and what is not, an informal institution. We see actors and networks as working in, through and against institutions but as separate to them. To be sure, networks will be more or less formalised, will be more or less institutionalised and can have *institutional effects*, but they are collectivities of *actors*, rather than being institutions themselves.

Studying informal institutions – their substantive characteristics and their gendered effects – requires the use of a variety of methods. We encourage a broad approach to the selection of methods, understanding that each provides a different insight and perspective to the multiple layered and often unpredictable processes and outcomes that institutions produce. We acknowledge that different methods will be more or less relevant depending on the temporal and contextual elements of the case at hand, and that researchers will need to be guided by these factors in their selection. One of the potential benefits of FI to the broader field of feminist political research is its methodological pluralism – the willingness of its adherents to engage with, test and extend mixed approaches to be able to gain insights into the gendered relations between formal and informal institutions, their reproductive mechanisms and effects.

What is in a name? A lot – and if we are to extend the reach of FI, we need to develop some core common language, and specification of concepts. Doing so is not easy: there is always a trade-off between empirical richness and the winnowing and simplification required to gain analytic purchase, and gender scholars are rightly cautious about parsimony given the messiness of gendered political life. But more careful specification is essential: it enables us to build and test theory and to consolidate the empirical findings and theoretical insights of the growing body of FI work that addresses the interactions between formal and informal institutions. In other words it enables FI scholars to speak to ourselves and to others. Our argument is that FI can remain a big tent, but should not serve merely as a flag of convenience.

REFERENCES

Acker, Joan. 1992. 'From Sex Roles to Gendered Institutions'. *Contemporary Sociology* 21(5): 565–69.

Annesley, Claire and Francesca Gains. 2010. 'The Core Executive: Gender Power and Change'. *Political Studies* 58(5): 909–29.

Annesley, Claire, Karen Beckwith and Susan Franceschet. 2015. 'Rules or Norms? The Gendered Nature of Cabinet Appointments'. Paper prepared for the 4th European Conference on Politics and Gender. University of Uppsala, Sweden. 28 June to 1 July 2015.

Azari, Julia R. and Jennifer K. Smith. 2012. 'Unwritten Rules: Informal Institutions in Established Democracies'. *Perspectives on Politics* 10(1): 37–55.

Beckwith, Karen. 2005. 'A Common Language of Gender?' *Politics & Gender* 1(1):128–37.

Beyeler, Michelle and Claire Annesley. 2011. 'Gendering the Institutional Reform of the Welfare State: Germany, the United Kingdom, and Switzerland'. In *Gender, Politics and Institutions: Towards a Feminist Institutionalism*, edited by Mona Lena Krook and Fiona Mackay. Houndmills, Basingstoke: Palgrave Macmillan, 79–94.

Bjarnegård, Elin. 2013. *Gender, Informal Institutions and Political Recruitment: Explaining Male Dominance in Parliamentary Representation*. Basingstoke: Palgrave Macmillan (2nd Edn 2015).

Bjarnegård, Elin and Meryl Kenny. 2015. 'Revealing the Secret Garden: The Informal Dimensions of Political Recruitment'. *Politics & Gender* 11(4): 748–53.

Bjarnegård, Elin and Meryl Kenny. 2016. 'Comparing Candidate Selection: A Feminist Institutionalist Approach'. *Government and Opposition* 51(3): 370–92.

Campbell, John 1. 2004. *Institutional Change and Globalization*. Princeton: Princeton University Press.

Chappell, Louise. 2002. *Gendering Government: Feminist Engagement with the State in Australia and Canada*. Vancouver: University of British Columbia Press.

Chappell, Louise. 2006. 'Comparing Institutions: Revealing the "Gendered Logic of Appropriateness"'. *Politics & Gender* 2(2): 223–35.

Chappell, Louise. 2016. *The Politics of Gender Justice at the International Criminal Court: Legacies and Legitimacy*. Oxford: Oxford University Press.

Chappell, Louise and Fiona Mackay. 2015. Critical Friends and De(con)structive Critics: Dilemmas of Feminist Engagement with Global Governance and Gender Reform Agendas. Paper presented at the European Consortium for Political Research 4th European Conference on Politics and Gender. Uppsala, Sweden, 11–13 June 2015.

Chappell, Louise and Georgina Waylen. 2013. 'Gender and the Hidden Life of Institutions'. *Public Administration* 91(3): 599–615.

Childs, Sarah. 2004. 'A Feminised Style of Politics? Women MPs in the House of Commons'. *British Journal of Politics and International Relations* 6(1): 3–19.

Claveria, Sílvia and Tània Verge. 2015. 'Post-Ministerial Occupation in Advanced Industrial Democracies: Ambition, Individual Resources and Institutional Opportunity Structures'. *European Journal of Political Research,* 54(4): 819–35.

Clemens, Elisabeth. 1993. 'Organizational Repertoires and Institutional Change: Women's Groups and the Transformation of American Politics, 1890–1920'. *American Journal of Sociology* 98(4): 755–98.

Connell, Raewyn W. 2000. *The Men and the Boys*. Cambridge: Polity Press.

Connell, Raewyn W. 2002. *Gender*. Cambridge: Polity Press.

Crewe, Emma. 2014. 'Ethnographic Research in Gendered Institutions: The Case of the Westminster Parliament'. *Politics and Gender* 10(4): 673–78.

Duerst-Lahti, Georgia. 2008. 'Gender Ideology: Masculinism and Feminalism'. In *Politics, Gender, and Concepts: Theory and Methodology*, edited by Gary Goertz and Amy G. Mazur. Cambridge: Cambridge University Press, 159–92.

Duerst-Lahti, Georgia and Rita Mae Kelly. 1995. 'Gender, Power, and Leadership'. In *Gender Power, Leadership, and Governance*, edited by Georgia Duerst-Lahti and Rita Mae Kelly. Ann Arbor: University of Michigan Press, 11–39.

Fox, Charles J. and Hugh T. Miller. 1995. *Postmodern Public Administration*. Thousand Oaks, CA: Sage.

Gains, Francesca and Vivien Lowndes. 2014. 'How Is Institutional Formation Gendered, and Does It Make a Difference? A New Conceptual Framework and a Case Study of Police and Crime Commissioners in England and Wales'. *Politics and Gender* 10(4): 524–28.

Grey, Rosemary. 2015. *Prosecuting Sexual and Gender Violence Crimes in the International Criminal Court: Historical Legacies and New Opportunities*. PhD Thesis, University of New South Wales.

Gryzmala-Busse, Anna. 2010. 'The Best Laid Plans: The Impact of Informal Rules on Formal Institutions in Transitional Regimes'. *Studies in Comparative International Development* 45(3): 311–33.

Hawkesworth, Mary. 2005. 'Engendering Political Science: An Immodest Proposal'. *Politics & Gender* 1(1): 141–56.

Hay, Colin. 2002. *Political Analysis: A Critical Introduction*. Houndmills, Basingstoke: Palgrave Macmillan.

Helmke, Gretchen and Steven Levitsky. 2004. 'Informal Institutions and Comparative Politics: A Research Agenda'. *Perspectives on Politics* 2(4): 725–40.

Helmke, Gretchen and Steven Levitsky. 2006. 'Introduction'. In *Informal Institutions and Democracy: Lessons from Latin America*, edited by Gretchen Helmke and Steven Levistsky. Baltimore, MD: Johns Hopkins University Press, 1–32.

Hern, Erin. 2016. 'The Trouble with Institutions: How Women's Policy Machineries Can Undermine Women's Mass Participation'. *Politics and Gender*: 1–27. First View doi: 10.1017/S1743923X16000519.

Hooper, Charlotte. 2001. *Manly States: Masculinities, International Relations and Gender Politics*. New York: Columbia University Press.

Kenny, Meryl. 2007. 'Gender, Institutions and Power: A Critical Review'. *Politics* 27(2): 91–100.

Kenny, Meryl. 2011. 'Gender and Institutions of Political Recruitment: Candidate Selection in Post-Devolution Scotland'. In *Gender, Politics and Institutions: Toward a Feminist Institutionalism*, edited by Mona Lena Krook and Fiona Mackay. Basingstoke: Palgrave Macmillan, 21–41.

Kenny, Meryl. 2013. *Gender and Political Recruitment: Theorising Institutional Change*. Basingstoke: Palgrave Macmillan.

Kenny, Meryl and Tánia Verge. 2016. 'Opening Up the Black Box: Gender and Candidate Selection in a New Era'. *Government and Opposition* 51 (3): 351–69.

Krook, Mona Lena. 2009. *Quotas for Women in Politics: Gender and Candidate Selection Worldwide*. New York: Oxford University Press.

Krook, Mona Lena and Fiona Mackay. 2011. 'Introduction: Gender, Politics and Institutions'. In *Gender, Politics and Institutions: Toward a Feminist Institutionalism*, edited by Mona Lena Krook and Fiona Mackay. Basingstoke: Palgrave Macmillan, 181–96.

Krook, Mona Lena, Joni Lovenduski and Judith Squires. 2006. 'Western Europe, North America, Australia and New Zealand: Gender Quotas in the Context of Citizenship Models'. In *Women, Quotas and Politics*, edited by Drude Dahlerup. London: Routledge, 194–221.

Lauth, Hans-Joachim. 2000. 'Informal Institutions and Democracy'. *Democratization* 7(4): 21–50.

Leach, Steve N. and Vivien Lowndes. 2007. 'Of Roles and Rules: Analysing the Changing Relationship between Political Leaders and Chief Executives in Local Government'. *Public Policy and Administration* 22(2): 183–200.

Levitsky, Steven and Dan Slater. 2011. 'Ruling Politics: The Formal and Informal Foundations of Institutional Reform'. In *Ruling Politics*, edited by Steven Levitsky and Dan Slater. Cambridge, MA: Harvard University Press.

Lovenduski, Joni. 1998. 'Gendering Research in Political Science'. *Annual Review of Political Science* 1: 333–56.

Lovenduski, Joni. 2005. *Feminizing Politics*. Cambridge: Polity Press.

Lovenduski, Joni. 2011. 'Foreword'. In *Gender, Politics and Institutions: Towards a Feminist Institutionalism*, edited by Mona Lena Krook and Fiona Mackay. Houndmills, Basingstoke: Palgrave Macmillan.

Lowndes, Vivien. 2010. 'The Institutional Approach'. In *Theory and Methods in Political Science*, 3rd edition, edited by David Marsh and Gerry Stoker. Houndmills, Basingstoke: Palgrave Macmillan.

Lowndes, Vivien. 2014. 'How Are Things Done around Here? Uncovering Institutional Rules and Their Gendered Effects'. *Politics & Gender* 10(4): 685–91.

Lowndes, Vivien and David Wilson. 2003. 'Balancing Revisability and Robustness? A New Institutionalist Perspective on Local Government Modernization'. *Public Administration* 81(2): 275–98.

Lowndes, Vivien and Mark Roberts. 2013. *Why Institutions Matter: The New Institutionalism in Political Science*. Basingstoke: Palgrave Macmillan.

Mackay, Fiona. 2004. 'Gender and Political Representation in the UK: The State of the "Discipline."' *The British Journal of Politics and International Relations* 6(1): 99–120.

Mackay, Fiona. 2008. '"Thick" Conceptions of Substantive Representation: Women, Gender and Political Institutions'. *Representation* 44(2):125–39.

Mackay, Fiona. 2011. 'Conclusion: Towards a Feminist Institutionalism?' In *Gender, Politics and Institutions: Toward a Feminist Institutionalism*, edited by Mona Lena Krook and Fiona Mackay. Basingstoke: Palgrave Macmillan, 181–96.

Mackay, Fiona. 2013. New Rules, Old Rules and the Gender Equality Architecture of the UN – the Creation of UN Women. Paper presented at the Annual Meeting of the American Political Science Association. Washington DC. 29 August–1 September 2013.

Mackay, Fiona. 2014a. 'Nested Newness, Institutional Innovation, and the Gendered Limits of Change'. *Politics and Gender* 10(4): 649–71.

Mackay, Fiona. 2014b. Global Governance and UN Women: Nested Newness and the Gendered Limits of Institutional Reform. Paper presented at International Studies Association Annual Conference. Toronto. 25–27 March, 2014.

Mackay, Fiona and Georgina Waylen. 2009. 'Critical Perspectives on Feminist Institutionalism'. *Politics & Gender* 5(2): 237–80.

Mackay, Fiona, Meryl Kenny and Louise Chappell. 2010. 'New Institutionalism through a Gender Lens: Towards a Feminist Institutionalism?' *International Political Science Review* 31(5): 1–16.

Mahoney, James and Kathleen Thelen. 2010. 'A Theory of Gradual Institutional Change'. In *Explaining Institutional Change: Ambiguity, Agency, and Power*, edited by James Mahoney and Kathleen Thelen. Cambridge: Cambridge University Press.

March, James G. and Johan P. Olsen. 1989. *Rediscovering Institutions: The Organizational Basis of Politics*. New York: Free Press.

McAdam, Doug and W. Richard Scott. 2005. 'Organizations and Movements'. In *Social Movements and Organization Theory*, edited by Gerald F. Davis, Doug McAdam, W. Richard Scott and Mayer N. Zald. Cambridge: Cambridge University Press.

North, Douglas. 1990. *Institutions, Institutional Change and Economic Performance*. Cambridge: Cambridge University Press.

O'Connor, Julia S., Ann Shola Orloff and Sheila Shaver. 1999. *States, Markets, Families: Gender, Liberalism and Social Policy in Australia, Canada, Great Britain and the United States*. Cambridge: Cambridge University Press.

Olsen, Johan P. 2009. 'Change and Continuity: An Institutional Approach to Institutions of Democratic Government'. *European Political Science Review* 1(1): 3–32.

Oosterveld, Valerie. 2014. 'Constructive Ambiguity and the Meaning of "Gender" for the International Criminal Court'. *International Feminist Journal of Politics* 16(4): 563–80.

O'Rourke, Catherine. 2014. 'Feminist Legal Method and the Study of Institutions'. *Politics and Gender* 10(4): 691–97.

Ostrom, Elinor. 2005. *Understanding Institutional Diversity*. New Jersey: Princeton University Press.

Owen-Smith, Jason and Walter W. Powell. 2008. 'Networks and Institutions'. In *Sage Handbook of Organizational Institutionalism,* edited by Royston Greenwood, Christine Oliver, Roy Suddaby and Kerstin Sahlin-Andersson. London: Sage Publications, 594–621.

Peters, B. Guy. 2012. *Institutional Theory in Political Science: The New Institutionalism*. New York: Continuum International.

Peterson, V. Spike. 2015. 'International/Global Political Economy'. In *Gender Matters in Global Politics*, edited by Laura J. Shepherd. London: Routledge, 173–185.

Piscopo, Jennifer M. 2015. 'States as Gender Equality Activists: The Evolution of Quota Laws in Latin America. Latin American'. *Politics and Society* 57(3): 27–49.

Piscopo, Jennifer M. 2016. 'When Informality Advantages Women: Quota Networks, Electoral Rules, and Candidate Selection in Mexico'. *Government & Opposition* 51(3): 487–512.

Puwar, Nirmal. 2004. *Space Invaders: Race, Gender and Bodies Out of Place*. Oxford: Berg Publishers.

Radnitz, Scott. 2011. 'Informal Politics and the State'. *Comparative Politics* 43(3): 351–71.

Raymond, Leigh, Laurel S. Weldon, Daniel Kelly, Ximena B. Arriaga and Ann Marie Clark. 2014. 'Making Change: Norm-Based Strategies for Institutional Change to Address Intractable Problems'. *Political Research Quarterly* 67(1): 197–211.

Schoenman, Roger. 2014. *Networks and Institutions in Europe's Emerging Markets*. Cambridge: Cambridge University Press.

Sheingate, Adam. 2010. 'Rethinking Rules: Creativity and Constraint in the House of Representatives'. In *Explaining Institutional Change: Ambiguity, Agency, and Power*, edited by James Mahoney and Kathleen Thelen. Cambridge: Cambridge University Press, 168–203.

Smith, Dorothy E. 2005. *Institutional Ethnography: A Sociology for the People*. Maryland: AltaMira.

Stetson, Dorothy and Amy Mazur, eds. 1995. *Comparative State Feminism*. London: Sage.

Stivers, Camilla. 2002. *Gender Images in Public Administration: Legitimacy and the Administrative State,* 2nd edn. Thousand Oaks, CA: Sage.

Thornton, Patricia H. and William Ocasio. 2008. 'Institutional Logics'. In *The Sage Handbook of Organizational Institutionalism*, edited by Royston Greenwood,

Christine Oliver, Kerstin Sahlin, and Roy Suddaby. London and Thousand Oaks, CA: Sage, 99–129.

Verge, Tánia and Ana Espírito-Santo. 2016. 'Candidate Selection and Quota Compliance in Portugal and Spain'. *Government and Opposition* 51(03): 416–39.

Waylen, Georgina. 2007. *Engendering Transitions: Women's Mobilization, Institutions and Gender Outcomes*. Oxford: Oxford University Press.

Waylen, Georgina. 2014a. 'Informal Institutions, Institutional Change, and Gender Equality'. *Political Research Quarterly* 67(1): 212–23.

Waylen, Georgina. 2014b. 'A Seat at the Table? Is It Enough: Gender, Multi-Party Negotiations and Institutional Design in South Africa and Northern Ireland'. *Politics and Gender* 10(4): 495–523.

Weldon, S. Laurel. 2014. 'Using Statistical Methods to Study Institutions'. *Politics and Gender* 10(4):661–72.

Chapter 3

Local Heroes and 'Cute Hoors': Informal Institutions, Male Over-Representation and Candidate Selection in the Republic of Ireland

Leah Culhane

Candidate recruitment and selection has been highlighted as a, if not *the*, key process that must be examined if we are to understand global patterns of male parliamentary over-representation (Hinojosa 2012; Bjarnegård 2013; Kenny 2013). A significant amount of feminist work has explored how this process produces gendered outcomes both internationally (Lovenduski & Norris 1993, 1995; Caul 1999; Kittilson 2006; Murray 2010; Hinjosa 2012; Bjarnegård 2013; Kenny 2013) and in the Irish context (Randall & Smyth 1987; Fawcett 1992; Galligan 1993; McGing & White 2012). This rich body of work has been integral in informing our understanding of parties as the 'gatekeepers' of political representation and has highlighted the myriad of ways in which these party processes distribute power and privilege to gendered actors. Emerging within this literature is recognition of the importance of the informal institutions that govern political recruitment and selection and shape political outcomes. Although candidate recruitment and selection is generally governed by a set of formal institutions, namely the electoral system, the legal system and internal party rules, the process in practice is usually another story, with actors on the ground working within more informal understandings of 'the way things are done' (Kenny 2013; Bjarnegård and Kenny 2015). In order to fully understand male parliamentary over-representation, a step has therefore been made to gender informal institutions, that is, to highlight the ways in which the unwritten rules, practices, norms and narratives work to preserve and reproduce male dominance and privilege in the political sphere (Beckwith 2005; Krook & Mackay 2011).

This chapter discusses how the 'informal rules of the game' shape political recruitment and selection in the Republic of Ireland, and how this has translated into male over-representation on party tickets and within Dáil Éireann, the lower house of the Irish legislature. The informal institution under scrutiny is localism, which, quite simply, can be defined as a preference for the local. It can be identified as an informal institution insofar as it is the defining political logic that underlies a series of rules, norms and narratives that shape political behaviour within Irish politics. Although largely unwritten in the formal rules, this privileging of 'the local' is widely known about and shapes political recruitment and selection in a number of ways, two of which are examined in this chapter.

First, it has shaped informal candidate recruitment criteria, such that the perception of what makes an electable and therefore 'good' candidate is one who is locally recognised and known by constituents. Second, it has shaped perceptions of *who* should select candidates, a power which is principally attributed to the local branch members as opposed to central strategy committees. Although the literature on candidate recruitment and selection generally focuses on parties as gendered organisations in themselves, whose internal rules and norms provide different opportunities to gendered actors, this chapter focuses on localism as a cross-party institution which informs decisions and behaviour at both local and central levels. It therefore makes a step towards looking more broadly at how informal institutions enable male over-representation, which, prior to the introduction of a legislative gender quota in 2016, has never fallen below the level of 84 per cent.

The chapter begins by outlining a feminist institutionalist (FI) approach to candidate recruitment and selection, and argues that a focus on both the formal and informal aspects of political institutions enables us to more fully understand the problem of male parliamentary over-representation. It then details the case study of the Republic of Ireland, outlining the institutions that govern candidate recruitment and selection, namely the electoral system and localism. Following this, it addresses the main aim of the chapter: to understand how informal localised recruitment and a localised and democratised selection process contribute to male over-representation.

The key argument of the chapter is that central to localism and to the above practices is the need for aspirants to have personal networks, both within the electorate and within the party, a requirement that has enabled the maintenance of male political dominance. I resist suggesting that the need for networks is inherently detrimental for women. Rather, I take the stance that the interaction between formal and informal institutions shapes what types of networks matter and how they matter, that is, their potential for determining political outcomes. The analysis therefore suggests two things. First, with regard to recruitment, the desire for general election candidates with large brokerage networks is gendered insofar as it privileges those who already have political experience in local politics, the majority of whom are men. However, the analysis also suggests that, due to a masculinised perception of politics, men are more likely to be seen as potential political brokers and encouraged to put themselves forward to be local councillors. Second, the need for pre-existing personal networks at the selection stage rewards longevity and thus bestows disproportionate preference and privilege to incumbents, reproducing the masculine nature of Irish politics. Thus, it is a requirement that largely protects the masculinised status quo, allowing those who have already succeeded in getting into a position of power to protect it. The chapter concludes by suggesting that in order to more fully understand the patterns of male parliamentary dominance, more research is needed which connects informal institutions, networks and gendered power dynamics.

CANDIDATE SELECTION, INFORMAL INSTITUTIONS AND MALE OVER-REPRESENTATION

This chapter, like others in this volume, adopts a FI framework to explain the problem of male over-representation. The central contention of such an approach is that institutions, understood here as the rules, norms and practices that shape behaviour, are gendered (Krook & Mackay 2011). FI work is therefore interested in both 'the gendered character and the gendering effects' of political institutions (Mackay 2011, 181). Following from new institutionalist literature, a large amount of this work has also contributed to the recognition of informal institutions and their role in shaping political actions and outcomes. Both feminist and mainstream neo-institutionalists have sought to explore 'how things really work' by focusing their attention on the 'hidden lives' of institutions (Cheng & Tavits 2009; Hinjosa 2012; Bjarnegård 2013; Chappell & Waylen 2013; Kenny 2013; Waylen 2014). Indeed, one of the primary traits of neo-institutionalist analysis is its acceptance of a more expansive definition of institutions to include these informal aspects that work to constrain or enable actors. The most frequently drawn upon definition is that of Helmke and Levitsky (2004, 727), who purport that informal institutions are 'socially shared rules, usually unwritten, that are created, communicated, and enforced outside of officially sanctioned channels'. Although there is still a general agreement that institutions are the 'rules of the game' (North 1990, 3) that shape human behaviour and interaction, these rules now include formal and informal dimensions.

Specifically focusing on the recruitment process, an emerging body of FI work has carried out micro-level analysis, which examines the role of the informal in reproducing male dominance within political parties and on party tickets. Candidate selection and recruitment operates within, and is influenced by, a matrix of informal and formal party rules, practices and norms that are explicitly and implicitly gendered (Lovenduski & Norris 1993; Norris & Lovenduski 1995; Murray 2010; Bjarnegård 2013; Kenny 2013). The aim of this chapter, however, is to highlight what really matters with regards to recruitment and selection, to reveal what experience, traits and resources are needed to become and be considered a legitimate and electable candidate and consequently to detail whom this privileges. Indeed, the absence of formal barriers to women's participation in politics has led male over-representation to be framed as an unfortunate consequence of a gender-neutral, fair and effective system, which produces the best people for the job. These arguments, however, fail to take into account the 'informal rules of the game' that bestow significant advantage to specific actors.

Existing research, for example, has highlighted that contrary to being gender neutral, formal and informal rules around suitability are often infused with a masculine bias that reflects a privileging of certain traits and experience over others (Lovenduski 1998). Because the underlying rules were created by men, they 'ensure that the qualifications of men [are] better valued and [lead] more reliably to power and rewards' (Lovenduski 1998, 347). Even when women do have the necessary qualifications or experience, this may not translate into political capital. Experimental methods that focus on recruitment in the labour market have shown that when qualifications are controlled for, gender plays a strong part in determining who will be considered appropriate for specific types of jobs. In formal parliamentary politics, that which is valued, power, competition and an aggressive leadership style, all reflect dominant notions of masculinity, which are traditionally associated with, and attributed to, male bodies. This association shapes perceptions of who would make a 'good' politician and filters into political recruitment and selection. Thus, although informal rules often privilege qualifications that men disproportionately hold, men are often assumed a priori to be more suitable politicians. Informal localised candidate criteria, for example, have often, in practice, translated into 'the local man' and have been used as an exclusionary discourse to 'other' both female and ethnic minority aspirants despite competing definitions and degrees of 'localness' (Evans 2012; Kenny 2013).

The issue of *who* selects has also been highlighted as an important aspect when analysing the maintenance and reproduction of male dominance (Hinojosa 2012; Bjarnegård & Kenny 2016) with gender scholars examining the effects of inclusivity (how many people are involved in the decision) and decentralisation (at what level the decision is made) on gendered patterns of representation. Largely, the role of local influence on selection has not been viewed positively for those interested in gendered change, with powerful local actors usually being powerful local men (Bjarnegård & Kenny 2016). Furthermore, a centralised selection system (combined with political will) is considered integral to the success of affirmative action measures, which aim to challenge male dominance (Lovenduski & Norris 1993; Kittilson 2006). Looking at the effects of institutional configurations, Hinjosa's (2012) extensive study found that centralised-exclusive selection is beneficial to female candidacies, while the combination of decentralised and inclusive selection impedes it. In the Irish context, the decentralised and inclusive nature of the process is generally pinpointed as a hindering feature with regards to more balanced representation, considering that local influence over selection inhibits central strategy committees and party leaders from promoting female candidates (Buckley et al. 2015).

Interest in networks and the role they play in influencing and gendering political outcomes is also burgeoning within FI analysis. Conceptualising networks, FI scholars have been careful to distinguish them from informal institutions in themselves (Bjarnegård et al. 2016; Chappell and Mackay this volume). As Chappell and Mackay argue in this volume, networks should be viewed as groups of actors, which maintain, deploy or carry informal institutions as opposed to informal rules, norms and practices in themselves. Networks here are similarly conceptualised as groups of actors, however, the emphasis is not solely on the plurality of actors or on the organising potential of political actors who group together, either formally or informally, to advance shared interests. Rather, the emphasis includes the personal connections between those actors. Thus, the terms connections and networks are often used interchangeably.

Although there is a broad consensus that networks matter, how they matter in particular institutional contexts is the subject of empirical analysis. In relation to political aspirants, the role of networks has been highlighted as key to ensuring selection in many contexts (Bjarnegård 2013; Franceschet & Piscopo 2013; Kenny 2013). Networks provide the necessary resources that are needed to be selected, be they human (Franceschet & Piscopo 2013) or financial. Access to strong networks is an informal precondition for becoming a candidate and who you know, as opposed to what you know, is a key determinant for securing a nomination (Bjarnegård 2013; Franceschet & Piscopo 2013). If who you know is essential for succeeding in certain political contexts, why then does this bestow advantage to men? Bjarnegård (2013) offers the concept of homosocial capital to explore the gendered nature of both trust and networks, arguing that men, who disproportionately hold positions of political power, tend to recruit and include other men. Homosocial capital, she argues, 'highlights both the fact that an interpersonal capital needs to be built up before an individual is included in a political network, and the fact that there are gendered aspects to this interpersonal capital: it is predominantly accessible for other men' (Bjarnegård 2013, 24). In Thailand (Bjarnegård 2013, 24) and Argentina (Franceschet & Piscopo 2013), for example, this has shaped unequal access to clientlist networks which are necessary in order to become political power brokers. A move has therefore been made to gender the nature of trust and networks, which is an important step in understanding the persistence of male political dominance. While this highlights that gender mediates access to (already male dominated) networks, this chapter makes an effort to highlight some of the ways in which the need for pre-existing personal networks bestows privilege to certain gender actors. The remainder of this chapter draws on these insights in order to understand and unpack the problem of male parliamentary dominance.

DATA AND METHODS

Despite acknowledgement of the distinctness of different institutional contexts, particularly the specific interplay between formal and informal rules, a comparative, yet qualitative, research agenda focusing on gender, political recruitment and informal institutions is beginning to emerge (Bjarnegård & Kenny 2016). Localism has been identified in a number of contexts (Randall & Smyth 1987; Evans 2012; Kenny 2013) and thus, the specific effect of this informal institution on recruitment and selection is of interest to a broad range of scholars. Ireland is a particularly interesting case study as it is a country in which localism is particularly pronounced and thus offers clear insights into its functioning and effects. The case study also aims, however, to contribute to a broader FI agenda by unpacking the relationship between institutions and networks and, thus, also has implications for other contexts where social connections are central to progressing.

In order to investigate the gendered and informal aspects of recruitment and selection, in-depth, semi-structured interviews were carried out. Although FI has thus far been marked by methodological pluralism, in-depth interviews were chosen as they provided a rich insight into the informal aspects of selection and recruitment, which other research methods could not provide. The data gathered from these interviews were compared with the formal rules set out in party rulebooks and constitutions and internal party documents to uncover the importance of the unwritten in guiding gendered recruitment and selection. In total, sixty-seven interviews were carried out with male and female affiliates of the four main Irish political parties in the Republic of Ireland: Sinn Féin, Fianna Fáil, Fine Gael and the Labour Party.[1] Those interviewed are characterised by their involvement in the selection process and included aspirants, candidates, incumbents and members of central election strategy committees. Further interviews were conducted with academics and members of the 50/50 campaign and Women for Election group considering the particular knowledge these actors have with regards to political recruitment and selection. Interviews have been anonymised so that actors could speak with ease about personal experiences and internal party procedures, without being identified. The fact that many participants requested this highlights that political recruitment and selection remain sensitive processes, a 'secret garden' for political parties that is regulated by rules outside those that are written down.

The interviews took place in the year preceding the 2016 general election, when the candidate selection process was taking place. This general election was the first one in the history of the state whereby a legislative gender quota was applied which obliged Irish political parties to run no less than 30 percent male and female candidates or face losing half of their state funding. New formal rules such as these have the potential to alter selection and recruitment methods and thus patterns of inequality. It is important, however, to understand the pre-existing context onto which this new rule is being layered in order to fully comprehend the outcomes of institutional change. This chapter therefore deals with the context preceding this new rule, a context whereby the level of male parliamentary representation has never fallen below 84 percent.

THE IRISH CASE

Political Parties and Male Over-Representation

The over-representation of men is an issue that pertains as much to Ireland as it does to the rest of the globe. After the 2011 elections, men made up 84 percent of Irish TDs,[2] with 480 male candidates running compared to eighty-six females (McGing & White 2012). Men won 141 of the 166 Dáil seats, with this decreasing to 140 following the 2014 by-elections. Following the last election, Ireland was therefore 83rd in the global ranking of women in parliament and 20th of the twenty-seven EU member states. The over-representation of men in parliament has thus been a key concern for Irish feminist activists, academics and politicians alike. Three parties have traditionally dominated parliamentary politics in the Republic of Ireland: Fianna Fáil, Fine Gael and the Labour Party. Although the latter rose in popularity in 2011, general elections have historically been a 'two horse race' between Fianna Fáil and Fine Gael. In contrast to other party systems, a strong right/ left divide does not characterise Irish political parties. Fianna Fáil and Fine Gael were both born out of nationalist concerns in the years following the signing of the Anglo-Irish Treaty (1921), which established the Irish Free State and eventually led to the consolidation of independence from Britain. The treaty split the radical nationalist party Sinn Féin, who spearheaded the struggle for independence, resulting in the establishment of pro-treaty and anti-treaty groups, which went on to become the basis for the two parties. The Labour Party is ideologically more distinct. A social democratic party of the centre-left, it was originally launched in 1912 as the political wing of the

Irish Trade Union Congress. In recent years, modern-day Sinn Féin has also become a realistic challenger in the Republic of Ireland, residing before on the sidelines of general elections. A left leaning nationalist party, concerned mainly with achieving a united and socially democratic Ireland, it is the only all-island party of the four.

The four main political parties have differed in their attempts to address gender imbalance in the past and consequently have had varying levels of male dominance on party tickets, demonstrating that internal party ideology and internal rules do matter in terms of representation. The Labour Party, for example, introduced soft quotas in the 1980s as a result of internal lobbying from the women's group within the party, Labour Women, and although these targets were often not met, they did produce a much higher number of female candidates in comparison to the other parties at a much earlier point in the party's history (Buckley 2013). The Labour Party has therefore traditionally had the most gender-balanced slates reaching a high of 27 percent female candidacy in 1997. The other three parties have introduced soft or rhetorical measures at various points in recent years yet have also failed to meet their own party targets and promises on numerous occasions. Prior to the introduction of the 2016 legislative gender quota, Fine Gael's highest percentage of female candidates on a general election party ticket stood at 18 percent (2002), Fianna Fáil's at 14.7 percent (2011) and Sinn Féin's at 24.4 percent (2007). This high number of men on party tickets has, of course, resulted in a higher number of men in parliament. How male dominance is maintained and reproduced in individual party settings and through what means should be explored in a broader analysis. The next section, however, attempts to give a general overview of the broader system–level institutions which affect recruitment and selection. In doing so, it highlights some features that are common across parties, which may be useful for broader comparative analysis.

PR-STV and Localism

The most notable feature of Irish politics is localism, an informal institution that is widely recognised by both Irish scholars (Gallagher 1980; Carty 1981; Chubb 1992; Gallagher & Komito 2010) and political actors[3] as central to Irish political culture. Localism, as a preference for and privileging of 'the local', is the defining political logic that guides Irish politics. With regards to recruitment and selection, localism manifests in cross-party preference for 'local candidates', that is, candidates who are from and known in the constituency they represent. Unlike other political contexts, Irish TDs are expected to reside in the locality they represent and are elected based on their ability to secure gains; for individual constituents and for the broader local area

(Chubb 1992; Gallagher 1980). Many descriptions of Irish politics detail this 'brokerage' relationship between politician and voters, whereby elected representatives are expected to act as a medium between local constituents and the state's administrative apparatus (Carty 1981; Gallagher & Komito 1992, 2010). This relationship is often distinguished from clientelism in the existing literature insofar as politicians rarely distribute that which constituents are not entitled to; rather they use their influence and knowledge to facilitate access to state resources. The elected representative is therefore more akin to a 'lawyer, who operates not by bribing the judge, but by ensuring that the case is presented better than the citizen would be able to present it' (Gallagher & Komito 1992, 140). Although brokerage relationships are viewed more favourably than clientelist, both political logics depend on the reproduction and maintenance of extensive local networks.

The localised (and personalised) nature of Irish politics has been shaped by Ireland's electoral system, the single transferable vote system of proportional representation (PR-STV). Indeed STV systems tend to foster this kind of personality-based, candidate-centred voting considering that the electorate must express a preference for candidates (Gallagher 1980). Running in multi-member constituencies that range from three to five seats, parties may run a number of candidates in any one district. Unlike both single member district and PR-List systems, there is also no party list. Considering that voters can vote across party lines with no restraint from the parties themselves, intra-party competition is exceptionally fierce with candidates often fighting for the remaining seat in a constituency with a member of their own party. Observers have remarked how, unable to distinguish themselves on party lines, aspirants must compete on a personal basis and must have a significant personal vote (Gallagher 1980; Carty 1981). One such way of creating this is through extensive local constituency work and the creation of local brokerage networks, thus reproducing the expectation from the electorate.

Localism also shapes perceptions of *who* should select. Within party politics, localism is often used to denote a preference for constituency-based ways of organising and decision-making. Consequently, candidate selection in the Republic of Ireland is largely decentralised, with those at the local branch level perceived as having the best knowledge on local interests and by extension potential candidates who can represent such interests. The process is often described as 'constituency-level selection, with national supervision and influence' (Gallagher & Marsh 1988, 125). Each party adheres to a three-tier system of branch, constituency and national-level organisation, with additional district-level structures existing within some regions/parties. Candidates are both nominated and selected at local selection conventions by party members through the one member, one vote system with each member of the associated constituency afforded voting rights so long as they are a standing member of the party for a specific length of time and they have paid their associated membership fees. The basic process in itself is also similar. Following the decision that a selection convention is to be held, party headquarters write to members from the relevant constituency and their associated branches. A nomination period is opened, usually a week or two, where any paid-up member can nominate party members for selection. After this period is complete, a list of aspirants is confirmed, who then have a further number of weeks to campaign the party membership in that area for member votes.

Although selection has been largely decentralised in practice, there has been an overall trend towards increasing central power (Gallagher 1988; Galligan 2003; Reidy 2011) with each of the parties now possessing a central committee or department through which selection is overseen and instructed. Even though nomination and selection is largely a local affair, the National Executive can influence outcomes in two ways. First, the central level has the power (in varying degrees) to appoint, veto, deselect and ratify candidates. Vetoing or deselecting a candidate, however, is rare for fear of local backlash. Appointing or 'adding' candidates to a locally selected panel is more common, although also a delicate process. Added candidates are rarely 'parachuted' in, completely unknown by the local organisation. Rather, they are often unsuccessful aspirants or local party members. The central imposition of an 'outsider' is considered in opposition to the 'spirit of the organizations' (Gallagher 1988, 131). Thus, although power is formally allocated to central committees, selection by local members is expected and considered legitimate.

Second, the central level exercises power through its ability to devise and issue convention directives. These guidelines specify to a convention how many candidates are to be selected and in some cases the candidate criteria. Despite the widely acknowledged existence of localism in the Irish context, few studies have sought to understand how this has shaped political recruitment and selection, and contributed to male over-representation. The next section looks at how localism has shaped first recruitment and then selection, and seeks to explain how this has privileged men and, particularly, existing incumbents.

GENDERING RECRUITMENT

Informal Candidate Criteria and Localism

Formal rules regarding the selection of candidates in Ireland are set out in the party rules books and constitutions and stipulate the guidelines that pertain to the process. These official rules largely set out who is responsible for selection by detailing the distribution of power between local branches and central committees, and outlining the procedure for local conventions. Furthermore, the party constitutions give more details on the selection of candidates, as opposed to their recruitment. Thus, a large amount of discrepancy exists in terms of how candidates are actually found, through what means and by what criteria. Consequently, the 'recruitment' of candidates in the Irish context is largely informal. Aspirants are largely drawn from local branch structures but there is no formal process whereby people are approached or asked to run. Rather, 'everyone is a recruiter'[4] and informal encouragement from local branch officials or the national level to seek a nomination is the norm. There are also no formal criteria that determine a candidate's suitability. Basic eligibility requirements state that aspirants must have been a party member for a specific amount of time and must take a partly pledge that states allegiance to the party. However, other determinants of suitability or definitions of merit, such as educational or political experience, are wholly absent across each of the parties' internal documents. Unlike comparative party processes that mimic corporate recruitment, there is also little to no process in measuring a candidate's suitability, either at the central or at the local level. With the exception of the Labour Party,[5] application forms, job descriptions and interview processes are absent in the Irish context. After securing two nominations from local members, aspirants have the task of contacting other members and branches personally and individually pleading their case as the best person for the job.

Despite the lack of formal criteria and screening process, those who have a hand in recruitment and selection, at both the local and central levels, have a strong sense of informal criteria. Due to the extent of localism in Irish political culture, it is widely acknowledged that an aspirant's local profile is key to determining 'a good candidate'. The preference for 'local heroes'[6,7] is a cross-party phenomenon, with the ideal candidate being one who is 'big in the community',[8] with 'extensive local connections' and 'name recognition'.[9] Although it was thought that local candidates could better represent the interests of those in their constituency, seeking a candidate with a local profile is more closely tied with the broader electoral concerns of political parties. As was outlined in the previous section, the expectation that candidates should know voters on a personal or local level is a strong determinant of electability. Localism does not, therefore, just represent a preference for candidates from the local area. Having a base within the local constituency is a necessary, but not sufficient criteria to be considered legitimate. Rather, a range of strong networks is integral to the perception of being local and has shaped ideas about what makes a good and electable candidate. The assessment of electability is not only uniform across parties but is also across party levels.

Commenting on who would make a successful candidate, a high central-level male strategist from Fianna Fáil remarked:

> Big in the community geography. But you do know when you meet a candidate whether a candidate's a candidate. It's a bit like if you're walking through 6th class in a primary school and you're watching the men . . . or the women playing football. Anyone who knows their football will walk up and say 'that girl will make the county team' . . . What determines that statement being made? Tis the same.[10]

The preceding statement illustrates two things. First, despite a lack of formal criteria, there is an institutionalised informal perception of electability. If you know politics, if you are aware of the rules of the political game, you know what is needed to succeed, namely local recognition and networks. Second, despite a lack of screening process, there is a perception that those involved in selection, at both the local and central levels, are able to personally judge who has local recognition and networks.

The desire for local recognition and networks need not privilege men. It has often been argued in fact that women's political engagement has been more concerned with the locality, with women opting to invest their energies in grassroots issues and organisations (Lovenduski 1993, 13). Thus, it might be hypothesised that a local orientation would offer women a gendered advantage. Unpacking why 'local women' were less frequently approached and encouraged, both within branch structures and in the local community, the explanation that 'women are invisible' was reoccurring. This begs the question as to which networks matter, and what local experience is valued.

Local Political Experience: Seeking Existing Brokers

Most discernibly, holding an elected post previously is desirable. Those who have already succeeded in becoming an elected representative have had time to build and maintain extensive brokerage networks in the constituency and thus have greater local name recognition. Furthermore, they have proven electability. It has long been argued that the desire for incumbents reproduces the status quo by favouring existing elites. For non-incumbent TDs, a track record in local government is key to being considered a legitimate candidate with local councillors holding the same advantages as incumbents but to a slightly lesser extent. Indeed, candidates for the general election are largely drawn from this pool of aspirants. Considering that incumbency is gendered insofar as both local and national government structures are and have historically been male-dominated, this criterion is readily met by a much larger number of male aspirants than female (Buckley et al. 2014, 2015).

Although local experience is important to candidate success in general elections (Gallagher 1980; Weeks 2008; Reidy 2011), the use of representative experience as one of the sole determinants of electability serves to devalue other criteria and thus acts as a mechanism of exclusion. Previous polling results or 'tallies' frequently act as hard evidence for electability and for aspirants with different experience and backgrounds, this evidence is impossible to supply. One explicitly feminist member of the central Labour Party remarked on the trouble of attempting to get a female aspirant accepted on to the ticket, despite the fact that she had no 'tallies' from the previous election:

> Every time you would talk about her winnability, track record, media profile, the tallies were just thrown on the table, physically, aggressively . . . that's what you were up against and no she hadn't got that, so culturally the patriarchy was maintained through the mechanism of maintaining that way of making decisions and not bringing in other criteria for making decisions, . . . her visibility to the electorate was much more significant, her policy capacity, but that didn't matter, numbers was how patriarchy maintained its power base.[11]

Therefore, as is articulated in the previous quote, local experience and incumbency are often used to maintain male dominance, even when other candidates may have broader local recognition without experience as a representative.

Local Recognition: Seeking Potential Brokers

Electoral experience aside, the dominant perception of the ideal candidate as a political broker is also gendered, with women less likely to be perceived as suitable political brokers. The colloquial term 'cute hoor'[12] is often used to denote the archetypal political figure in the Irish context (O'Carroll 1987; Collins & Butler 2001). He is the wheeler and dealer, the crafty rogue who can 'get things done' with a wink and a nod. With the onset of the financial crash in 2008 and revelations of extensive political corruption, the 'cute hoor-dom', which characterised the politics of Celtic Tiger Ireland, has become subject to scrutiny. Through a number of public tribunals and enquiries, a political system that was embedded with corruption and cronyism has been revealed. The now-infamous 'Galway tent' has become a particular symbol of this political zeitgeist. The annual fundraiser saw Fianna Fáil elites entertain and rub shoulders with elite property developers and bankers at the Galway horse races each year. The 'cute hoor' therefore has gained negative connotations and has now come to be associated with political corruption, the Irish banking crisis and the unsavoury relationship between politicians and their political funding. The term, however, is far from new and has often been used to describe the ideal political 'broker' in the past. In 1987, O' Carroll remarked:

> . . . to be successful in politics aspirants to office have to be able to show they have power. Those who can deliver material favours are said to have 'pull'. In the continuous, intense competition necessitated by the electoral system, 'pull' indicates an ability to 'deliver' more than other competitors for political office. The fact that most of that which is delivered is imaginary in no way lessens the degree of confidence in the person who is seen to have 'pull' . . . In local parlance the actions which most strikingly demonstrate power, however, are termed 'strokes'. The perpetrator of a stroke is called a 'cute hoor', a term which denotes a certain admiration for the way in which he outmanoeuvres his [emphasis added] competitors'. (O'Carroll 1987, 82)

If the ideal politician reflects a masculine bias, so too does the 'cute hoor.' Implicit in the notion of the local Irish broker is the wink-and-elbow language of masculinity and homosociality. It is a way of doing politics that depends on the ability to wield power through informal networks of influence. The ability to 'play the game' in this way was seen as incompatible with femininity, presenting politics as a dirty and sometime cut-throat business. 'Visibility' is not therefore an issue of presence; rather it is one of recognition. Although women may have local recognition and indeed local networks, they are not seen to have the right sort of networks, nor to be able to wield their networks in the appropriate way. This tells us more about why local structures are male-dominated and sheds some light on who is viewed more generally as having brokerage capacity.

On a practical level, attention must also be paid to sites of recruitment in terms of potential local brokers. Traditionally, there has been a strong inclination towards approaching men who have played hurling or Gaelic football[13] for their counties (Gallagher 1980). This is partially due to the instant name recognition that local sporting heroes have in their constituencies, much akin to 'celebrity candidates' in other contexts. Indeed, the reoccurring description of the ideal candidate as one involved in the GAA (Gaelic Athletic Associations) is unsurprising considering the unparalleled importance of these local sporting clubs in Irish (particularly rural) communities. However, local GAA clubs in themselves are extensive, pre-established loyalty networks so that those who are sufficiently active within them at a local level are already in positions to access a broad range of contacts in the local community and by extension have 'pull.' They either already are, or have potential to be brokers.

Although women and men are involved in Gaelic sports, as both members and players, local sporting organisations remain largely a 'male preserve' and are gendered in terms of the distribution of resources, recognition and particularly in terms of leadership positions (Liston 2006). Furthermore, sporting experience does not, however, seem to be as valuable to women here with sporting capital translating much more readily into political capital for men. In McMurrow's book, *Dáil Stars* (2010), for example, he highlights how the GAA has been a breeding ground for Irish politicians for over a century, devoting each of the fifteen chapters to men who have transitioned from the organisation into politics.

Furthermore, the GAA club acts as a space whereby trust, loyalty and friendships can be established and developed. The local GAA club is an 'in-group', and involvement in it already expresses a common local identity and sense of belonging with those involved. Membership and participation in the GAA was considered a signifier of activism and commitment to the local community, despite the fact that local organisations are non-partisan and not explicitly political. Furthermore, it allows dedication and hard work to be demonstrated. As one male candidate remarked on this:

> You have to know people to know they're committed. If you work with them in that or see them they are committed. It's parochialism really too, if you're involved in the GAA you would say that person is one of our own and we want one of our own as a councillor.[14]

The preceding statement highlights the necessity to be trusted, to be considered 'an insider' when entering Irish politics. In a system where informal networks, interpersonal capital and who you know are so important, the GAA is a space where those connections can be made, and where trust, loyalties and friendships can be built up.

GENDERING SELECTION

Local Selection, Networks and Male Dominance

The localised and democratised nature of selection in Ireland has already been identified as contributing to gendered outcomes in the Irish context (Randall & Smyth 1987; McGing & White 2012). Being selected at a convention is dependent on getting votes from local members. This of course favours incumbents, most of whom are male, who are able to depend on their long-standing supporters for votes. Indeed, many supporters within branch structures are explicitly loyal to a particular aspirant, something that is fostered by the fact that incumbents often install personally loyal supporters and relatives in the local organisation over time who often then obtain official positions of power within the branch. Elected representatives therefore create 'personal machines' that work to preserve the power of their chosen TD (Carty 1981) and hinder potential competitors. Furthermore, the 'stuffing' of selection conventions with relatives and personal supporters is a widely known and common informal practice. This involves aspirants signing up members to the local party organisation, who remain inactive until the night of the convention, when they then 'come out of the woodwork' to cast a vote. Formal criteria surrounding voting rights state that members must have been signed up (and paid up) for at least two years, a rule that is aimed at preventing this practice. As opposed to halting it, however, these criteria again serve to advantage those who have been there the longest.

Central Intervention and Male Dominance

Although local selection has been pinpointed in the Irish context as key to reproducing male dominance, central intervention, through the use of formal rules, has also served this function. The priorities of the selectorate at the local level are often deemed at odds with that of the central level, the presumption being that local influence tends to foster strong personal loyalties that subvert broader party priorities such as producing a balanced slate of 'electable candidates'. As was previously highlighted however, 'electability' is a highly gendered concept and thus, the local well-networked man is often as appealing to central-level strategists as to the local constituency. In practice, the formal rules are often used at the selection stage to protect the position and interests of incumbents. Incumbents, having already proved their electability, are valuable assets to the party. Furthermore, if an incumbent defects to a different party or decides to run as an independent candidate, this could result in the loss of a seat for the party, as loyal voters may vote for the incumbent regardless of partisan allegiances. Using electability as a bargaining tool, the value placed on incumbents therefore enables them to protect both their own positions and those within their personal networks through central intervention. As one male Fine Gael candidate remarked about previously competing against an incumbent:

> He [the incumbent] would have been very friendly and still is with . . . one of our chief electoral strategists at the time . . . there was a huge aversion to having anyone run with him. It was felt, or so it seemed to me, that he needed to be protected and if he had a running mate he would potentially lose his seat to his running mate, if there was only going to be one Fine Gael seat in that constituency it would be whoever wasn't him basically. So at all costs they said no way, you are not going in there.[15]

Although it was perceived that the party could have maintained a seat with another candidate, the incumbent was protected as the 'tried and tested' model, and was able to maintain his position and power through central intervention. Thereby, open competition was hindered for other aspirants who could potentially have displaced him. The above statement points to the importance of intra-party networks in advancing aspirants at the selection stage. Although it is rare that the interests of incumbents are protected over the chance of winning a seat, 'all things equal', personal loyalties, friendship and kinship have significant sway in determining which electable aspirant benefits from the formal rules and central intervention. In this case, a long-standing friendship with a person of influence enabled the exclusion of other aspirants from the selection process. This does not just advantage incumbents, but also those who they wish to be their successors, allowing systems of patronage to be realised at the selection stage. As one female Fine Gael aspirant remarked:

> The selection convention was set up so that the members I had signed up wouldn't have been members for two years. I asked them to delay it by a few weeks but he [the incumbent] said no. His best man was running against me so blood is thicker than water.[16]

The formal rules and informal personal networks therefore interact with social connections conditioning political strategies, central decisions and the use of formal rules. This calls into question the tension between the priorities of the central and local levels, a presumption that is evident in both mainstream and feminist literature regarding candidate selection. Strong local influence over selection does hinder the opportunity for central strategy committees and party leaders to intervene with regards to gender; however, it is important to acknowledge that central intervention has also at times reproduced male dominance as opposed to challenge it. The issue of gender, therefore, calls into question the supposed dichotomy between the two, pointing to the importance of both shared gendered perceptions of electability and personal networks, which connect actors at different levels of the organisation.

The experience of being 'shafted' or 'blocked' is certainly not a practice that pertains only to female party members. However, considering that central intervention has been wielded on gendered criteria of 'electability' and furthermore on the basis of personal loyalties, which must be built up over time, newcomers to the game, particularly female newcomers, are disadvantaged. These practices at both the central and locals level raise questions not only about gender but about the transparency and fairness of the selection system. The stifling of aspirants, at both the local and national levels, was not perceived to be problematic for the functioning of a democratic or meritocratic selection system, rather it was seen as 'politics as usual':

> The problem is they say they shafted someone but the reality is there's someone there already. What actually happens is there someone else in situ. You can't be the captain of the team if there's a captain already, even though you want to be the captain. But what happens then is that people who surround the captain don't want the competition for the captain so they stop competition. That is the world over.[17]

Hindering open and fair competition was also not perceived as a structural or institutional problem. Respondents across Fine Gael, Fianna Fáil and the Labour Party referenced notable female aspirants who had been 'blocked' by existing TDs, but who had left and built a successful career in another party, thus overcoming the barriers they had faced. Speaking about the blocking of female candidates, the previous respondent continued:

> You have to believe yourself that you want it – man or woman – and if you are good enough you will make it. If you are good enough in any political party you will make it.[18]

As the preceding comment illustrates, an unfair playing field is widely accepted in the Irish context and if not legitimised, at least normalised.

CONCLUSION

This chapter set out to identify how an informal institution, localism, has shaped candidate recruitment and selection and how this has (re)produced male dominance on party tickets and within the Irish parliament. Through data obtained from in-depth qualitative interviews with political actors, it has highlighted how, in the absence of formal criteria, informal and localised criterion of the electable candidate has favoured experience disproportionately held by men. It also argues, however, that the stereotypical political broker is masculinised in itself, such that men are more likely to be perceived to be able to do a certain type of networking. They are more likely to be considered both local heroes and 'cute hoors'. This allows us to unpack who is informally encouraged at the local level. Also, the need for influential and numerous personal connections rewards those who have been there the longest, and who have had the chance to install and build personal networks at both the local and central levels. This raises questions about how easy it is to access a political career as a newcomer to the game and will obviously have implications with regards to attempts at institutional change. Indeed, further research is needed to examine how formal attempts to challenge male dominance, through the introduction of the recent gender quota, will interact with and change a largely informal yet institutionalised system. Furthermore, with regards to both recruitment and selection, this chapter largely details the importance of personal networks for advancing political aspirants and makes an effort towards outlining some of the gendered implications of an institution that rewards and values who, as opposed to what, you know. It therefore offers insights into other informal institutions that rely on networks such as clientelism and patronage and calls into question gendered definitions of merit and its role in determining political success. Further research is needed in this area if we are to more fully understand male political over-representation.

NOTES

1. The breakdown of interviewees by sex was twenty-five men and forty-three women.

2. TD is an abbreviation of Teachta Dála, a member of Dáil Éireann, the lower house of the Oireachtas (the Irish Parliament). It is the Irish equivalent of an MP.

3. Whether viewed positively or negatively, the importance of localism was mentioned by all of the interviewees.

4. Interview no. 27, female party strategist (central level) for the Labour Party, March 2015.

5. A notable difference between the parties is the use of Candidate Selection Boards by the Labour Party, which screen aspirants prior to the selection convention. The Labour Party is therefore the only party who has an official screening process and the right to intervene before a convention. There are however no objective criteria that these panels attempt to measure. Thus, although the Labour Party has a process, what that process is trying to assess is undefined.

6. Interview no. 12, female party strategist (central level), February 2015.

7. Interview no. 66, female candidate for Sinn Féin, November 2016.

8. Interview no. 37, male party strategist (central level) for Fianna Fáil, July 2015.

9. Interview no. 12, female party strategist (central level), February 2015.

10. Interview no. 37, male party strategist (central level) for Fianna Fáil, July 2015.

11. Interview no. 12, female party strategist (central level), February 2015.

12. This is slang for the term, cute whore, which is evidently a gendered term in itself.

13. A type of football played mainly in Ireland.

14. Interview no.49, male local councillor for Sinn Féin, October 2015.

15. Interview no. 7, male local councillor for Fine Gael, January 2015.

16. Interview no. 51, female candidate for Fine Gael, November 2015.

17. Interview no. 37, male party strategist (central level) for Fianna Fáil, July 2015.

18. Interview no. 37, male party strategist (central level) for Fianna Fáil, July 2015.

REFERENCES

Beckwith, Karen. 2005. 'A common language of gender?' *Politics & Gender* 1(1): 128–137.

Bjarnegård, Elin. 2013. *Gender, Informal Institutions and Political Recruitment: Explaining Male Dominance in Parliamentary Representation.* Houndmills, Basingstoke: Palgrave Macmillan.

Bjarnegård, Elin and Meryl Kenny. 2015. 'Revealing the "Secret Garden": The informal dimensions of political recruitment'. *Politics & Gender* 11(4): 748–753.

Bjarnegård, Elin and Meryl Kenny. 2016. 'Comparing candidate selection: A feminist institutionalist approach'. *Government and Opposition* 51(3): 370–392.

Bjarnegård, Elin, Meryl Kenny and Tánia Verge. 2016. 'Conceptualizing informal networks within feminist institutionalism,' Paper prepared for the 24th World Congress of Political Science, IPSA, Poznan, 23–28 July.

Buckley, Fiona .2013. 'Women and politics in Ireland: The road to sex quotas'. *Irish Political Studies* 28(3): 341–359.

Buckley, Fiona, Mack Mariani and Timothy White. 2014. 'Will legislative gender quotas increase female representation in Ireland? A Feminist Institutionalism analysis'. *Representation* 50(4): 471–484.

Buckley, Fiona, Mack Mariani, Claire McGing and Timothy White. 2015. 'Is local office a springboard for women to Dáil Éireann?' *Journal of Women, Politics & Policy* 36(3): 311–335.

Carty, R.K. 1981. *Party and Parish Pump: Electoral Politics in Ireland.* Waterloo, Ontario: Wilfrid Laurier University Press.

Caul, Miki. 1999. 'Women's representation in parliament: The role of political parties'. *Party Politics* 5(1): 79–98.

Chappell, Louise and Georgina Waylen. 2013. 'Gender and the hidden life of institutions'. *Public Administration* 91(3): 599–615.

Cheng, Christine and Margit Tavits. 2009. 'Informal influences in selecting female political candidates'. *Political Research Quarterly* 64(2): 460–471.

Chubb, Basil. 1992. *The Government and Politics of Ireland,* 3rd ed. Harlow: Longman.

Collins, Neil and Patrick Butler. 2001.'Cute hoors as local heroes: Politicians and public service delivery'. *Irish Journal of Management* 22(1): 113.

Evans, Elizabeth. 2012. 'Selecting the "Right Sort": Patterns of political recruitment in British by-elections'. *Parliamentary Affairs* 65(1): 195–213.

Fawcett, Liz. 1992. 'The recruitment of women to local politics in Ireland: A case study'. *Irish Political Studies* 7(1): 41–55.

Franceschet, Susan and Jennifer Piscopo. 2013. 'Sustaining gendered practices? Power, parties, and elite political networks in Argentina'. *Comparative Political Studies* 47(1): 85–110.

Gallagher, Michael. 1980. 'Candidate selection in Ireland: The impact of localism and the electoral system'. *British Journal of Political Science* 10(4): 489–503.

Gallagher, Michael and Lee Komito. 1992. 'Dail deputies and their constituency work'. In *Politics in the Republic of Ireland*, 1st edition, eds. John Coakley and Michael Gallagher. Galway: PSAI press.

Gallagher, Michael and Lee Komito. 2010. 'The constituency role of Dáil deputies'. In *Politics in the Republic of Ireland,* 5th edition, eds. John Coakley and Michael Gallagher. London: Routledge and PSAI Press.

Gallagher, Michael and Michael Marsh (eds.). 1988. *Candidate Selection in Comparative Perspective: The Secret Garden of Politics.* London: Sage.

Galligan, Yvonne. 1993. 'Party politics and gender in the Republic of Ireland'. In *Gender and Party Politics,* eds. Joni Lovenduski and Pippa Norris. London: Sage, 147–167.

Galligan, Yvonne. 2003. 'Candidate selection: More democratic or more centrally controlled?' In *How Ireland Voted 2002,* eds. Michael Gallagher, Michael Marsh and Paul Mitchell. Houndmills, UK: Palgrave Macmillan.

Helmke, Gretchen and Steven Levitsky. 2004. 'Informal institutions and comparative politics: A research agenda'. *Perspectives on Politics* 2(4): 725–740.

Hinojosa, Magda. 2012. *Selecting Women, Electing Women: Political Representation and Candidate Selection in Latin America.* Philadelphia: Temple University Press.

Kenny, Meryl. 2013. *Gender and Political Recruitment: Theorizing Institutional Change.* Basingstoke: Palgrave Macmillan.

Kittilson, Miki Caul. 2006. *Challenging Parties, Changing Parliaments: Women and Elected Office in Contemporary Western Europe.* Columbus OH: Ohio State University Press.

Krook, Mona Lena and Fiona Mackay. 2011. *Gender, Politics and Institutions: Towards a Feminist Institutionalism.* Basingstoke: Palgrave Macmillan.

Liston, Katie. 2006. 'Women's soccer in the Republic of Ireland: Some preliminary sociological comments'. *Soccer and Society* 7(2–3): 364–384.

Lovenduski, Joni.1993. 'Introduction: The dynamics of gender and party'. In *Gender and Party Politics,* eds. Joni Lovenduski and Pippa Norris. London: Sage.

Lovenduski, Joni. 1998. 'Gendering research in political science'. *Annual Review of Political Science* 1(1): 333–56.

Lovenduski, Joni and Pippa Norris (eds.). 1993. *Gender and Party Politics.* London: Sage.

Lovenduski, Joni and Pippa Norris (eds.). 1995. *Political Recruitment: Gender, Race and Class in the British Parliament.* Cambridge: Cambridge University Press.

Mackay, Fiona. 2011. 'Conclusion'. In *Gender, Politics and Institutions: Towards a Feminist Institutionalism,* eds. M.L. Krook and F. Mackay. Basingstoke: Palgrave Macmillan, 181–196.

McGing, Claire and Timothy White. 2012. 'Gender and electoral representation in Ireland'. *Études Irlandaises* 37 (2): 33–48.

McMorrow, Conor. 2010. *Dáil Stars: From Croke Park to Leinster House.* Mentor Books: Dublin.

Murray, Rainbow. 2010. *Parties, Gender Quotas and Candidate Selection in France.* Basingstoke: Palgrave Macmillan.

North, Douglass C. 1990. *Institutions, Institutional Change and Economic Performance.* Cambridge: Cambridge University Press.

O'Carroll, J.P. 1987. 'Strokes, cute hoors and sneaking regarders: The influence of local culture on Irish political style'. *Irish Political Studies* 2(1): 77–92.

Randall, Vicky and Ailbhe Smyth. 1987. 'Bishops and bailiwicks: Obstacles to women's political participation in Ireland'. *Economic and Social Review* 18(3): 189–214.

Reidy, Theresa. 2011. 'Candidate selection'. In *How Ireland Voted 2011: The Full Story of Ireland's Earthquake Election*, eds. Michael Gallagher and Michael Marsh. London: Palgrave Macmillan.

Waylen, Georgina. 2014. 'Informal institutions, institutional change, and gender equality'. *Political Research Quarterly* 67(1): 212–223.

Weeks, Liam. 2008. 'Candidate selection: Democratic centralism or managed democracy?' In *How Ireland Voted 2007: The Full Story of Ireland's General Election*. London: Palgrave Macmillan UK, 48–64.

Chapter 4

Excavating Informal Institutional Enforcement through 'Rapid' Ethnography: Lessons from the Australian Construction Industry

Louise Chappell and Natalie Galea

Feminist institutionalists have long recognised that informal institutions are key to understanding gender change and stasis in political organisations. As the chapters in this volume illustrate, informal institutions – operating as rules, practices and norms – can operate to reinforce, undermine or displace formal rules in ways that can entrench or, sometimes, transform the gender status quo.

Despite a growing awareness of the centrality of informal institutions to (gendered) political outcomes, little attention has been paid to the mechanism through which sets of rules and practices are *enforced* and *sanctioned*, primarily through penalties and rewards. This chapter aims to bring fresh perspective to the notion of enforcement of informal political institutions by drawing on experiences of actors in another highly masculinised environment – professionals in the Australian construction sector – and using an innovative method, 'rapid' ethnography. In terms of gender, the profile of professionals in the Australian construction sector has much in common with that of Australian politicians – the sector is male dominated, perpetuates male advantage and produces highly gendered outcomes in terms of appointments and policies (or legislation) (Galea and Chappell 2015). Given these similarities, it is possible to hypothesise that mechanisms of enforcement also operate in a similar, though, given the different contexts, not identical ways. If this is so, lessons from the construction industry are relevant to future research into informal political institutions and their enforcement, including their gendered processes and effects.

Using the Australian construction sector as a case, this chapter pursues two core questions: what are the key enforcement mechanisms of informal institutions and how do they operate 'on the ground'? And, what are the best methods for 'seeing' gendered institutions and mechanisms that operate 'under the surface' in male-dominated environments?

The chapter will proceed in four parts. Part one briefly defines what we understand informal institutions to be, and then focuses on one particular trait – enforcement. Part two details the benefits of the 'rapid ethnography' approach used in the case study of professionals in the Australian construction sector (Loosemore et al. 2015) to interrogate enforcement mechanisms. Part three provides a series of vignettes from the case study to identify informal institutions, mechanisms of sanctioning and reward, and their gendered effects. Part four concludes by highlighting the value of paying closer attention to institutional enforcement mechanisms, and discusses the advantages and limitations of using rapid ethnography for studying these processes in other male-dominated political sites including parliaments, state bureaucracies and institutions of global governance.

IDENTIFYING THE FEATURES AND ENFORCEMENT OF INFORMAL INSTITUTIONS

The basic premise of new institutionalism is that 'rules matter', structuring social interaction and shaping behaviour of people, organisations and politics (Helmke and Levitsky 2004). Moreover, there is general agreement in the literature that institutions exist in both a formal and an informal guise, and that the interaction between the two is central to understanding organisational processes, effects and outcomes (Raymond et al. 2014). In our chapter, we treat formal and informal institutions as distinct entities but closely related (Waylen 2014). As Radnitz notes, the informal can work to 'weaken, substitute for, or work in parallel with' formal institutions (2011, 352). Formal institutions are rules and practices that are consciously designed and clearly specified (Lowndes and Wilson 2003). By contrast, we see informal as operating at a submerged level, as enduring rules, norms and practices, and in ways that also shape shared expectations and collective behaviour (see Azari and Smith 2012; Helmke and Levitsky 2004; Lauth 2000). Whereas formal rules are identifiable through codes of conduct, contracts, procedures, policies and laws, informal institutions usually operate through more opaque means – including norms, practices and narratives (Helmke and Levitsky 2004; Lowndes and Roberts 2013).

Most authors agree that enforcement is a critical distinguishing feature of all institutions, whether formal or informal (Lowndes and Roberts 2013, 51). The literature suggests that regardless of the type of institution, enforcement tends to be 'triadic' in nature, stemming from a third party (Helmke and Levitsky 2004; Lowndes and Roberts 2013). It is also generally argued that whether talking of formal or informal institutions, actors recognise that enforcement mechanisms exist, and are aware when they are breaking them (Lowndes and Roberts 2013, 51). However, there are some important differences between enforcement of formal and informal institutions. For instance, the enforcement of formal institutions is relatively easy to 'see' in operation: sanctions are usually clearly articulated and codified and take place through official channels – including adjudicative bodies such as commissions, courts and tribunals (Helmke and Levitsky 2004). By contrast, the enforcement of informal rules can be harder to identify as these mechanisms can take more subtle forms – such as criticism, surveillance or sarcasm – which can easily be hidden from view.

Importantly, enforcement helps to delinate institutions from other general forms of behaviour – such as raising an umbrella when it rains – which is an individual practice, and one that has no collective effect. As Azari and Smith suggest, to meet the definition of an informal institution, there is a 'sanction imposed by an agent upholding some collective expectation of right conduct' (2012, 40). For Azari and Smith, enforcement is a defining feature of all informal institutions, a necessary feature to avoid them becoming a 'catch all category': the enforcement dimension constrains the subject matter and distinguishes unwritten rules from related concepts such as ideas, culture and networks (2012, 40).

The existing literature mostly conceives of institutional enforcement mechanisms in a negative sense – focusing particularly on the application of sanctioning through penalties and punishments for those who deviate from the rules. Helmke and Levitksy for instance suggest that sanctions exist along spectrum from minor to major interventions against non-compliant actors, ranging from 'hostile remarks, gossip, ostracism, and other displays of social disapproval to extrajudicial violence' (2004, 733). Similarly, Lowndes and Robert (2013, 60) in their discussion on enforcement highlight the range of penalties faced by rule breakers, 'from expressions of disapproval, to social isolation of the offenders, to in extreme cases verbal intimidation and threats of violence'.

Given much less emphasis in literature, but, we would argue, especially important in the enforcement of gender rules, are those more 'positive' aspects of enforcement. These appear in the guise of a *reward* for those who comply with the rules, be they formal or informal, that operates to maintain the (gendered) status quo. These rewards have a similar effect to penalty-based sanctions: countenancing and reinforcing the existing logic of appropriateness. Rewards for 'doing the right thing' and maintaining the rules can be legal, such as being granted increased status (Azari and Smith 2012), conferred through job promotion or other measures. Equally, rewards can be illegal or 'shady' transactions, for example the payment of bribes and back-handers to politicians for maintaining a particular policy agenda on behalf of a set of interests, or the provision of prostitute services to business-men to celebrate the closing of a contract.

Whether enforced via rewards or penalties, Lynne Zucker (1999) makes the interesting point that the more institutionalised an informal rule, the less need there may be for sanctioning. Based on her ethnographic organisa-tional research, Zucker suggests the 'more institutionalised, the greater the maintenance without direct social control' (1999, 102). If Zucker is right, an empirical question arises as to whether the opposite may also be the case: where informal rules are undergoing a process of instantiation or deinstitu-tionalisation, driven through exogenous or endogenous change processes, is sanctioning asserted more forcefully? This has resonance for work on gender and institutions, where feminist actors are often seeking to disrupt the status quo to bring about change.

Institutional power relations are one reason enforcement practices may be more obvious at some moments than another. As Sheingate suggests (2010, 200), '[r]ules generate inequalities, not only because rules govern the distribution of resources but also because the capacity to negotiate complex rules is in itself a valuable resource'. Enforcing institutions – whether formal or informal – will always favour some actors over oth-ers: sanctioning creates winners and losers. For Sheingate those with institutional power are the actors who have the authority to make, break, interpret (2010, 170) and, we would add, *enforce* the rules. Where there are signs of institutional change, and threats to the institutionalisation of particular rules, the chances are that those who benefit from the applica-tion and maintenance of these rules will seek to enforce them. This could occur via increased penalties for those who are spearheading change, or rewards for those who are working towards the maintenance of the status quo. However, we are mindful of Mahoney and Thelen's (2010, 14) argu-ment that enforcement itself can also be contested. Such contestation can blur the boundaries between winners and losers, and rather than shoring up the status quo, it can open up an avenue to pursue institutional change (Mahoney and Thelen 2010, 14).

Gender and Enforcement

In the emerging work on gender and informal institutions there has been some limited discussion about enforcement and its gendered impact. For instance, Fiona Mackay's work on the Scottish parliament highlights how old ways of doing things, including the reintroduction of party discipline of members of parliament through the informal practice of 'whipping', is used to keep members in line, and disrupt efforts for more collaborative – read feminine – committee-based decision-making (Mackay 2014, 563). Attention has also been paid as to which actors are able to be 'rule makers' and 'rule breakers', and the gendered costs and benefits of such behaviour. Meryl Kenny's work focused on Scottish Labour Party pre-selection processes has shown how certain men in leadership positions have allowed other men to flout the formal rules to reinforce old practices, including promoting 'favoured sons' to safe seats at the expense of women, and thereby reinforcing the existing gender status quo in electoral competition (2013).

Despite this important work, very little attention has been given in the feminist institutionalist literature to the specific gender dimensions of enforcement mechanisms, be they rewards or penalties. Understanding how formal institutional enforcement is linked to gender is a relatively straightforward task as sanctions tend to be written into the design of these institutions. For example, official sanctions imposed for breaches of political party gender quotas are traceable because the rules tend to be explicit and codified. A more significant research challenge, and the one we grapple with in this chapter, is how to identify the way in which unwritten informal institutions are enforced and sanctioned in ways that interact with entrenched gender norms and practices and produce gender outcomes.

In undertaking this challenge of excavating informal enforcement mechanisms, we suggest that it is necessary to pursue three levels of investigation. The first level is to investigate the gendered *actors'* dimension of rule enforcement. As Gains and Lowndes (2014) remind us, institutional actors are not automatons but design, interpret and adapt rules on a daily basis. How they do this is shaped by their gender – including their sexed bodies, intersection with other identities and expectations about their masculine or feminine behaviour (Gains and Lowndes 2014, 529). It is important not only to identify the categories of men and women who are rule makers, breakers and takers, but to pay attention to *which* men and women can enforce and are rewarded or penalised for maintaining or changing the rules. The second level of investigation considers how gender rules, norms and practices adhere to the *substance* of an enforcement mechanism. By this we mean the extent to which the reward or punishment has a gender dimension itself – that is, are enforcement rules coded to give preference to certain gendered forms of behaviour than others? The third layer is to consider how these actors and the substance of the rule contribute to the gendered *outcome* of the enforcement process. In the next section, 'Seeing' sanctions through 'rapid ethnography', we apply this framework to professionals in the Australian construction sector to illuminate the gender dimensions of the enforcement of informal rules, and gendered outcomes. But before doing so, we discuss the utility of 'rapid ethnography' as a way to 'see' the operation and effects of sanctioning on the ground.

'SEEING' SANCTIONS THROUGH 'RAPID ETHNOGRAPHY'

It is widely acknowledged in the literature on informal institutions that identifying informal institutions and their enforcement mechanisms is difficult to do, and requires close evaluation of the arena in which they operate. In Helmke and Levtisky's (2004, 733) view:

> Identifying the shared expectations and enforcement mechanisms that sustain informal institutions is a challenging task, requiring in most cases substantial knowledge of the community within which the informal institutions are embedded. Hence there is probably no substitute for intensive fieldwork in informal institutional analysis.

Sheingate agrees, suggesting that it is important to see actors at work as they 'interpret, elaborate, bend or even break the rules' (2010, 184). One of the most promising methods – still underutilised in political science – for 'seeing' the engagement of institutional actors with the rules is through ethnographically focused research (Radnitz 2011; Rhodes 2002, 2005).

In simple terms, ethnography is a set of methods which involves the researcher participating in the daily lives of people for an extended period of time, observing what happens, listening to what is said, asking questions, undertaking follow-up interviews and collecting any relevant data that can throw light on issues of interest (Hammersley and Atkinson 1995). In ethnography, the researcher effectively acts as a translator between the group or culture under study and the reader (Millen 2000). Ethnographic research is typically more intensive than other forms of social research and is holistic, descriptive and reflective in nature (Ybema et al. 2010). It tends to avoid causal relationships – in favour of inductive explanations of explanatory theories – and generally relies on a limited number of case studies that are investigated intensively in both highly personalised and field-based contexts using primarily qualitative methods. This enables the researcher to capture the social meanings, 'unarticulated attitudes' and ordinary activities of people in their natural settings – including, we suggest, the operation of informal institutions and their enforcement (Busby 2013).

The use of ethnography to reveal gendered dimensions of social life has a long history, but as Chappell and Waylen (2013) note, ethnography has rarely been used in new-institutionalist research in specifically gendered ways, or as a gendered lens on informal institutions. However, feminist ethnographer of the British Parliament, Emma Crewe (2014, 678) suggests that the method has utility for feminist institutionalist scholars because it encourages them: 'to pay more attention to their own assumptions and their informants' cultural specificity and context, to diversity between informants and within social groups, and to social change'.

This claim was borne out in our research on professionals in the Australian construction sector. Our study, undertaken by a five-member team, is interested in the intransigence of gender inequity in professional careers in construction (Galea et al. 2015) – in terms of the attraction, promotion and retention of women professionals in the sector – despite the introduction of an extensive suite of formal 'rules about gender' (Gains and Lowndes 2014) such as the provision of 'family friendly' work practices including parental leave, the provision of childcare facilities and women's leadership training. In our research, we have been interested in interrogating how these formal rules have been displaced, undermined or reinforced by informal rules – which we have found often have 'gendered effects' (Gains and Lowndes 2014). Our study is based on research over a three-year period of two multinational construction firms operating in Australia: Company A is a privately owned multinational contractor, which operates in the commercial, residential, engineering and infrastructure markets; Company B is a publicly listed multinational contractor, which operates in the commercial, residential, engineering and infrastructure markets.

In deciding to use an ethnographic approach to better understand 'everyday practices' related to recruitment, progression and retention in the construction section, the team decided to eschew traditional ethnography and explore what has been coined 'rapid' ethnography. This decision was based on a few issues including the project-based nature of construction activity across multiple locations and for finite periods of time, and the time-pressured and commercial aspects of the job which made it unlikely we could get 'buy in' from the companies (Galea et al. 2015).

In contrast to the wide-angled, explorative and time-intensive nature of the traditional approach, rapid ethnographers work in teams to undertake short, intensive and focused investigations using multiple and iterative methods to gain a deep understanding of the work setting they are studying (Isaacs 2013; Millen 2000). In rapid ethnography, open-ended interviews and explorative observations are replaced with condensed equivalents that are more focused on specific issues of interest identified from existing literature and theory, the later providing a framework to aid the researcher in their exploration (Baines and Cunningham 2013). Furthermore, broad conversations and interactions with numerous random informants are replaced with targeted and deliberative interviews with sampled respondents at key intervals and moments where data is the richest and most relevant to the questions of interest. For some, rapid ethnography is seen as a 'quick and dirty', second-rate approach to ethnography (Isaacs 2013; Millen 2000). However, it was ideal for the purposes of our project, and for overcoming the various hurdles we confronted.

Our rapid ethnographic study was a two-stage process. The first stage of the ethnography was less intrusive and aimed at building rapport and trust between the researchers and respondents. It involved pairs of researchers observing events related to the recruitment, retention and promotion of professionals such as engineers, architects, project managers and the like, including formal and informal meetings, diversity training, new employee inductions, graduate assessment centres, leadership and skills training, mentoring initiatives, management 'road shows' and diversity-specific events. Where appropriate the researchers participated in these events and conducted informal conversation with attendees asking questions such as 'Is this event/ activity typical?' 'Is it important to attend events like this?' 'What would happen if you did not take part in this activity/event?' These questions were aimed at identifying what the informal rules were, and how they were enforced. Participants were also invited to take part in an interview if the conversation became more personal. Interviews that formed part of the rapid ethnography were designed to complement the observations, and as such they explored narratives around career history, recruitment, and pathways, promotion processes and strategies, mentoring and networks, and work practices (such as work hours and work-life balance).

The second stage of the rapid ethnography involved observation of a number of construction project sites and involved two researchers spending three to five days, depending on the size of the project, shadowing and interviewing professional employees across range of positions including engineers, project managers, design specialists, construction managers and site foremen. Observations on site focused on the roles and relationship of actors, daily work practices, engagement with head office and subcontractors, demarcations between the project site and the site office and group dynamics. Researchers paid particular attention to reoccurring narratives and (non)compliance with formal rules and sanctioning practices. Shadowing provided an excellent opportunity for informal conversations and 'walking interviews' (Clark and Emmel 2010) with participants and included questions such as 'Was that a typical site meeting?' 'Is it important to arrive on site at this time?' 'What happens if you're late, or sick or have urgent caring responsibilities?' 'Who is most valued on this site, Why?' If the conversation became more personal, participants were invited to take part in a more formal interview. To address concerns around confidentiality, we took care to anonymise all responses, and where this was not possible, reflected on the processes we were observing, rather than individuals.

Where possible, the two-member research teams involved in the observations were twinned – an 'insider' with an 'outsider'. The insiders were members of the research team with extensive experience and established relationships in the construction sector, while the outsider researchers were gender experts from sociology and political science. This combination allowed the researchers to overcome challenges associated with being both an outsider – potentially not understanding issues – and an insider – missing important messages because they are taken for granted (Baines and Cunningham 2013; Bjarnegård 2013). Our research team comprised both men and women and we actively tried to maintain this mix throughout the research, in recognition that as gendered actors ourselves, our involvement may impact on the field and our interpretation of data. Indeed, this did appear to make an important difference, for example male researchers being exposed to conversations about sex and pornography on different sites, while these topics were never raised with the female researchers.

An important aspect of the process was debriefing sessions for the pair of researchers undertaking the observation. In line with good ethnographic practice (Pink and Morgan 2013), in the post-observation phase, members of the research team reflexively considered how empirical insights link with theory throughout the research process. These debriefing sessions, and researchers' field notes and analytical memos, were important in addressing the challenges of analysis in a multi-researcher ethnography, where there are bound to be perceptual differences and various points of (dis)agreement.

The overwhelming view of the research team, many of whom had never used ethnographic methods before, was that the method was an excellent way to 'see' informal institutions at work, including sanctioning processes – both rewards and punishments. Our strong sense was that compared to relying on interviews alone, even spending a relatively short period shadowing participants made them more relaxed, open and willing to reveal aspects of their working lives through informal conversations and in formal interviews. It also gave us the opportunity to identify patterns of behaviour and micro-practices that would not have otherwise been possible to witness, revealing a great deal about the operation of gender practices, norms and narratives. Each researcher was both touched and surprised by the number and nature of the personal stories participants shared about the stress of working in the industry including their (lack of) work-life balance, caring responsibilities, relationship challenges both on site and at home, and the mental and physical health effects of this stress.

Our team approach and our debriefing sessions have proven to be particularly valuable. Not only have they helped us speed up the ethnographic process, as required, but we have had the ability to compare observations, and overtime, build up a picture of informal institutions and sanctioning practices that travel between different levels of each site and across different work sites. Using rapid ethnography we have been able to identify a range of informal rules, norms and practices operating in these construction organisations, which are discussed in detail in next section.

CAPTURING INFORMAL INSTITUTIONS THROUGH RAPID ETHNOGRAPHY

In the field, we observed a variety of informal institutions that were repeated across construction sites. Three of the most notable institutions observed were: homosocial loyalty, presenteeism and total availability. Reflected through norms, practices and narratives, we see these as informal institutions in that they were repeated across sites, had a collective effect and had an enforcement mechanism attached, if not adhered to (also see Chappell and Mackay, this volume). Homosocial loyalty draws on the work of Bjarnegård (2009), among others, by acknowledging the social and political bond between people of the same sex. In male-dominated environments, adherence by men to expected codes of masculinity builds trust, essential in uncertain environments such as construction (Collinson and Hearn 2005; Kanter 1977). The practice of homosocial loyalty is 'an investment in predictability' (Bjarnegård 2009, 25), operating through the selection and advancement of men willing to maintain the homogenous position of the group. Total availability and presenteeism are similar in that they are both grounded in the notion of reliability. The expectation at the heart of total availability is that work is prioritised above all else – including family and non-career demands. By contrast, presenteeism is the expectation of bodily presence on the job, reflected through the celebration of long working hours, whether work requirements exist or not. In the vignettes to follow, and in Table 4.1, we detail how sanctioning occurs and by whom, and the outcome for the individual and the gendered effect overall. While each vignette provides an individual story, it has been selected because it is representative of a pattern observed across a number of sites, and is intended to give a flavour of how the enforcement of informal rules takes place.

Informal Institution 1: Homosocial Loyalty

The first informal institution observed operating across construction sites was homosocial loyalty. Often subtle and working in conjunction with formal promotion procedures, in the Australian construction sector homosocial loyalty is enforced by men through the granting of opportunities and endorsements to some, but not others, in exchange for their allegiance and support. Homosocial loyalty is an example of sanctioning happening through *rewards*, in some instances, and *penalties* in others.

Table 4.1 Observed informal institutions

Informal Rule	Observation Context	Substance of Enforcement Mechanism	Gendered Actor Doing the Enforcing	Gendered Outcome	Gendered Effect
Homosocial loyalty	1. William is taken to project meetings with senior management	Endorsement, opportunity and sponsorship	Male project manager	Visibility in front of power brokers	Maintenance of homosocial networks that sustain the gender power status quo
	2. Emanuela is expected to work over and above the formal rules for a promotion	Lack of recognition of performance; allocation of additional tasks	Male project leader	Despondence and frustration	Reinforces who is considered a legitimate construction professional Impacts retention and progression of women
Total availability	3. Rejection of Jacqueline's staged return from maternity leave	Hostile remarks and complaints	Male peers, male project leader	Jacqueline forced to return to her pre-maternity work hours operating as a warning to other women on the site	Non-compliance of work practices undermines actors' legitimacy Rigid work practices force a choice between work or family Devalues care work
	4. Expectation that Jay will not set his hours of work and will work from home	Disapproval and speculation	Senior male leaders Male project leader	Pressure to conform to work after hours	Actors forced to prioritise work over care responsibilities Reinforces traditional gender roles, e.g. male breadwinner
Presenteeism	5. Expectation for Ingrid to work long hours even when work is completed and the company states otherwise	Repeated inquiry, public shaming and reprimand	Male line manager Male project director	Adherence to the long work hours	Rules in and out who can/cannot participate in a construction profession
	6. Ronald is publicly reprimanded and reminded of the informal work hours	Public shaming and reprimand	Male project director	Adherence to the informal work hours	Hours on site count no matter whether you have work or not

---

OBSERVATION 1

The site office window looked out to the construction site; an inner city residential block. The most important people in the team sit closest to the construction site. James, the project manager, sits closest to the window and spends most of his day looking out to the site as he talks to subcontractors. William, the project engineer, sits next to him. Quietly spoken and ambitious to get ahead, William suggests, you have to 'have the right attitude, be a go getter, do your work and know what you want'. This is the second project William and James have worked on together. James picked William for this project. Thanks to James, William has started to cut his teeth on tasks that a project manager would do. The previous day, he took William to head office for a monthly project meeting. As a result, William was seen by senior company executives. Despite the regional manager making a few jokes at William's expense – reminding him he was at the bottom of the rung – William was there: to listen, to learn and, most importantly, to be visible to those who were important.

OBSERVATION 2

Of all the site sheds we visited, this is the bleakest. A thick film of yellow dust forms a shadow around the base of the desk and under the chair. No surface is free from un-kept papers except the grey bookshelves that stand empty. Sparsely spaced grilled windows do little to attract the natural light leaving the rows of fluorescent lights to cast shadows over the room. It is also the smallest office (twelve staff) and quietest. There is no room for personal conversations in this shed, not unless you wanted your colleagues to hear it. In the middle of the site office sit Emanuelam a graduate, and Jeremy, a site engineer. Their desks face each other but are separated by a low-level partition that has a single unopened beer bottle sitting atop of it, left over from a Friday drinks session.

Both Emanuela and Jeremy were recruited into the company three years ago on the same graduate intake. New university graduates are recruited into the company through a vigorous selection process. Once employed, graduates are rotated through different work areas including quality control, safety, design and services. Within these areas they are required to complete a range of tasks that are signed off and graded from one to four by their direct line manager. A mark of one is considered a fail and marks from two to four are recognised as a pass. Emanuela shows me her checklist. It is full of threes and fours, so she is doing really well but there are plenty of empty spaces left in her checklist. It is different to Jeremy's checklist which my colleague was shown yesterday; a completed checklist populated with twos and threes. Yet, six months ago, Jeremy was promoted to a site engineer.

Emanuela is keen to talk to me about her experience. As we leave the office to survey the site, Emanuela opens up to me about her frustration with the promotion process. She senses that the pace of progress through the checklist is highly dependent on the graduate's relationship with their line manager. It is evident that Emanuela is ambitious and is very keen to be promoted to a site engineer. Progression has both a financial and career value for the quietly spoken yet very friendly and open twenty-eight-year-old. As she checks the ceiling panels, she tells me that Jeremy's recent promotion happened very quickly. She puts this down to his relationship with his line manager and the other guys on site. She tells me that senior men pick their teams and that Jeremy has been picked and promoted; 'he is part of the team'. 'I haven't made the team yet', says Emanuela, although she notes that some things have slowly improved for her on this site. When she arrived, she was the only woman and allocated a desk in the corner of the site shed, well away from the rest of the team. Now there are three women on site and her desk is more centrally located. Yet, her frustration at her lack of progression is obvious. After Jeremy's promotion, Emanuela arranged a meeting with her project manager to seek his advice on gaining promotion. He suggested that in addition to completing the tasks on the grad program, Emanuela should take on additional responsibilities and organise a workshop for company graduates. This would involve her in designing the event, costing it, sending emails to participants, flying graduates to the site and arranging presentations. Her manager explained that this would demonstrate her initiative and would aid her promotion to site engineer.

Observation 1 illustrates homosocial loyalty is well understood between male actors in construction as a practice necessary for career progression. As a reward for demonstrating loyalty and commitment to the male manager and to the project's success, male underlings were introduced to the chief power brokers and given opportunities for the accrual of important skills and networking.

For women, as shown in Observation 2, homosocial loyalty is rarely on offer, not least because of the absence of women managers and leaders on construction sites. The normalisation of male competency and place in construction shapes perceptions of (male) managers about who is 'right for the job', reinforced by rewards for loyal men, and punishments for women. These punishments appear in the form of having to meet a higher or different standard, which, as in the case of Emanuela and others in our study, required them to take on an additional task – as administrator/organiser of an event – which is a gendered task in itself. By contrast, for men such as William and Jeremy, homosocial loyalty provided a slip-stream to promotion. In addition to creating 'gendered' winners and losers, the cumulative effect of homosocial loyalty in the Australian construction sector operates to preserve the gender power status quo and the reinforcement of men as legitimate – and women as illegitimate – construction professionals.

Informal Institution 2: Total Availability

The informal institution of total availability is the shared expectation among construction workers and managers that their construction work will be prioritised above all else, as and when needed. This institution is rooted in the gendered notion of the unencumbered male worker who has no care responsibilities. In this industry, it is also a side effect of the construction contract that stipulates financial penalties for late project completion. Over the course of our project, we observed that the closer a project comes to completion, the 'greedier' the institution becomes in terms of total availability (Mackay and Rhodes 2013), and the more strongly it is enforced.

OBSERVATION 3

Jay, a site manager, joined the company the week after his first child was born. His baby boy is now twelve weeks old. I have been following Jay since 6.45 am. This was later than the 6.30 am arranged time, but Jay explained in a matter-of-fact tone when he met me that he'd been distracted by a visit from local and interstate union officials that delayed his slab pour scheduled to commence at 6 am. After collecting my safety gear – hard hat, high visibility vest and protective glasses, Jay paced off to the construction site across the road. I trailed behind him struggling to keep up, tangling myself in my safety gear. Once through the hoarding and onto the site, the familiar pungent smell of glue accompanies us to the fifth floor. In between persistent phone calls, Jay explained to me that he was relatively new to the company and got in on his second try. At the first interview – with two senior male site managers – Jay had mentioned his new born baby and specified the hours he was able to work, from 6 am to 5 pm Monday to Saturday (66 hours per week, despite being contracted to a 37.5 hour week). This would allow Jay to be home at night to put his boy to bed. Jay didn't get the job. He suspects that the older site manager was turned off by him because he stipulated the hours he wanted to work. 'He thought I was wanting to work flexible hours', Jay said. Soon after Jay was called back in for a second interview, this time with Mark, the more senior project director. During this discussion, Jay tells me that he and Mark found they had something in common: small children. Mark made it clear during the interview that he understood Jay's predicament and that he himself tried to leave at 5 pm every day to be home to see his three children before they went to bed. Jay got the job. However, after a short time in the position, Jay realised his understanding of leaving at 5 pm was different to Mark's. On the second week of the job, as Jay was leaving the office to head home, Mark said to Jay, 'What? You don't take your laptop home with you at night?' Jay knew Mark did. After this chiding, Jay started to take his laptop home. He tells me he receives emails from Mark late into the night, which he is expected to respond to. During our week on site neither man left the office at 5 pm; most days they left well past it.

OBSERVATION 4

Phoebe, a well-dressed woman in her early 30s, suggested we grab a coffee offsite so that she could speak to me about gender issues. It was clear that this topic was sensitive and not something she wanted to address in the site office. As we slip through the heavy site gates of the medium-sized public works project and make our way to the nearby café, Phoebe explains that she is looking to have children in the future but foresees a huge issue in negotiating her maternity leave. This is despite the fact that Phoebe has been working in a close-knit team for fifteen years with Cameron, the project leader, and Grant, the site manager. Phoebe tells me she thinks retention of women, particularly around pregnancy, is a real problem for the company. She has seen that women are not supported before or after they go on maternity leave. 'If they are not pushed out of the industry altogether and decide to return, they are relegated to the development or the commercial side of the business'. As we leave the noise of the site behind us, Phoebe notes that, currently, their site has two women on maternity leave: one unplanned and one planned. The woman who fell pregnant unexpectedly told Phoebe, 'Once I have a baby, I am dead to them' [the construction company]. Phoebe tells me she calls this woman monthly while she is on leave, to make her feel wanted and valued, as part of a new initiative developed in their region.

As we entered the café, I broach the issue of Phoebe's colleague Jacqueline's staged return from maternity leave, which I'd learnt about the previous day. Jacqueline is an engineer who sits diagonally opposite Phoebe. Returning from maternity leave ten months earlier, Jacqueline, a project engineer, had negotiated with Paul, the Operations Manager who oversees all the resourcing of projects, to continue to work her formal contracted hours (37.5 hours per week) 'flexibly' for three months. For Jacqueline, this included three ten-hour days on site and the remainder of hours made up over two days working from home. Jacqueline was told by the Operations Manager not to broadcast her 'flexible' arrangement which was then terminated after three months by Cameron, the project manager who had fielded multiple complaints from the male site team. They thought it was unreasonable that Jacqueline was not physically on site during her shifts and were aggrieved that she was not working every second Saturday, like them. Cameron gave Jacqueline a choice: work part-time in a commercial role or put your child into full-time childcare. Jacqueline chose the latter. Phoebe tells me that she doesn't really know Jacqueline well, but that she has watched how Jacqueline was not supported after she returned from maternity leave. For Phoebe, it was the negative comments made by the site team about Jacqueline and her competency as an engineer that she found most unfair.

I asked Phoebe if her male colleagues had experienced this issue when they had returned from paternity leave. 'There's no issues . . .' She explained that the men don't see having children as an issue in their world; they don't think about negotiating parenting with work. As we walk back to the site, Phoebe says, 'I shouldn't say this but they all do the same, you know. They get married young. They have kids. They're all clones of each other. Very similar. They are from very similar education backgrounds. Private school boys that have two kids, who don't rock the boat'. After a moment of silence, I ask, 'What about the guys who do rock the boat? The guys who do step up and parent, who do care, you know, take time off for care responsibilities?' Phoebe replies, 'They aren't supported either.' It also impedes their next job opportunity. 'They are not considered for higher positions on the next job. They are seen as not being capable of stepping up to a higher role or a higher responsibility.' With that, she takes hold of the heavy site gate and inches it open for us to pass through to the site office.

Observations 3 and 4 demonstrate the full spectrum of sanctioning undertaken by powerful individuals and peer groups towards workers who are unable to, or do not want to, prioritise work at all times above their care commitments. The sanctions for those who attempt to break the rules by demonstrating a commitment to caring responsibilities take the form of punishments, from off-handed jibes and hostile complaints to outright rejection shown through lack of promotion. They are also used to draw into question the workers' capability and commitment to their jobs. For those with caring responsibilities but who remain totally available, no punishment exists; indeed they are rewarded by being treated as 'one of the team'; they appear to continue with their career progression without skipping a beat, including being offered jobs on the next big contract. Ongoing perceptions by rule makers and peers about the need for total availability reinforces gendered notions about the legitimacy of 'breadwinner' worker model, about the undervaluation of care roles and responsibilities, and ultimately deters most men, and some women, from ever challenging the rule.

Informal Rule 3: Presenteeism

Connected to the same drivers of total availability, the institution of presenteeism directs construction workers to be physically present on site and work long hours, even if there is no actual work to do, and regardless of whether longer hours run counter to formal company rules and staff contracts. Presenteeism is contextual and operates rigorously on construction sites, where failure to complete the construction works on time attracts high financial penalties under the contract that will eat away at the company's profit.

OBSERVATION 5

Having chosen to study engineering on a whim, mainly because she enjoyed maths, Ingrid found her way into the construction industry through a combined engineering/commerce degree. The double degree ensured she had a backup plan – just in case she did not like construction, or it did not like her. Now a site engineer on a large construction site, much of Ingrid's day is spent at her computer. Only once in the middle of the day do we venture on to site. On site, Ingrid marks off on an A3 drawing the recently erected steel members. As we stand overlooking the giant steel structure, our conversation drifts to the topic of working hours. Ingrid tells me that she's in the process of testing the boundaries in relation to the long hours that are expected, even though her formal contract requires her to work 37.5 hours. Generally, Ingrid works Saturdays, mainly because her project engineer asks her every Friday, 'Are you coming in tomorrow?' She understands this to mean that working Saturdays is expected of her, regardless of the stage of the project or her workload. There have been times that she has turned up to work on Saturday and had no work to do. The only time that Saturday work has been officially discussed on site was in relation to rostered days offs (RDOs). RDOs occur every month but they specifically apply to blue-collar construction workers, not white-collar workers like Ingrid. The company standard, Ingrid understands, is that if someone works Saturdays, they can take half the RDOs off when they occur. However, no one on her site seems to follow this in practice. Ingrid tells me that she decided to challenge the company practice by not coming to work when the next RDO fell due having worked every Saturday. The response was swift and public; at the next team meeting, the project director sought to embarrass Ingrid stating: 'If you need help, grab Ingrid. She clearly doesn't have enough work to do if she is taking an RDO'. I asked Ingrid, 'What happened at the next RDO?' and she said, 'I didn't take it off. It [the message] is not very subliminal'.

OBSERVATION 6

Standing at his desk that was positioned at the other end of the long site office, the project director yelled across the rows of heads: 'See you on Monday Ronald. Make sure your start time has an 8 at the front of it.' In unison, faces looked up from their computer screens and heads turned towards Ronald, the project lawyer. Acknowledging the comment with a waved hand, Ronald left for his long weekend. This event capped off a day of public ribbing for Ronald by his peers regarding the time he arrived to work in the mornings. Earlier in the day, he had told me that it was unusual to have a lawyer permanently based on site, but this project was large and took all his time so he relocated himself from head office to site. But since basing himself on site, Ronald had been repeatedly told by the project leader that he must arrive to site before 8 am, just in case the site team had an issue that needed his assistance. Ronald acknowledged that over the last few weeks he had made an effort to arrive earlier than his usual head office start time at 9–9.30 am. It was hard for him, however. He was a night person and was used to working late hours. I asked Ronald whether since arriving earlier in the morning the team had sought his attention. 'No, they are used to me coming in late', he replied.

Like total availability and homosocial loyalty, presenteeism is adhered to and enforced by site leaders, who in our research were always male. That is not to say men are the only actors enforcing informal institutions; we observed women enforcing them too, by joining in with the humour, jibes and ridicule for example, but as they were always in more junior positions they tended not to lead the sanctioning. As with these other informal institutions, presenteeism was also mostly sanctioned through punishments. Presenteeism appeared to be institutionalised within most sites we visited and as our observations show, it was only new team members, like Ingrid, or those who had a secure position and could shift back to Head Office, like Ronald, that needed to be brought into line with humour, public shaming, confrontation and reprimand. This links to Zucker's point outlined earlier that the more highly institutionalised a practice, the less need for its enforcement.

The gendered effects of presenteeism are similar to those of total availability, in that they intersect with participants' care commitments. For women who remain primary care givers, it places a great obstacle to their capacity to maintain a career in construction. But as our observations also found, it had a detrimental impact on men too. The burden of meeting these demands affected their personal lives, with high rates of relationship breakdown, drug and alcohol abuse and mental and physical health issues. While each company through their formal policies acknowledged some of these problems, none were linked back to the cause of the problem – presenteeism – and no recognition was given to the gendered effect of such informal rules.

THE ADVANTAGES AND DISADVANTAGES OF RAPID ETHNOGRAPHY

Our project using rapid ethnography provides some lessons for those seeking to understand informal rules and their enforcement in other male-dominated contexts such as parliaments, courts, bureaucracies, international organisations. Rapid ethnography enables the researcher to gain deep insights into the specific environments in which institutions develop: in this case, through experiencing the noise, silence, heat, cold, dust, pressure and smell of different construction sites. Experiencing these contextual elements first hand gives researchers important background signals about what institutions are at play, who takes responsibility for enforcing them and helps us to make better sense of why they are in operation.

Rapid ethnography also enables researchers to build a rapport with participants in a much deeper way than interviews alone allow. In our study, this has meant we have been better able to interrogate what sanctioning mechanisms are in place in terms of rewards and punishments, which actors are responsible for enforcing the rules and what happens to those who uphold or who break the rules. Aside from identifying specific sanctioning mechanisms, by witnessing the operation of these mechanisms we have been struck by how effective they can be and by their gendered effects. Sanctioning through *punishments* has stopped people breaking and displacing the rules – such as in Ingrid's case when she challenged working hours. But we have also seen how important *rewards* can be in reinforcing the rules. Our observations on homosocial loyalty are a case in point: ongoing sponsorship of 'favored sons' maintains the existing order and ensures those who do not fit the profile remain marginalised in institutional power play. 'Seeing' informal rules and these sanctioning mechanisms has helped us understand why institutional change can be so difficult, and to discover who is involved in its contestation – these are important pieces of the puzzle to identify in studying any organisation.

Rapid ethnography has also been important for better understanding informal rules with gender effects. One of the advantages of this method has been to allow us experience up close the clash that occurs between the demands of the workplace and caring responsibilities. In the Australian construction industry, the rules around workplace performance are particularly heavily enforced through punishments for those who break the informal rules – such as extended work hours – and rewards for those who uphold them. It is this enforcement that helps to maintain the gender status quo in this sector, downplaying care responsibilities and emphasising careers at all costs; these findings are likely to also be at play in other male-dominated organisations. One of the important discoveries of our work has been not only how the enforcement of these rules impedes women's careers, but the high cost they impose on men, including in terms of their relationships and well-being.

We acknowledge that rapid ethnography also has its limitations – limitations that are likely to be evident in political research contexts too. Due to the short time periods spent in each location, the ability of researchers to blend in can be impaired, particularly in contexts with few participants. This might not be such a problem in parliaments where 'strangers' can slip as if a staffer, but it could be more difficult in more intimate settings such as in political party head offices, or small party branch meetings, or behind the scenes in courtrooms for instance. The short time spans in the field make it easier for actors to put on a 'performance' – something that some of the participants were accused of by their colleagues – or quarantine the researcher's access to the field. This can potentially skew the researcher's understanding of the operation and enforcement of the rules. Despite these limitations, we think rapid ethnography does have many advantages over interviews alone, and is an important tool to be added to the methodological kit of feminist researchers.

CONCLUSION

Our chapter has attempted to shed light on the issue of enforcement – an important constitutive element of formal and informal institutions – but which remains underdeveloped in the literature, including feminist institutionalist scholarship. Focusing on gender and the attraction, promotion and retention of professionals in the Australian construction sector, the chapter has paid particular attention to the enforcement of informal institutions, which are harder to identify than formal mechanisms that are usually codified and clear-cut. Our chapter has shown that sanctioning is the key enforcement mechanism for informal institutions, and that while many of these sanctions take the form of punishments including sarcasm, ridicule and biting humour, we have also noted the importance of rewards for maintaining the status quo, including the existing gender logic of appropriateness.

We are convinced that rapid ethnography is a powerful method for 'seeing' informal institutions, their enforcement and gendered effects in male-dominated environments. Although the construction site is a unique venue, we are confident that this method can travel and would be equally valuable in other male-dominated environments such as legislatures or political party headquarters for instance. We suspect that this approach may well also be useful for those studying gender and executives, where issues of attraction and promotion are also obvious. Indeed, given the hidden nature of informal institutions, we suggest that these ethnographic approaches should be used more frequently to better understand why formal institutions, to bring about gender equality, often falter at the coalface, and to identify institutional gender effects. We suspect that much of what we discovered about the operation of informal rules and their enforcement carries not only across construction sites in one country, but also across different sectors – political, social, economic – in similar settings. Ethnographically driven comparative research across sectors and across countries is a promising path to be explored to get to understand not only the existence of informal institutions, but their enforcement, and what this means for gendered institutional stasis and change. As Emma Crewe (2014) suggests, '[g]endered differences may be universal, but the forms they take are endlessly varied.' Better understanding this variation is an important research task, one made possible, we argue, through the employment of ethnographic techniques.

REFERENCES

Azari, Julia R. and Jennifer K. Smith. 2012. 'Unwritten rules: Informal institutions in established democracies'. *Perspectives on Politics* 10(01):37–55.

Baines, Donna and Ian Cunningham. 2013. 'Using comparative perspective rapid ethnograpy in international case studies: Strengths and challenges'. *Qualitative Social Work* 12(1):73–88.

Bjarnegård, Elin. 2009. *Men in Politics: Revisiting Patterns of Gendered Parliamentary Representation in Thailand and Beyond*. Uppsala, Sweden: Uppsala University.

Bjarnegård, Elin. 2013. *Gender, Informal Institutions and Political Recruitment: Explaining Male Dominance in Parliamentary Representation*. New York: Palgrave Macmillan.

Busby, Amy. 2013. '"Bursting the Brussels bubble": Using ethnography to explore the European parliament as a transnational political field'. *Perspectives on European Politics and Society* 14(2):203–222.

Chappell, Louise and Georgina Waylen. 2013. 'Gender and the hidden life of institutions'. *Public Administration* 91(3):599–615.

Clark, Andrew and Nick Emmel. 2010. *Using Walking Interviews*. National Centre for Research Methods, Morgan Centre, University of Manchester.

Collinson, David L. and Jeff Hearn. 2005. 'Men and masculinities in work, organizations and management'. In *The Sage Handbook of Men and Masculinities*. London: Sage.

Crewe, Emma. 2014. 'Ethnographic research in gendered organizations: The case of the Westminster parliament'. *Politics & Gender* 10(04):673–678.

Gains, Francesca and Vivien Lowndes. 2014. 'How is institutional formation gendered, and does it make a difference? A new conceptual framework and a case study of police and crime commissioners in England and Wales'. *Politics & Gender* 10(04):524–548.

Galea, Natalie, Abigail Powell, Martin Loosemore and Louise Chappell. 2015. 'Designing robust and revisable policies for gender equality: Lessons from the Australian construction industry'. *Construction Management and Economics* 33(5–6): 375–389.

Galea, N. and Chappell, L. (2015) The Power of Masculine Privilege: Comparing Male Overrepresentation in the Australian Political and Construction Sectors. *ECPR Joint Sessions Workshop* Warsaw, Poland.

Hammersley, Martyn and Paul Atkinson. 1995. *Insider accounts: Listening and asking questions. Ethnography: Principles in practice*: London: Routledge 124–156.

Helmke, Gretchen and Steven Levitsky. 2004. 'Informal institutions and comparative politics: A research agenda'. *Perspectives on Politics* 2(4):725–740.

Isaacs, E. 2013. 'The value of rapid ethnography'. In *Advancing Ethnography in Corporate Environments: Challenges and Emerging Opportunities*, eds. B. Jordan and Walnut Creek, CA: Left Coast Press.

Kanter, Rosabeth Moss. 1977. *Men and Women of the Corporation*: New York: Basic Books.

Kenny, Meryl. 2013. 'Reforming recruitment: Gender and newness in the candidate selection process'. In *7th ECPR General Conference*. Sciences Po Bordeaux, Bordeaux, France.

Lauth, Hans-Joachim. 2000. 'Informal institutions and democracy'. *Democratization* 7(4):21–50.

Loosemore, Martin, Abigail Powell, Megan Blaxland, Natalie Galea, Andrew Dainty and Louise Chappell. 2015. *Rapid Ethnography in Construction Gender Research*. ARCOM, Lincoln, UK.

Lowndes, Vivien and David Wilson. 2003. 'Balancing revisability and robustness? A new institutionalist perspective on local government modernization'. *Public Administration* 81(2):275–298.

Lowndes, Vivien and M. Roberts. 2013. *Why Institutions Matter*. Basingstoke: Palgrave.

Mackay, Fiona. 2014. 'Nested newness, institutional innovation, and the gendered limits of change'. *Politics & Gender* 10(04):549–571.

Mackay, Fiona and RAW Rhodes. 2013. 'Gender, greedy institutions, and the departmental court'. *Public Administration* 91(3):582–598.

Mahoney, James and Kathleen Thelen. 2010. *Explaining Institutional Change: Ambiguity, Agency, and Power*. New York: Cambridge University Press.

Millen, David R. 2000. 'Rapid ethnography: Time deepening strategies for HCI field research'. In *Proceedings of the 3rd Conference on Designing Interactive Systems: Processes, Practices, Methods, and Techniques*. ACM, New York.

Pink, Sarah and Jennie Morgan. 2013. 'Short-term ethnography: Intense routes to knowing'. *Symbolic Interaction* 36(3):351–361.

Radnitz, S. 2011. 'Informal politics and the state'. *Comparative Politics* 43(3):351–371.

Raymond, Leigh, S. Laurel Weldon, Daniel Kelly, Ximena B. Arriaga and Ann Marie Clark. 2014. 'Making change: Norm-based strategies for institutional change to address intractable problems'. *Political Research Quarterly* 67:197–211.

Rhodes, Roderick A.W. 2002. 'Putting people back into networks'. *Australian Journal of Political Science* 37(3):399–416.

Rhodes, Roderick A.W. 2005. 'Everyday life in a ministry public administration as anthropology'. *The American Review of Public Administration* 35(1):3–25.

Sheingate, Adam. 2010. 'Rethinking rules: Creativity and constraint in the US House of Representatives'. *Explaining Institutional Change: Ambiguity, Agency, and Power*: 168–203.

Waylen, Georgina. 2014. 'Informal institutions, institutional change, and gender equality'. *Political Research Quarterly* 67(1):212–223.

Ybema, Sierk, Dvora Yanow, Harry Wels and Frans Kamsteeg. 2010. 'Ethnography'. *Encyclopedia of Case Study Research* 2:348–352.

Zucker, Lynne. G. 1999. 'Institutionalization and cultural persistence'. In *The New Institutionalism in Organizatioal Analysis,* eds. Walter W. Powell and Paul J. DiMaggio. Chicago: University of Chicago Press.

Chapter 5

Party Office, Male Homosocial Capital and Gendered Political Recruitment

Tània Verge and Sílvia Claveria

Despite the political gains made by women in the last decades, both legislative and executive offices remain male dominated (Jalalzai and Krook 2010). Strongly skewed parliaments and all-men cabinets have gradually disappeared, but parity is still rather exceptional. While sociocultural and institutional factors may partially account for cross-country differences, political parties are crucial actors in making or breaking women's political presence in public office (Kittilson 2006; Claveria 2014a). The role of political parties in hindering the feminisation of political institutions is well established (Lovenduski and Norris 1993; Norris and Lovenduski 1995). Yet, more research is needed to shed light on the operation of the gendered patterns of inclusion and exclusion within political parties, and to unveil the informal norms and practices that lie behind political recruitment processes (Bjarnegård and Kenny 2015).

Given that political parties are the main distributors of elective and appointive positions, party members, and particularly party officers, count as a key 'organizational resource' in political recruitment processes (Kopecký and Mair 2012). Indeed, party patronage is a formal institution – a formal prerogative codified in laws – through which political parties can field positions in public institutions (legislative and cabinet office, regulatory agencies, executive boards of public companies, etc.). While the distribution of party patronage is a formal prerogative of political parties, it should be noted that doing so to their members and officers is not a codified rule thereby providing a broad leeway for informal practices to emerge (see Franceschet, this volume), which might well entail gendered effects.

This chapter adopts a feminist institutionalist approach (Mackay, Kenny and Chappell 2010; Krook and Mackay 2011) to investigate whether in the last stages of the ladder of political recruitment holding a position within the ranks of the party organisation has gendered implications for political advancement. As posited by Annesley and Gains (2010, 912), 'Formal and informal rules in one institutional setting influence outcomes in another.' These institutional arrangements shape the ways in which resources and influence are made available to, and exchanged between, political actors. Therefore, by operating in 'selective and partial ways' political recruitment may advantage some office holders at the expense of others (ibid., 913).

More specifically, using a mixed-method approach we uncover the gendered institutionalised processes through which individuals can take advantage of the opportunities, resources and recognition derived from holding party office in advanced industrial democracies. In doing so, we pay attention to parliamentary candidacy, ministerial appointments and the post-ministerial offices in public and semi-public life that are also in the hands of political parties to distribute. After showing through a large-scale cross-national analysis that men are much more likely than women to benefit from holding party office in their ascendant political careers, we turn to examining the gender power dynamics capable of simultaneously subordinating or empowering individuals with similar positional power within political parties. Our qualitative meta-analysis of extant research on gender and political recruitment unfolds a specific gendered institutional logic: despite contextual differences, party office gives men privileged access to party patronage through a variety of informal norms and practices that build on male 'homosocial capital', a type of interpersonal capital generated among men for benefit of other men (Bjarnegård 2013, 24).

Focusing on *who is privileged* enables us to identify how *exclusionary mechanisms* operate in political recruitment processes (see Bjarnegård and Kenny, this volume). Simultaneously, identifying the gendered effects of holding party office allows us to pinpoint how formal and informal institutions form a continuum. Party patronage is a formal institution but is distributed in informal ways to party members and officers. We argue that the informal norms and practices upon which patronage is distributed build on the gendered composition and operation of (typically male) informal networks within the party organisation, which constitute themselves a bearer of informal institutions underpinned by (male) homosocial capital. While based on the formal positional power derived from holding party office, this political resource is riddled with informality and most crucially is overridden by gender: party office is not only more accessible to men but is also more valued in men, all else being equal, thereby rendering women party officers outsiders on the inside.

The remainder of the chapter is organised as follows. We start by conceptualising party office as a political resource within gendered political party organisations. After presenting the data and methods used in this study we move to the empirical analysis. We discuss, first, the results of the quantitative analysis and then provide a qualitative meta-analysis of extant research on gender and political recruitment. The last section discusses the main findings and concludes.

PARTY OFFICE: A GENDERED POLITICAL RESOURCE?

Political parties are central to representative democracy. Besides aggregating and representing societal interests and socialising citizens into democratic politics, they recruit political leaders and run organised election campaigns. Even where independent candidacies are allowed, most candidates compete in elections under a party label. Indeed, the candidate pool is largely made of parties' rank-and-file members (Gallagher and Marsh 1988). The assignment of leadership functions within parliaments (whips, spokespersons, etc.) also tends to be made by the party in central office.

Political parties also play a crucial role in appointments to the executive branch. While formally the selection of ministers is an exclusive competence of the prime minister or president, political parties do not play a negligible role. Prime ministers and presidents tend to be the party leaders, and heavy weights of the party usually occupy prominent positions within the government, which leads to the fusion of party and ministerial elites, particularly under bipartisan systems (Blondel 2000) and coalition cabinets (Warwick and Druckman 2001). In addition, party criteria such as geographical spread or factional diversity are present in the appointment of ministers (see Kopecký, Mair and Spirova 2012).

Political parties can also facilitate ex-ministers' post-office political career in the higher ranks of the public administration, in advisory committees and regulatory bodies, as well as in the governing boards of public enterprises. Party patronage may also reach processes of privatisation and marketisation, with heavy weights of the party often being appointed to the corporate boards of these companies (Kopecký and Mair 2012, 13). Similarly, partisan senior bureaucrats typically have longer tenures than departing ministers with no such background (Ennser-Jedenastik 2014). Departing ministers can also obtain safe seats or winnable positions in party lists in subsequent elections (Stolz and Kintz 2014).

What all these elective and appointive positions have in common is that they tend to require from aspirants a close connection to their respective political parties. Party membership and, more specifically, party office can thus be characterised as an 'organizational resource' that provides loyal members with access to the patronage parties use to control policy design and implementation (Kopecký and Mair 2012, 3). Party patronage is thus a 'key mechanism of elite recruitment' (p. 12). To what extent are the benefits carried by party office distributed equally across sex?

Gender and politics scholars have shown that political parties are gendered institutional spaces with organisational structures, procedures and practices 'saturated with gender' (Lovenduski 2005; see also Kenny and Verge 2016). Thus, it might well be that party office produces a differential access to party patronage for female and male actors. As posited by Kenney (1996, 456), the experiences of individuals within an institution vary according to gender, including access to circumscribed opportunities and the definition of the qualities and characteristics that are valued in order to be entitled to such opportunities. Gender is often 'done' in institutions through informal rules on masculinity and femininity that maintain the asymmetry of institutional power relations (Mackay, Kenny and Chappell 2010; Krook and Mackay, 2011).

Even when men and women hold the same elected or appointed positions, this power imbalance may be sustained by the gender power entrenched in the institutional gendered ethos and the interpersonal relationships 'infused with sex-role ideology, sex-role socialisation, and stereotypes about which behaviours, styles, and attitudes and beliefs each particular sex will manifest' (Kelly and Duerst-Lahti 1995, 59). In this vein, socially shared values and norms, conventions, routines and practices, de facto guide institutional processes and interactions and may eventually undermine gender reforms, such as gender quotas, when formal rules are not actively maintained or enforced (Helmke and Levitsky 2004; Chappell and Waylen 2013). These non-codified but still important rules, norms and practices shield male dominance through a 'gendered logic of appropriateness' (Chappell 2006) along with institutional narratives of gendered behaviour that legitimise gendered outcomes (Lowndes 2014; Waylen 2014).

How is party office, and more generally the operation of political parties, gendered? Whereas positional power in party executive bodies paves the way for a political career in public office, women's progress in party politics is 'a contested, slow, uneven, and incomplete process' (Kittilson 2013, 546). Although party office has been increasingly feminised over time (Kittilson 2006), party executives have seen gender reinscribed in different ways through patterns of inclusion and exclusion in the inner circles of informal power (Verge and de la Fuente 2014). Women party officers are often elected in contexts of poor party popularity but are still expected to deliver unrealistic achievements (Trimble and Arscott 2003, 71). Gender differences are also found in regard to rate of acclamation and percentage of the vote received by the victorious candidate, with women leaders being more contested than men and presenting a lower survival rate (O'Neill and Steward 2009, 747; Sawer 2013, 59). Women have a greater likelihood of stepping down when their parties lose seat share (O'Brien and Rickne 2014; O'Brien 2015). Women's higher turnover is also closely related to the gendered informal norms and practices that operate within political parties, such as being held to higher standards, facing continuous super-surveillance and receiving scarce recognition for their work (Verge and de la Fuente 2014, 72).

Other gendered experiences at party elite level include the gendered division of labour in the distribution of top party offices (Jennings and Farah 1981; Threlfall 2005; Verge 2015). Women assume more frequently labour intensive roles or routine functions while men take up more visible and rewarding positions (Fowlkes, Perkins and Tolleson-Rinehart 1979), which produces an asymmetric disposition of resources, visibility and influence. This constitutes a remainder that gender is 'oppositional and hierarchical' (Kenney 1996, 458). Consequently, although party office is a political resource that provides those seeking a political career with privileged access to the distribution of public positions, it might well be that the 'rules-in-use' (Leach and Lowndes 2007) render it a gendered organisational resource that yields higher benefits for men vis-à-vis women in their ascendant political career. Shedding light on this theoretical expectation requires examining both political recruitment processes and the broader party institutional setting wherein they take place.

DATA AND METHODS

As posited by Mackay, Armitage and Malley (2014, 104), 'answering the questions raised by gendered institutionalism requires a multi-method approach'. First, to uncover whether party office produces heterogeneous effects across sex, we undertake a cross-national comparative analysis following Weldon's (2014) call to using statistical methods to study institutions. In examining the effect of party office on parliamentary candidacy, we make use of the Comparative Candidate Survey database (CCS 2014). We select twelve countries for which there is available data on party office for candidates competing in the most recent election – Belgium, Czech Republic, Denmark, Finland, Germany, Greece, Hungary, Netherlands, Norway, Portugal, Sweden and Switzerland. To capture party office, we have created a dichotomous variable measuring whether candidates held (1) or did not hold (0) a position within the party leadership at any level of the party (local, regional or national). In exploring the gender distribution of executive and post-ministerial positions, we turn to Claveria's (2014b) cross-sectional database of cabinets in twenty-two advanced industrial democracies with strong political parties (Australia, Austria, Belgium, Canada, Denmark, Finland, France, Germany, Greece, Iceland, Ireland, Italy, Japan, Luxembourg, Netherlands, New Zealand, Norway, Portugal, Spain, Sweden, Switzerland and the United Kingdom). Party office is measured in this case as ministers holding (1) or not holding (0) an office within the national party decision-making bodies.

Although information for the whole pool of aspirants and eligible candidates for parliamentary, ministerial and post-ministerial offices does not exist, we can focus on individuals having achieved these positions and explore whether holding party office made a difference in their election or appointment. Therefore, we treat party office as our main independent variable (at any party level for parliamentary candidacy and at the national level for ministerial and post-ministerial appointments, where decisions on such positions are likely to be made). The elective and appointed positions under examination are our dependent variables. In order to unfold whether party office is a gendered political resource, we interact the variables party office and sex. With a view to easing the interpretation of the interaction term the empirical analysis exclusively provides the predicted probabilities of occupying the various political positions under examination by party office and sex. The calculus of marginal effects is based on logistic regressions – with errors clustered on country – that include other control variables (see Appendix 5A for variable description).

Second, to identify the causal mechanism behind the genderedness of party office, we adopt a qualitative approach. Particularly, using qualitative meta-analysis, while retaining the focus on meaning in context, we search for a synthesis of the interpretations provided by previous studies in light of how they translate into one another (see Noblit and Hare 1988). This synthetic secondary analysis allows for a comparative understanding that goes beyond individual accounts, thereby producing novel interpretations of findings or identifying 'the underlying conceptual relations signified, albeit not necessarily explicitly expressed, in the findings' (Sandelowski and Barroso 2007, 200). As highlighted by Bjarnegård and Kenny (2016), second-order interpretations of extant research carried out diachronically in seemingly very different contexts still allow pulling common insights that help us identify common causal mechanisms. Our target finding is the gendered implications of party office for the advancement of political careers.

THE DIFFERENTIAL EFFECT OF PARTY OFFICE ACROSS SEX

Our examination of the potential heterogeneous effect of party office across sex focuses on viable candidacy for parliamentary office, ministerial appointments to the most prestigious or 'inner' portfolios[1] and political post-office occupations. In our sample, women account for 35.8 percent of candidates in the most recent national elections, 31.3 percent of ministers, 18.9 percent of ministers in inner portfolios and 28.6 percent of departing ministers in political post-office occupations. The first goal of the empirical analysis is to prove that party office matters in recruitment processes, that is that political parties use their formal prerogative to distribute patronage in ways that benefit their members and officers, although this practice is not usually codified in national legislation or party documents. To put it differently, if party office is a political resource, holding such position should increase an individual's chance to get selected or appointed. Is this the case?

We start our survey with the analysis of viable candidacy for parliamentary office. Political parties shape candidates' chances of getting elected through their assignment to either safe, competitive or hopeless seats – under plurality systems – or their rank order in electoral lists – under PR systems (Norris 2004). The allocation of viable candidacy has been found to be highly gendered in both PR and plurality systems (Murray 2013; Luhiste 2015). To examine whether party service provides a comparative advantage to obtain winnable positions or safe seats we use the Comparative Candidate Survey (CCS) database. While the CCS database does not include a variable specifying whether candidates run in such electable spots, we can use, as a proxy, the variable capturing whether the candidate was elected or not in the most recent national election. Therefore, being elected is closely associated to having competed in a winnable position in party lists or in a safe seat.

The percentage of individuals with party office at any level of the party are higher among elected candidates (92 percent) than among non-elected candidates (80.3 percent), with differences being statistically significant at the 1 percent level. Elected men are more likely to have this organisational resource than women (88.3 percent vs. 93.4 percent, difference statistically significant at the 5 percent level). As illustrated in Figure 5.1, when also controlled by other variables such as seniority in public office, average number of monthly hours devoted to party work, educational level and age of candidates, holding or not holding party office leaves untouched women's predicted probability of being elected while men's probability increases from 3.5 percent to 7.2 percent.

Party office, as has been discussed, is also relevant for ministerial appointments. Using Claveria's (2014) database, we find that while most ministers are affiliated to a political party, only about a third of them (27.4 percent) hold, or have held in the past, an office in their party's national executive bodies. Female and male ministers are rather alike in their having this political background, with no significant gender differences found (26.3 percent vs. 30 percent, respectively). However, access to the most prestigious portfolios shows a different picture. Using Borrelli's (2002) classification, we see that 34.5 percent of ministers in inner portfolios (defence, treasury, economy, home office and foreign office) hold party

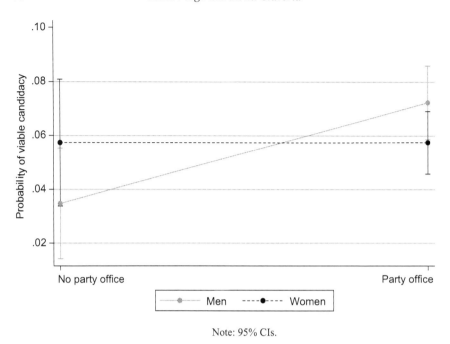

Note: 95% CIs.

Figure 5.1   Predicted probability for viable parliamentary candidacy by party office and sex.

office as compared with 24.2 percent of ministers in outer portfolios – difference statistically significant at the 5 percent level. Party office matters differently across sex groups. 34.3 percent of men in inner portfolios hold national party office as compared with 21.9 percent of men in outer portfolios – statistically significant at the 5 percent level. In contrast, the share of women with party office in inner and outer portfolios does not present statistically significant differences – 37.5 percent vs. 28.3 percent.

The interaction term between party office and sex, as illustrated in Figure 5.2, confirms that party office yields heterogeneous effects in the case of inner portfolios. Controlling for other political factors such as seniority in public office, policy expertise in the purview of the portfolio and educational level, we can see that holding an executive position in the party national leadership strongly increases men's likelihood of landing into an inner portfolio, but it has barely any effect on women's chances. Women's probability increases marginally from 16.8 percent when not holding party office to 23.5 percent when this organisational resource is possessed. Conversely, men's predicted probability of being appointed to such a portfolio when not holding party office is 32 percent, and it climbs to 48.5 percent when party office is held.

Last, we turn to post-ministerial occupations in the field of politics, the one more likely to be shaped by political parties through the distribution of

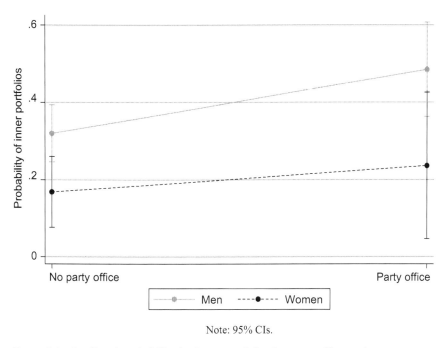

Note: 95% CIs.

Figure 5.2 Predicted probability for inner portfolios by party office and sex.

new positions in the top echelons of the public administration, the governing boards of public enterprises, advisory committees or regulatory bodies, as well as viable candidacy in the next elections. 31.8 percent of ex-ministers getting a new political position after cabinet termination[2] hold party office as compared to 21.5 percent who do not hold it – with differences statistically significant at the 5 percent level. Gendered patterns also emerge here. The share of party officeholders is lower among female ex-ministers keeping active in politics (27.3 percent) than those starting other non-political occupations (28.6 percent), with no significant differences found. Alternatively, 33.6 percent of male departing ministers landing in another political office when cabinet service terminates hold party office while this resource is only possessed by 18 percent of male ex-ministers who obtain other (non-political) post-office occupations – difference statistically significant at the 1 percent level.

As shown in Figure 5.3, the marginal effects at average values controlling for other variables, such as seniority in public office, policy expertise in the purview of the portfolio, country levels of party patronage and type of ministerial recruitment, indicate that male ex-ministers with party office are much more likely to continue their political career upon termination of cabinet service than those lacking this political resource, with their probability boosting from 42.5 percent to 63.6 percent. Yet, experience in national party office

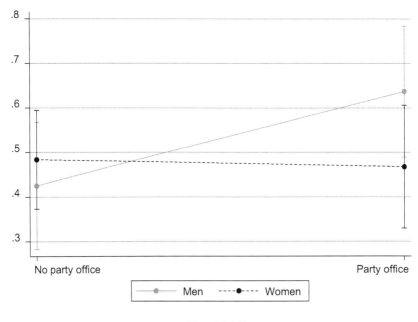

Note: 95% CIs.

Figure 5.3 **Predicted probability for post-ministerial occupation in politics by party office and sex.**

provides no comparative advantage to female departing ministers, with their probability slightly decreasing from 48.3 percent to 46.7 percent. Thus, party office exclusively expands men's post-tenure options in politics.[3]

PARTY OFFICE, HOMOSOCIAL CAPITAL AND MALE NETWORKS

The quantitative analysis has shown that party office does produce a significant differential effect across sex. This suggests that gender power is well established within political parties. Which are the gender power dynamics capable of simultaneously subordinating or empowering individuals with similar party positional power? With a view to identifying the causal (exclusionary) mechanism behind this gendered pattern we turn to a qualitative analysis of extant scholarship on gender and political recruitment. Through a comparative understanding of the gendered and institutional dimensions of the opportunity structures within political parties, we are able to trace women's discrimination in political recruitment processes back to the ways in which party service and, more specifically, party office operate.

The emerging common line of argument of our meta-analysis suggests that holding party office gives men more access to party patronage through a myriad of informal norms and practices entrenched in male 'homosocial capital'. As developed by Bjarnegård (2013, 24) in her groundbreaking research of male power in Thai parties' political recruitment shaped by clientelist practices, homosocial capital is an interpersonal capital 'predominantly accessible for other men as well as more valuable when built between men'. This concept translates very well into studies of political parties in advanced industrial democracies. In this vein, several works highlight the existence of 'male informal networks' (Verge and de la Fuente 2014; Annesley 2015), 'old boy networks' (Galligan, Clavero and Calloni 2007; Verge 2010) and 'male power monopolies' (Jones 2008; Hinojosa 2012; Johnson 2016). Other studies note women's absence from 'party gatekeepers,' 'social networks' (Cheng and Tavits 2011) and the 'back rooms of the party' (Sawer 2013, 60).

Male homosocial networks are generally built at the local or constituency level (Hinojosa 2012; Kenny 2013; Verge and de la Fuente 2014) but operate as well at the national party level (Jones 2008). They should not be seen as a single structure since they are often reproduced across party factions (Johnson 2016). This form of men's complicity is never put into question nor considered political, although it plays a crucial role in parties' decision making and in the building of support when aspirants decide to run for office (Verge and de la Fuente 2014, 76). The role of mentors and sponsors is also highlighted in several works. As pointed out by Childs and Murray (2014, 82), male incumbents 'often groom their successors, with a colleague from local politics often primed to replace them upon retirement'. Similarly, Lillefeldt (2011, 26) notes that 'borrowing social capital from a sponsor means getting informal support from a trusted, established insider'. Mentors and networks can thus be seen as a source of gender power at the level of interpersonal interactions and relationships within institutions (Kelly and Duerst-Lahti 1995, 48).

While connections among network members may be long-standing, even pre-dating party membership and originating in university, jobs or trade unions (see, for example, Lovenduski 2013), similar male homosocial networks are found within the youth party organisations.[4] These gendered patterns of participation in political parties and their collateral organisations have thus become deeply institutionalised in the political party culture. Women's relative historical exclusion from party politics in terms of membership and especially leadership positions entails that women's entry at both levels encounters a 'set of male-centred institutional practices' (Lovenduski 2005, 27) that create an uneven field for half the population.

The very existence of a network requires separating those who are members from those who are not, that is 'for collective norms and information-sharing purposes, a certain degree of closure is needed' (Bjarnegård 2013, 24).

The exclusionary 'membership' is not just granted by means of biological sex, that is by simply being a man. Rather, it is also protected by other gendered dynamics. Some studies report that the 'blokey' and 'laddish' culture of the inner circles of power hinders women's access to high-trust networks (Annesley and Gains 2010). Exclusionary practices also include the time when these networks tend to be built and sustained, and the spaces where they operate. Informal male networking typically takes place outside the formal decision-making arenas (Sawer 2013, 60), very often in bars or restaurants, after the formal meeting has ended (Verge and de la Fuente 2014, 74). It also tends to occur at 'unsocial' (late night) hours (Kolinsky 1993, 144), which reflect male schedules and may only adjust to those network participants that count with 'wifely or maternal supports' (Franceschet 2005, 90). This masculine hegemonic practice establishes an informal intensive dedication norm to party service, which is instrumental in recruitment processes and that discriminates against women due to the sexual distribution of labour and pervasive gendered roles in society (Verge and de la Fuente 2014, 74). Therefore, gendered norms and practices accommodate and reinforce existing social ideologies of gender and arrangements between the sexes (Verge 2015, 755).

One may argue that for women to overcome their political disadvantage, caring responsibilities allowing, they should 'infiltrate' these informal networks. Yet, when women occasionally join these informal decision-making arenas they tend to be shut down from the conversations (Verge and de la Fuente 2014, 73), making visible their status as 'space invaders' (Puwar 2004), despite holding similar party offices than their male peers. Indeed, women's entry would alter the implicit gendered presumptions (Borrelli 2000, 189). Therefore, homosociality leads to the ritualisation of predominant male practices and to the political exclusion of women. Thus, it goes beyond having the spare time to join the network, and it is about being or not being 'one of us', 'one' with whom solidarity ties and trust built on masculinity can be established (Galligan, Clavero and Calloni 2007, 101), as further developed below.

On the few occasions that women use informal means of organisation, significant differences emerge. On the one hand, they tend to use informal practices to force the party leadership to uphold the party's gender equality commitments, such as an effective implementation of electoral gender quotas. On the other hand, the party women engaged in these practices usually build cross-party informal networks or align with external party actors – such as female journalists or the women's movement (see Verge and Espírito-Santo 2016; Piscopo 2016). Such networks thus seek to compensate the absence of effective party positional power very often experienced by women.

According to Bjarnegård (2013, 28), all-men networks distribute 'instrumental resources', especially advantageous access to political positions and information exchange among their members. Thus, male homosocial networks are key distributors of office rewards. Yet, homosocial capital is also 'about more psychological considerations' that provide 'expressive resources' associated to stereotypical gender roles (ibid.: 29). The hegemonic masculinity leadership style is recognised by network members as deploying competence and likeability, and as facilitating communication and mutual understanding. This paves the way for 'men's sense of entitlement', leading to the promotion of men and the informal obstruction of women (Annesley 2015, 632). As Sawer notes (cf. 2013, 60), if deals continue to be made among men, it is unsurprising that they benefit men more than women.

The expressive resources underpinning homosocial capital provide participants with the familiarity and confidence for extracting cues to select candidates for party executives, electoral lists, parliamentary and executive office, and beyond. This yields an 'ingrained ethos of masculinity', making highly qualified and politically well-connected women less likely to be recruited to run for public office than men sharing similar traits (Fox and Lawless 2010). As posited by Franceschet and Piscopo (2014, 96), 'Gender is a strong predictor of the value that party leaders assign to candidates.' It seems too much of a coincidence that female candidates' profile typically matches that of non-winning male candidates in local party selections (Chapman 1993), whereas it is stereotypically masculine characteristics that party gatekeepers 'see' in 'good' candidates (Niven 1998; Tremblay and Pelletier 2001).

Women are often perceived as parachuted 'outsiders', whereas the 'favorite sons', namely local male candidates, are protected (Childs and Webb 2012; Kenny 2013; Culhane this volume). Men have more name recognition and access to party resources, and women are less likely to be encouraged to stand by party selectors (Dittmar 2015). The counterfactual does also exist. Women candidates are more likely to be selected when the local party gatekeeper, typically the local party president, is a woman, even after controlling for incumbency and the district and party contexts where electoral competition takes place (Niven 1998). Likewise, the more feminised party executives are, the more gender-neutral the allocation of safe positions in party lists appears to be (Kittilson 2006; Verge 2010).

We do also observe a transferability of recognition. Informal norms about a 'good candidate' travel to evaluations of a 'good leader', and vice versa (Cheng and Tavits 2011). The aspirants encouraged to run or to integrate the top positions of party lists are likely to be those with whom homosocial capital is already shared within the party organisation. Positions on electoral lists reflect candidates' prominence within the party hierarchy (Franceschet and Piscopo 2014, 96) as well as their density of networks within the party (Childs and Murray 2014, 83). As posited by Threlfall (2005, 137), 'the composition of the constituency candidate lists, being the nexus between internal party life and public office, reflects the overall gender balance of power throughout a party'. In other words, 'data on leading candidates closely reflects women's role in internal party politics' (ibid.: 138). Therefore, monopolising the positions at the top of the lists is not only instrumental to securing (re)election but also to maintaining positional power within parties (Childs and Murray 2014, 81).

While party office has been increasingly feminised, men still occupy the most prominent leadership positions. Thus, the lion's share of top positions in party lists, especially position number one, tends to be allocated to men, usually party officials with a strong hold in the district – predominantly local party leaders (Verge and Espírito-Santo 2016). Simultaneously, top-ranked candidates in party lists are typically awarded the most desirable appointment in the local party executive (O'Brien and Rickne 2014, 15). As highlighted by Childs and Murray (2014, 86), 'While women have gained access to less powerful positions in large numbers, men have used their positions of power within parties and elected politics to ensure that the most important offices have largely resisted parity.' Therefore, the informal norms underlying the selection of candidates for position number one reinforce patterns of women's exclusion and men's dominance in both party and elective positions.

While 'male power monopolies' tend to be built at the party local level (Hinojosa 2012; Kenny 2013) the cumulative effects derived from membership in the network reaches different political arenas such as the executive branch. As noted by Annesley and Gains (2010, 915), 'Aspirant ministers also need to be loyal to the party leadership and prime minister, play the favours game and be well networked.' The expressive component of homosociality is illustrated by the fact that presidents and prime ministers, who are typically men, tend to rely more on other men. While appointees' credentials are relevant, presidents and prime ministers also 'want certain "chemistry" in their cabinet' (Borrelli 2002, 5). As highlighted by Annesley (2015, 632), 'There is evidence that women are excluded – either overtly or covertly – from the crucial networks around the PM that set up opportunities for ministerial office.'

Ministers' presidential connections exclusively increase the chances of being appointed to a prestigious portfolio in the case of men (Escobar-Lemmon and Taylor-Robinson 2016). These connections derive to a large extent from the party, with a widespread 'tradition' mandating that 'ministers are drawn from the party leadership' (Franceschet and Thomas 2015, 651). It is no surprise then that 'party insider' presidents appoint fewer women to their cabinet than 'free-wheeling independent' presidents do, as shown by Escobar-Lemmon and Taylor-Robinson's (2008, 362) comparative study of Latin American cabinets. The inner circle of confidence thus travels from political parties to cabinets.

Simultaneously, regional and national party leadership positions are the main recruiting fields for ministers with party office. Annesley (2015, 632) points that few women manage to secure the 'leadership positions in political parties which set up ministerial opportunities'. Threlfall (2005, 132) finds that most of the women rising to a regional leadership post do not get a policy portfolio at all in the party executive but are rather brought in as lower-tier junior members or are appointed to either 'soft' or 'feminized' portfolios (welfare, environment or culture). These second-order positions of power within the party decision-making bodies are less likely to facilitate progressive political careers (Verge and de la Fuente 2014, 7). In a similar vein, previous research has noted that for men there is a positive association between integrating the party 'shadow cabinet', whose members tend to be appointed by the leader of the main opposition party to mark cabinet members, and occupying prestigious portfolios within the government when the party wins the election. Women tend to occupy fewer relevant positions within the party shadow cabinet, unless party quotas are applied to these positions – in which case the size of the shadow cabinet may increase to accommodate more women in without leaving men out (Karam and Lovenduski 2005, 200; see also Annesley 2015). Therefore, the over-representation of men in ministerial positions, especially in core portfolios, lies in the gender dynamics of political parties.

Male homosocial networking also produces 'discursive strategies of gendered Othering and gendered practices of rule-making and rule-breaking' (Kenny 2013, 155). As highlighted by Franceschet and Thomas in their study of parity cabinets (2015, 661), 'Informal norms are more visible when they are violated or challenged rather than routinely respected.' Homosociality can break female aspirants' ambitions since the meaning of ambition when displayed by men and women varies, especially if it threatens male power. In this vein, the capacity to sanction 'transgendered' behaviours (Duerst-Lahti and Kelly 1995) is identified as part of the male networks' expressive resources, which often translates into the capacity to establish informal norms regarding legitimate competition from female aspirants.

For example, Verge and de la Fuente (2014, 73) report that when two men compete to head a district-level party list, after the membership vote has taken place, the winner will typically take position number one and the front runner will get the second position. If the losing contestant is a woman, she is likely to be displaced to an unwinnable position in the party list. Similar gendered sanctions are found under plurality systems (Kenny 2013). Women party officers who publicly show their political ambition may also experience a subtle weakening of the competencies assigned to their position (Verge and de la Fuente 2014, 73). This suggests that while ambition is seen as a positive trait when found in men, it is generally perceived as a negative trait and even as a threat when found in women.

Homosocial networks of male peers should then be seen as bearers of informal institutions that underpin the operation of party office and party service more broadly by providing men with more expressive and instrumental strategic resources (recognition, opportunities, capacity to reward and to sanction) as compared with women, thereby keeping party machine politics deeply male dominated. Such (male) informal networks multiply men's positional power within the party organisation.[5] They can be conceived as an underlying structure of party politics that creates and naturalises, that is, that institutionalises advantage and disadvantage, as summarised in Table 5.1. It can be argued that male homosocial networks 'encompass (e)valuation of things, behaviors, and ways of being' (Duerst-Lahti and Kelly 1995, 20). If institutions 'are the means by which group actors inherit, accumulate and consolidate power' (Lowndes and Roberts 2013, 86), male homosocial networks within political parties allow conferring power and legitimacy to men at the expense of women. These networks become the 'locus of formal and informal decision-making' (Galligan, Clavero and Calloni 2007, 101).

Table 5.1 Meta-analysis synthesis: concepts, second- and third-order interpretations

Concepts	Second-Order Interpretation	Third-Order Interpretation
Network composition (who integrates the network): Male informal networks; male power monopolies; party gatekeepers' social networks	Informal norm for access (including restricting access to outsiders or space invaders) based on homosocial capital	Male homosocial networks as a bearer of informal institutions within political parties that sustain gender power relations
Settings and times (where and when male networking takes place): Unsocial hours; back rooms; places alien to formal party politics (bars, restaurants, etc.)	Masculine political repertoires as the norm Informal norms underpinning party service (like intensive dedication norm) that count against recruitment chances	
Expressive resources (psychological considerations related to gender roles): Likeability and confidence among male peers	Informal norms for being more positively (e)valuated and not held to constant scrutiny	
Instrumental resources (advantageous access to political positions): Capacity to reward and sanction	Transferability of recognition between different arenas as an informal selection criteria Informal norms and practices regarding 'legitimate' ambition and competition	

Overall, our synthetic secondary analysis of previous scholarship in the field of gender and political recruitment indicates that party office is a political resource in as much as it is held by men who share with male peers a specific type of (homo)social capital within the party organisation. The gendered composition of these networks, the settings in which such networks are built and sustained and the type of social capital developed among their members informally produce different entitlements of party office across sex through a myriad of informal norms and practices. Belonging to these male homosocial networks yields a higher capacity for rule-making and rule-breaking, and for enjoying the rewards associated to holding party office, such as access to party patronage. So, as highlighted by Childs (2013, 93), female party actors may not have 'gained power relative to where power lies', which has strong implications for the evaluation of internal party democracy.

CONCLUSION

Party office is a crucial political resource through which individuals can benefit from the capacity of political parties to select and appoint people to a myriad of public and semi-public offices. Riding on party coat-tails, office-seeking politicians can obtain new positions. Our empirical analysis confirms that holding party office gives politicians an advantageous access to party patronage. However, we also show that party office is a gendered political resource because it produces a differential access for women and men to viable candidacy for parliamentary office, ministerial (inner portfolios) appointments as well as post-ministerial political career opportunities. The cross-national quantitative analysis undertaken in this study allows us to sustain that these are robust findings. Our results also speak about the real influence and power women have within the party structure: gender seems to override the (formal) positional power derived from holding party office in the case of women.

In the second part of the chapter, through a qualitative meta-analysis we have argued that the underlying causal mechanism lies in the ways in which male homosocial capital underpins party membership and party office, making men's and women's experiences within political parties vary significantly. The power differential is not explained by the proportion of offices held by men and women within political parties but rather by the asymmetrical density of informal networks in which office-seeking men and women participate and the type of interpersonal relationships they can establish. The pervasiveness of male homosocial networking favours the recruitment of more men than women in the various stages of political recruitment through a variety of informal norms and practices, which allows the in-group (men) to safeguard its privileges against the legitimate aspirations of the out-group (women). Such informal networks can then be characterised as power multipliers for men.

Overall, the foundations of gender power relations in both the party organisation and in elective and appointive positions extend beyond a purely distributive logic – which sex holds a larger share of party offices. Intra-party institutionalised masculinity unequivocally empowers men and disempowers women in regards to access to elective and appointive offices through 'often-subtle cumulation of often-small advantages', as posited by gender politics scholars (Burns 2005, 138). Therefore, in order to unveil the norms, organisational practices and relations patterned through gender, we must pay greater attention to the micropolitics of the daily functioning of political parties that ultimately bias recruitment processes.

APPENDIX 5.1: DATA SOURCES AND VARIABLES

1. Comparative Candidate Survey (CCS, 2014)

Dependent variable. A4b1. Elected in the most recent national election: 1 = Yes; 0 = No.

Independent variables:

*A8a. Number of years in local party office
*A8b. Number of years in regional party office
*A8c. Number of years in national party office

* Combined in a single dichotomous variable

A12. Number of hours devoted to party activities in an average month
E1. Gender: 1 = Women; 0 = Men.
E2. Year of birth
E6a. Level of education: 1 = Incomplete primary; 2 = Primary completed; 3 = Incomplete secondary; 4 = Secondary completed; 5 = Post-secondary trade/vocational school; 6 = University incomplete; 7 = University completed.

2. Cabinet ministers (Claveria, 2014b)

Dependent variable 1. Type of portfolio: 1 = Inner portfolios (defence, treasury/economy, home office and foreign office); 0 = Outer portfolios (all remaining portfolios).
Dependent variable 2. Post-ministerial occupation: 1 = Politics, such as positions in the top echelons of the public administration, advisory and regulatory bodies and governing boards of public or recently privatised

companies; 0 = Other post-office occupations (including ministerial re-appointments).

Independent variables:

Sex: 1 = Women; 0 = Men.

Party office: 1 = Ministers holding or having held national party office (sitting members of national executive bodies) before or during their tenure in cabinet; 0 = Otherwise.

Seniority: Number of years a minister accumulates in any (appointed or elective) public office at any tier of government prior to cabinet entry.

Policy expertise: 1 = Ministers having university education or previous (non-political) professional experience in the purview of their portfolio; 0 = Otherwise.

Educational level: 1 = Primary education; 2 = Secondary education; 3 = Tertiary education.

Ministerial recruitment: 1 = Specialist systems; 0 = Generalist systems.

Patronage level: 1 = High or medium levels; 0 = Low levels or virtually none.

NOTES

1. Inner portfolios, which are found in every cabinet and in every country and do not tend to combine with other ministerial areas, including defence, treasury, economy, home office and foreign office (Borrelli 2002).

2. Following Claveria and Verge (2015) we exclude here government re-appointments, which are classified as a post-office occupation on its own right.

3. The variables 'party ideology' and 'party quotas' produce no statistically significant effect and the coefficients of the rest of variables hold virtually the same, so they have not been included in the final model. This result is not surprising since the genderedness of party organisations has also been identified for left-wing parties (see, among others, Lovenduski 2005; Kenny 2013; Verge and de la Fuente 2014). Left-wing parties typically count with higher numbers of party officers and field more women in public office vis-à-vis center or right parties but the gender-biased allocation of portfolios within party executives and cabinets is still a pervasive practice.

4. This was reported by young women party members in Verge and de la Fuente's research (2014).

5. We thank Fiona Mackay for this idea on informal networks constituting power multipliers for male actors and representing power compensators for equality entrepreneurs.

REFERENCES

Annesley, Claire. 2015. 'Rules of ministerial recruitment'. *Politics & Gender* 11(4): 618–642.

Annesley, Claire, and Francesca Gains. 2010. 'The core executive: Gender, power and change'. *Political Studies* 58.5: 909–929.

Bjarnegård, Elin. 2013. *Gender, informal institutions and political recruitment. Explaining male dominance in parliamentary representation*. Basingstoke: Palgrave Macmillan.

Bjarnegård, Elin, and Meryl Kenny. 2015. 'Revealing the "Secret Garden": The informal dimensions of political recruitment'. *Politics & Gender* 11(4): 748–753.

Bjarnegård, Elin, and Meryl Kenny. 2016. 'Comparing candidate selection: A feminist institutionalist approach'. *Government and Opposition* 51(3): 370–392.

Blondel, Jean. 2000. 'A framework for the empirical analysis of government-supporting party relationships'. In *The nature of party government. A comparative European perspective*, edited by Jean Blondel and Maurizio Cotta, 96–116. New York: Palgrave.

Borrelli, MaryAnne. 2000. 'Gender, politics, and change in the United States cabinet: The Madeleine Korbel Albright and Janet Reno appointments'. In *Gender and American politics. Women, men, and the political process*, edited by Sue Tolleson-Rinehart and Jyl J. Josephson, 189–204. New York: ME Sharpe, Inc.

Borrelli, MaryAnne. 2002. *The President's cabinet: Gender, power, and representation*. Boulder: Lynne Rienner.

Burns, Nancy. 2005. 'Finding gender'. *Politics & Gender* 1(1): 137–141.

CCS. 2014. Comparative Candidates Survey Module I – 2005–2012 [Dataset – cumulative file]. Distributed by FORS, Lausanne.

Chapman, Jenny. 1993. *Politics, feminism and the reformation of gender*. London: Routledge.

Chappell, Louise. 2006. 'Comparing political institutions: Revealing the gendered "logic of appropriateness"'. *Politics & Gender* 2(2): 223–235.

Chappell, Louise, and Georgina Waylen. 2013. 'Gender and the hidden life of institutions'. *Public Administration* 9(3): 599–615.

Cheng, Christine, and Margit Tavits. 2011. 'Informal influences in selecting female political candidates'. *Political Research Quarterly* 64(2): 460–471.

Childs, Sarah. 2013. 'Intraparty democracy: A gendered critique and a feminist agenda'. In *The challenges of intra-party democracy*, edited by William Cross and Richard Katz, 81–99. Oxford: Oxford University Press.

Childs, Sarah, and Paul Webb. 2012. *Sex, gender and the conservative party. From Iron Lady to Kitten Heels*. New York: Palgrave.

Childs, Sarah, and Rainbow Murray. 2014. 'Feminising political parties'. In *Deeds and words: Gendering politics after Joni Lovenduski*, edited by Rosie Campbell and Sarah Childs, 73–90. Colchester: ECPR Press.

Claveria, Sílvia. 2014a. 'Still a "male business"? Explaining women's presence in executive office'. *West European Politics* 37(5): 1156–1176.

Claveria, Sílvia. 2014b. *Women in executive office in advanced industrial democracies: Presence, portfolios and post-ministerial occupation*. PhD diss., Universitat Pompeu Fabra.

Claveria, Sílvia, and Tània Verge. 2015. 'Post-ministerial occupation in advanced industrial democracies: Ambition, individual resources and institutional opportunity structures'. *European Journal of Political Research* 54(4): 819–835.

Dittmar, Kelly. 2015. 'Encouragement is not enough: Addressing social and structural barriers to female candidate recruitment'. *Politics & Gender* 11(4): 759–765.

Duerst-Lahti, Georgia, and Rita Mae Kelly. 1995. 'On governance, leadership, and gender'. In *Gender power, leadership, and governance*, edited by Georgia Duerst-Lahti and Rita Mae Kelly, 11–37. Ann Arbor: University of Michigan Press.

Ennser-Jedenastik, Laurenz. 2014. 'Party politics and the survival of Central Bank governors'. *European Journal of Political Research* 53(3): 500–519.

Escobar-Lemmon, Maria and Michelle M. Taylor-Robinson. 2008. 'How do candidate recruitment and selection processes affect the representation of women?'. In *Pathways to power: Political recruitment and candidate selection in Latin America*, edited by Peter M. Siavelis and Scott Morgenstern, 345–368. Pennsylvania: Pennsylvania State University Press.

Escobar-Lemmon, Maria, and Michelle Taylor-Robinson. 2014. 'Women in presidential cabinets: Power players or abundant tokens?' New York: Oxford University Press.

Fowlkes, Diane L., Jerry Perkins and Sue Tolleson Rinehart. 1979. 'Gender roles and party roles'. *American Political Science Review* 73(3): 772–780.

Fox, Richard L., and Jennifer L. Lawless. 2010. 'If only they'd ask: Gender, recruitment and political ambition'. *Journal of Politics* 72(2): 310–326.

Franceschet, Susan. 2005. *Women and politics in Chile*. Boulder, CO: Lynne Rienner.

Franceschet, Susan, and Gwyn Thomas. 2015. 'Resisting parity: Gender and cabinet appointments in Chile and Spain'. *Politics & Gender* 11(4): 643–664.

Franceschet, Susan, and Jennifer Piscopo. 2014. 'Sustaining gendered practices? Power and elite networks in Argentina'. *Comparative Political Studies* 47(1): 85–110.

Gallagher, Michael, and Michael Marsh (eds.). 1988. *Candidate selection in comparative perspective: The secret garden of politics*. London: Sage.

Galligan, Yvonne, Sara Clavero and Marina Calloni. 2007. *Gender politics and democracy in post-socialist Europe*. Leverkusen Opladen: Barbara Budrich Publishers.

Helmke, Gretchen, and Steven Levitsky. 2004. 'Informal institutions and comparative politics: A research agenda'. *Perspectives on Politics* 2(4): 725–740.

Hinojosa, Magda. 2012. *Selecting women, electing women*. Philadelphia: Temple University Press.

Jalalzai, Farida, and Mona L. Krook. 2010. 'Beyond Hillary and Benazir: Women's political leadership worldwide'. *International Political Science Review* 31(1): 1–19.

Jennings, M. Kent, and Barbara G. Farah. 1981. 'Social roles and political resources: An over-time study of men and women in party elites'. *American Journal of Political Science* 25(3): 462–482.

Johnson, Niki. 2016. 'Keeping men in, shutting women out: Gender biases in candidate selection processes in Uruguay'. *Government & Opposition* 51(3): 393–415.

Jones, Mark P. 2008. 'The recruitment and selection of legislative candidates in Argentina'. In *Pathways to power: Political recruitment and candidate selection in Latin America*, edited by Peter M. Siavelis and Scott Morgenstern, 41–75. Pennsylvania: Pennsylvania State University Press.

Karam, Azza, and Joni Lovenduski. 2005. 'Women in parliament: Making a difference'. In *Women in parliament: Beyond numbers*, edited by Julie Ballington and Azza Karam, 187–213. Stockholm: International IDEA.

Kelly, Rita Mae, and Georgia Duerst-Lahti. 1995. 'The study of gender power and its link to governance and leadership'. In *Gender power, leadership, and governance*, edited by Georgia Duerst-Lahti and Rita Mae Kelly, 39–64. Ann Arbor: University of Michigan Press.

Kenney, Sally J. 1996. 'New research on gendered political institutions'. *Political Research Quarterly* 49(2): 445–466.

Kenny, Meryl. 2013. *Gender and political recruitment: Theorizing institutional change*. Basingstoke: Palgrave Macmillan.

Kenny, Meryl, and Tània Verge. 2016. 'Opening up the black box: Gender and candidate selection in a new era'. *Government & Opposition* 51(3): 351–369.

Kittilson, Miki Caul. 2006. *Challenging parties, changing parliaments. Women and elected office in contemporary Western Europe*. Columbus: The Ohio State University Press.

Kittilson, Miki Caul. 2013. 'Party politics'. In *The Oxford handbook of gender and politics*, edited by Georgina Waylen, Karen Celis, Johanna Kantola and S. Laurel Weldon, 536–553. Oxford: Oxford University Press.

Kolinsky, Eva. 1993. 'Party change and women's representation in Unified Germany'. In *Gender and party politics*, edited by Joni Lovenduski and Pippa Norris, 113–146. London: Sage.

Kopecký, Pter, and Peter Mair. 2012. 'Party patronage as an organizational resource'. In *Party patronage and party government in European democracies,* edited by Pter Kopecký, Peter Mair and Maria Spirova, 3–16. Oxford: Oxford University Press.

Kopecký, Pter, Peter Mair and Maria Spirova (eds.). 2012. *Party patronage and party government in European democracies*. Oxford: Oxford University Press.

Krook, Mona L., and Fiona Mackay. 2011. 'Introduction: Gender, politics, and institutions'. In *Gender, politics and institutions*, edited by Mona L. Krook and Fiona Mackay, 1–20, Basingstoke: Palgrave Macmillan.

Leach, Steve, and Vivien Lowndes. 2007. 'Of roles and rules: Analysing the changing relationship between political leaders and chief executives in local government'. *Public Policy and Administration* 22(2): 183–200.

Lillefeldt, Emelie. 2011. *European party politics and gender*. PhD diss., Stockholm University.

Lovenduski, Joni. 2005. *Feminizing politics*. Cambridge: Polity Press.

Lovenduski, Joni. 2013. 'United Kingdom: Male dominance broken?' In *Breaking male dominance in old democracies*, edited by Drude Dahlerup and Monique Leyenaar, 72–96. Oxford: Oxford University Press.

Lovenduski, Joni, and Pipa Norris (eds.). 1993. *Gender and party politics*. London: Sage.

Lowndes, Vivien. 2014. 'How are things done around here? Uncovering institutional rules and their gendered effects'. *Politics & Gender* 10(4): 685–691.

Lowndes, Vivien, and Mark Roberts. 2013. *Why institutions matter. The new institutionalism in political science*. New York: Palgrave.

Luhiste, Maarja. 2015. 'Party gatekeepers' support for viable female candidacy in PR-List systems'. *Politics & Gender* 11(1): 89–116.

Mackay, Fiona, Faith Armitage and Rosa Malley. 2014. 'Gender and political institutions'. In *Deeds and words: Gendering politics after Joni Lovenduski*, edited by Rosie Campbell and Sarah Childs, 93–112. Colchester: ECPR Press.

Mackay, Fiona, Meryl Kenny and Louise Chappell. 2010. 'New institutionalism through a gender lens: Towards a feminist institutionalism?'. *International Political Science Review* 31(5): 573–588.

Murray, Rainbow. 2013. 'Towards parity democracy? Gender in the 2012 French legislative elections'. *Parliamentary Affairs* 66(1): 197–212.

Niven, David. 1998. 'Party elites and women candidates: The shape of bias'. *Women and Politics* 19(2): 57–80.

Noblit, George W. and R. Dwight Hare. 1988. *Meta-ethnography: Synthesising qualitative studies*. London: Sage.

Norris, Pippa. 2004. *Electoral engineering*. Cambridge: Cambridge University Press.

Norris, Pippa, and Joni Lovenduski. 1995. *Political recruitment: Gender, race and class in the British parliament*. Cambridge: Cambridge University Press.

O'Brien, Diana Z. 2015. 'Rising to the top: Gender, political performance, and party leadership in parliamentary democracies'. *American Journal of Political Science* 59(4):1022–1039.

O'Brien, Diana Z., and Johanna Rickne. 2014. 'Gender quotas and women's political leadership'. *IFN Working Paper No.1043*. Stockholm: Research Institute of Industrial Economics.

O'Neill, Brenda, and David K. Stewart. 2009. 'Gender and political party leadership in Canada'. *Party Politics* 15(6): 737–757.

Piscopo, Jennifer. 2016. 'When informality advantages women: Quota networks, electoral rules, and candidate selection in Mexico'. *Government & Opposition* 51(3): 487–512.

Puwar, Nirmal. 2004. 'Thinking about Making a Difference'. *British Journal of Politics and International Relations* 6(1): 65–80.

Sandelowski, Margarete, and Julie Barroso. 2007. *Handbook for synthesizing qualitative research*. New York: Springer Publishing Company.

Sawer, Marian. 2013. 'New South Wales: Entering too late? Women in parliamentary politics'. In *Breaking male dominance in old democracies*, edited by Drude Dahlerup and Monique Leyenaar, 49–71. Oxford: Oxford University Press.

Stolz, Klaus, and Melanie Kintz. 2014. 'Post-cabinet careers in Britain and the US: Theory, concepts and empirical illustrations'. Paper prepared for the ECPR General Conference, Glasgow, 3–6 September.

Threlfall, Monica. 2005. 'Towards parity representation in party politics'. In *Gendering Spanish democracy*, edited by Monica Threlfall, Christine Cousins and Celia Valiente, 125–161. New York: Routledge.

Tremblay, Manon, and Rejean Pelletier. 2001. 'More women constituency party presidents: A strategy for increasing the number of women candidates in Canada?' *Party Politics* 7(2): 157–190.

Trimble, Linda, and Jane Arscott. 2003. *Still counting: Women in politics across Canada*. Peterborough: Broadview.

Verge, Tània. 2010. 'Gendering representation in Spain: Opportunities and limits of gender quotas'. *Journal of Women, Politics & Policy* 31(2): 166–190.

Verge, Tània. 2015. 'The gender regime of political parties: Feedback effects between supply and demand'. *Politics & Gender* 11(4): 754–759.

Verge, Tània, and Ana Espírito-Santo. 2016. 'Interactions between party and legislative quotas: Candidate selection and quota compliance in Portugal and Spain'. *Government & Opposition* 51(3): 416–439.

Verge, Tània, and Maria de la Fuente. 2014. 'Playing with different cards: Party politics, gender quotas and women's empowerment'. *International Political Science Review* 35(1): 67–79.

Warwick, Paul V., and James N. Druckman. 2001. 'Portfolio salience and the proportionality of payoffs in coalition governments'. *British Journal of Political Science* 31(4): 627–649.

Waylen, Georgina. 2014. 'Informal institutions, institutional change, and gender equality'. *Political Research Quarterly* 67(1): 212–223.

Weldon, S. Laurel. 2014. 'Using statistical methods to study institutions'. *Politics & Gender* 10(4): 661–672.

Chapter 6

Disentangling Informality and Informal Rules: Explaining Gender Inequality in Chile's Executive Branch

Susan Franceschet

Women's unequal participation in political institutions and the challenges of advancing feminist policy cannot be explained by looking only at the formal rules of politics. Democratic countries around the world have reformed their laws and constitutions to give women full rights to participate in politics. In today's democracies, there are no longer any legal barriers to voting, standing for elected office or being appointed to high-level posts in the executive or judicial branches. Gender scholars have thus had to look elsewhere to explain why, in the absence of formal barriers, women continue to be underrepresented in political institutions and why feminist policy goals, like ending violence against women and tackling the gender wage gap, remain on the margins of public policy agendas.

Over the past decade, gender scholars have produced a rich theoretical and empirical literature examining the deeper sources of women's inequality in public life. In particular, feminist researchers have drawn on historical and sociological institutionalism in order to explain gender inequality. This research highlights two aspects of institutions: First that the rules that comprise institutions are both formal, that is, codified and legally sanctioned, and informal, that is, unwritten and not enforced through law. The second aspect highlighted in this research is that rules create and reinforce advantages and disadvantages for differently situated social groups. In other words, institutional rules are not neutral. To the contrary, rules have gendered consequences that can reinforce or challenge a status quo in which men enjoy greater access to and power within the political arena. To date, most feminist research has focused on legislative institutions, bureaucratic arenas and discrete policy issues. Fewer researchers have examined the executive branch, an arena in which there has been minimal progress towards gender equality.

There are good reasons for feminist institutionalists to turn their attention to the executive branch. Gender scholars have long wanted to know whether elected women serve as substantive representatives, that is, whether they are more likely to pursue women's interests in their legislative work (Escobar-Lemmon and Taylor-Robinson 2014). But some note that even if female parliamentarians are more likely to want to pursue women's rights policies, their ability to do so is limited in political systems where the executive branch is the real source of power and therefore sets the policy agenda (Atchison 2015; Franceschet and Piscopo 2008). In most countries, the executive branch is the true locus of power in politics. This is particularly true for Latin America's presidential systems. Cabinet ministers 'have a near monopoly in the design of policy', they are key actors in getting a president's policy agenda through Congress and they oversee policy implementation, all with little oversight from the legislative branch (Martínez-Gallardo 2010).

At a theoretical level, studying the executive branch is valuable because of the way it differs from the legislative branch. Parliaments are governed by formal rules both for recruitment of members and how they do their work; courts and other official political authorities can sanction violations of these rules. Parliaments also do their work in the public eye. Chamber debates, committee deliberations and votes are recorded and sometimes televised. In contrast, the executive is organised and governed by rules that are not visible and, in many cases, not even written down. Gender scholars can gain much by exploring the relative lack of formal rules in the executive. But the exploration is more difficult precisely because whatever rules do exist are not codified or publicly visible. Scholars must dig deeper to account for gender inequality and explore how unspoken expectations, taken-for-granted practices and deeply ingrained ideas about appropriate roles and behaviour affect women and men's opportunities to participate fully in public life. This task is fraught with conceptual and methodological challenges, however. Just because behaviour is patterned does not mean that it is governed by rules. In other words, habits and routine practices are not the same as rules (Helmke and Levitsky 2006). The relative absence of formal rules requires scholars to think about how patterned behaviour nonetheless emerges, but also whether these patterns owe to rules that are simply informal (i.e. unwritten), or whether the patterns are not actually governed by rules at all. In this chapter, I refer to the absence of any types of rules, whether formal or informal, as *informality*.

In this chapter, I adopt a three-part distinction among formal rules, informal rules and informality – the absence of formal or informal rules. As noted, studying informal rules and informality poses methodological challenges. This is because we need to gain access to individuals with insider knowledge about what the unwritten rules are or how people behave in the absence of rules. In this chapter, I use a case study of Chile's executive branch to reveal the advantages of keeping informal rules conceptually separate from informality. In Chile, it is not just informal rules but the absence of rules or informality that accounts for gendered outcomes that keep women on the margins of political power.

The chapter has two sections: First, I outline the conceptual distinctions between informal rules and informality to capture the challenges and obstacles that women face. Second, I outline how informality and informal rules reinforce gender inequality in Chile's executive branch. What we see is that gender inequality is expressed in two ways: First, in men's over-representation among cabinet ministers, and particularly the most high-profile ministers; and second, the difficulty for women to access those executive arenas where the central policy agenda is set.

CONCEPTUAL AND METHODOLOGICAL CHALLENGES: IDENTIFYING INFORMALITY, INFORMAL RULES AND THEIR GENDERED EFFECTS

A key insight of the new institutionalism is that rules matter (Lowndes and Roberts 2013; March and Olsen 1989; Thelen and Steinmo 1992). Rules distribute power and therefore make some outcomes more likely and others more difficult to achieve (Thelen and Steinmo 1992). From the very beginning, institutionalists recognised that rules are not neutral, making the approach useful for gender scholars wishing to explain a wide array of political and policy outcomes, like why so few women are appointed to cabinet or why electing more women has not produced significant policy transformations. But gender scholars brought to institutionalism a key insight of feminist political science, namely that many of the rules and organising principles of institutions are not entrenched in constitutions, laws or written policy documents. The obstacles women face in getting elected, exercising power or pursuing gender-friendly policies no longer derive primarily from formal statutes and policies. Indeed, many of the goals of second-wave feminism have been achieved: legal reforms to prohibit sex-based discrimination and mandate equal opportunities are in place in most of the democracies around the world. Yet gender scholars have shown that unequal outcomes persist due to the stickiness of unwritten rules, customs, norms and practices that reinforce men's advantages in public life (Krook and Mackay 2011; Waylen 2014).

Of course, some of the emerging institutionalist scholarship also pays attention to the unwritten dimensions of social and political organisation. But few do so systematically, instead conceptualising institutions so broadly that empirical researchers have little guidance in identifying the relevant rules and practices, and separating them from *any* behaviour or outcome that appears patterned. More recently, efforts have gotten under way to produce more rigorous definitions, particularly for informal institutions, a term that risks becoming a meaningless residual category encompassing almost everything (Chappell and Waylen 2013). According to Lowndes, 'Feminist researchers should beware of expansive understandings of institutions that import into their definition broad notions of culture and custom' (2014, 687). If the goal for gender scholars is to understand how informal rules reinforce (or in some cases challenge) masculine privilege, then researchers must be able to separate out these rules from broader social structures like the gender division of labour (see also Thelen and Steinmo 1992). But scholars must also be able to separate rule-bound behaviour from behaviour that is not governed by rules at all.

It is important to acknowledge that the absence of formal rules does not automatically lead to the emergence of informal rules to fill the void. Researchers must take care not to elide informal rules with the absence of formal rules. Sometimes, rules (even unwritten ones) simply do not emerge. The two concepts – formal rules and informal rules – are far more useful if we think about how each of them creates different dynamics for reinforcing or challenging gender inequalities in politics. Informal rules share at least two key features with formal rules. First, they are both rules and thus they are followed most of the time. If the rules are violated, the actor(s) breaking them will face negative consequences. The key difference between formal and informal rules, according to Helmke and Levitsky (2006), is whether they are written or unwritten and whether sanctions for non-compliance occur through official, public channels or not. Sanctions for breaking informal rules are not codified and do not occur through official channels, and hence they vary tremendously. Sanctions may be strong, like being passed over in candidate nomination or being shut out of information networks that are critical to political effectiveness. Other sanctions are weaker, like public criticism or disapproval. Because some sanctions for rule breaking are weak, political actors may decide to bear the cost, especially if they consider it necessary to the pursuit of some other political objectives.

A second shared characteristic of formal and informal rules is that both can be identified and talked about by political actors. Of course, formal rules are easier to identify because they are written down somewhere. But while informal rules are unwritten, political insiders should be able to identify them and explain them to researchers. Sanctions, too, must be identifiable, although not necessarily empirically observed. According to Lowndes, for something to be a rule, it must be 'subject to some sort of third-party enforcement' and it should be 'able to be described and explained to the researcher' (2014, 686). Clearly, when a rule is strong, sanctions may never need to be invoked because violating the rule is unthinkable. At the very least, however, for something to be considered an informal rule, political actors must be able to imagine – and describe to researchers – the possibility of a sanction. What is most important is that because rule breaking involves sanctions, both formal and informal rules constrain actors' behaviour. Yet the degree to which rules constrain actors varies because rules are messy and complex rather than hierarchical and straightforward. According to March and Olsen, 'Although rules bring order, we see sets of rules as potentially rich in conflict, contradiction, and ambiguity, and thus as producing deviation as well as conformity' (1989, 38). This ambiguity creates space for political agents to reinterpret the meaning of rules in ways that may challenge the status quo. Likewise, Thelen and Mahoney write that whether formal or informal, rules are always 'subject to interpretation, debate, and contestation' (210, 8).

In contrast, arenas or situations that are governed neither by formal nor by informal rules create a permissive environment for the emergence of behaviour that is not subject to sanctions. Actors are thus not constrained by rules. This is what comes to mind when gender scholars talk about informality and particularly the presence of informal networks (like 'old boys' clubs') that exclude women. The role of male networks as a barrier to women's entry into politics has been extensively documented in gender and politics scholarship (Bjarnegård 2013; Franceschet and Piscopo 2014). Often, these networks are described as informal. This descriptor is entirely appropriate when networks comprise individuals whose influence is not necessarily derived from their official position, like cabinet minister, party leader or vice president of senate. The power and influence of individuals in informal networks is often unconnected to their official posts. Sometimes, members of informal networks are influential because they have the ear of people who actually do occupy key posts, like the president or party leader. But other times, it is unclear why individuals are influential; it is enough that others describe them that way and everyone knows who they are and believes them to be influential. It is not helpful, however, to consider informal networks and the role that they play in political recruitment or policymaking as institutions. Although some aspects of informal networks, particularly their membership, may be governed by informal rules about access, we need to separate how informal networks are formed and governed from the role that they play in political institutions. Or, at the very least, whether the role of informal networks in politics is governed by rules is an empirical question that should not be assumed at the outset but instead should be explored and established through research.

Distinguishing informal rules from informality is particularly important because each poses different sorts of barriers to change. Informal rules differ from formal rules in terms of how difficult or easy they are to change. Because formal rules are visible and codified, political actors can launch public campaigns to change them and direct their efforts to individuals with formal authority. But the stakes are often quite high: if existing rules reinforce benefits for some group, members of that group can block change. Informal rules, on the other hand, may be trickier to challenge: they are unwritten, and there are no identifiable individuals with the authority to change them. But this very challenge can become an opportunity. The fact that informal rules are less visible (since they are not codified) means that they contain more space for resistance or minimal compliance, especially when actors consider the sanctions for rule breaking worth bearing (Waylen 2014). In this same way, informality creates both challenges and opportunities for change. Without formal rules, it is difficult for advocates to lobby for change, since it is not clear where efforts should be directed. But it also creates space for actors with power and influence to effect change, namely to alter practices and behaviour that have disadvantaged women. But informality poses fewer constraints, since there are no sanctions for introducing changes to existing practices. Thus, when empowered actors want to promote equality, they can do so more easily.

The usefulness of distinguishing informality from informal rules, and the different possibilities for change, is evident when examining the executive branch, an understudied political arena. The lack of knowledge about the executive branch stems from the fact that so much of its work is hidden. Peter Siavelis notes the importance of informality in the executive, which he equates with the networks of 'advisors that help [leaders] structure relations with congress, protect their image, and navigate difficult political waters' (2010, 3). Although some of the advisors hold official positions, others do not. More significant for Siavelis, the influence or power that advisors (whether in formal posts or not) exercise is not governed by formal or informal rules, but by personal relationships with the president. Yet presidential advisors do not constitute a unified or coherent network whose membership and behaviour is organised by informal rules or shared purposes and beliefs. On an individual level, access to presidential advisory posts is primarily determined by prior relationships of friendship, trust or loyalty with the president. Presidents appoint advisors whom they trust and often that trust emerges from past experiences of working together or serving together in political parties or government offices. Because criteria such as friendship and trust are not considered to be the appropriate basis on which political appointments are made, the role played by presidential advisers is difficult to research: 'Presidents themselves seek to mask the influence of these networks for a variety of political reasons' (ibid). What is more, when it comes to rules, while there are some formal and informal rules that determine how executives are staffed, there are neither formal nor informal rules about how they take decisions, and how their various parts are related. Constitutions say surprisingly little about how presidents or prime ministers form their cabinets, or what sorts of power ministers and presidential advisors can wield. As such, looking at a country's constitution or laws will tell us little about how its most powerful political arena actually works.

We need different concepts and methods to reveal the role of executive actors in policymaking, and to determine how different parts of the executive are related to each other. Qualitative methods, particularly elite interviews, are well suited to revealing informal rules and the gendered consequences of both informal rules informality. Getting the right kind of information from political experts and insiders is difficult, however. Informal rules are taken for granted, requiring researchers to get insiders and observers to talk about and 'name' things that are rarely discussed explicitly. The privilege of certain groups is reinforced and protected by the public invisibility of existing informal rules and the absence of rules – that is, informality. In this case, men, who are the likely insiders within that privileged group, may be less than forthcoming, or even try to obfuscate when describing the processes and practices that they are being asked about. These challenges mean that researchers need to carefully design their interview guides and encourage respondents to clarify underlying assumptions and reasons for doing things in certain ways. Researchers should also avoid automatically taking interview respondents' remarks at face value. In order to shed light on how informality and informal rules in the executive branch create both challenges and opportunities for gender equality, researchers must seek a wide range of supporting data, whether from other interviews or other sources.

The remainder of the chapter draws on elite interviews conducted in Chile between 2013 and 2015 to outline how informal rules affect women's access to cabinet and how informality, that is, the absence of rules, pervades the functioning of the executive branch, particularly when it comes to the relationships between cabinet and presidential advisors.[1] My goal is to show how the rules, norms and day-to-day practices that structure executive institutions, like cabinet and the presidency, and the network of advisers and coordinating bodies that surround the chief executive, determine women's presence and their ability to place feminist issues at the centre of policymaking.

INFORMALITY, INFORMAL RULES AND GENDER IN CHILE'S EXECUTIVE BRANCH

Chile's constitution is often described as strongly presidentialist, concentrating extensive formal powers in the executive branch (Shugart and Carey 1992; Siavelis 2000). Although both branches of government enjoy the formal right to introduce legislation, there are restrictions on the type of bills that members of Congress may introduce, and the executive has vast agenda-setting powers. The constitution prevents members of Congress from introducing bills that involve spending or that affect the budget, and the executive is formally empowered to declare 'urgencies' that have the effect of fast-tracking committee and full-chamber discussion of a bill. The executive branch also possesses far greater resources in the legislative process, namely, access to congressional committees and greater human and technical resources (Haas 2010). In addition to its formal legislative powers, the president enjoys extensive powers of appointment, filling hundreds of posts throughout the state. What is more, the president's appointments need not be confirmed by another political branch, as do high court judges or cabinet ministers in the United States. Finally, the executive's rule-making powers include regulatory decrees: All laws passed by Congress require executive regulations that spell out how the laws are to be implemented. Notably, Congress cannot oversee policy implementation, and even if the executive is supposed to ensure that the regulatory decrees are in keeping with the spirit of the laws adopted by Congress, there is no mechanism for ensuring such correspondence (Martínez-Gallardo 2010). In brief, the formal powers of the Chilean executive are vast.

Yet the Chilean political institutions' formal rules are a poor guide for understanding how and why political actors behave the way they do. This is because, in addition to the formal rules, myriad entrenched informal rules guide political action. Most important, some of the informal rules have the effect of mitigating the concentration of power in the executive branch. Peter Siavelis (2006) shows that while the constitution concentrates great *formal* power in the executive, a series of *informal* institutions have developed to constrain presidents. Two of the informal rules of post-transition Chilean politics have profound gendered consequences. The first is the practice of consensus seeking, or 'politics by agreement'. According to this rule, presidents must seek consensus among the parties of the governing coalition,[2] and sometimes even with key opposition political actors, before formally introducing a new policy issue on the agenda. The other relevant informal rule governs executive recruitment. This is the practice of distributing posts proportionally across the parties of the coalition (see Siavelis 2006). Both rules aim to maintain coalition unity but have the effect of constraining presidents, particularly when it comes to appointing cabinet ministers and other top executive offices (like sub-secretaries, governors and intendants). Taken together, these informal rules affect recruitment to executive offices as well as the way that the executive branch actually functions, specifically, where power and policymaking influence are located. Both rules are gendered in ways that create opportunities and obstacles to women and to the pursuit of feminist policy goals.

Executive Recruitment

To a large extent, one cannot separate cabinet appointment from appointment to other high-ranking executive posts. In terms of formal rules, there is just one: presidents have the legal authority to appoint whomever they wish to executive posts.[3] But there are two important informal rules that work together to create different opportunities for men and women to access executive office: (1) the *cuoteo*,[4] which refers to achieving a numerical balance in executive posts across the parties of the coalition; and (2) *tranversalidad* (transversality), which means ensuring that the key posts are distributed across the parties, both horizontally and vertically.

The *cuoteo* can be best conceived as an informal rule that requires the president to distribute executive posts, which include not just cabinet posts, but also sub-secretaries and regional administrators (governors and intendants), across the coalition parties in relative proportion to the parties' electoral strength (Altman 2008; Dávila 2011). The rule about horizontal tranversalism means that the *cuoteo* does not just apply to the cabinet as a whole, but also to its most important subgroup, the political committee. The ministers that make up the political committee – namely the ministers of finance, interior, secretariat general of the presidency (SEGPRES) and secretariat general of government (SEGOB) – cannot all go to the same party, but must be shared across the main parties of the coalition. Vertically, the rule of transversalism means that the minister and sub-secretary, the two top posts in all ministries, must come from different parties.

These two practices have been observed for every single government since 1990, and thus it is relatively uncontroversial to categorise them as strong informal rules whose violation would elicit costly sanctions. As the rules are informal, the sanctions for breaking them would be political rather than judicial. Likely, they would take the form of political parties openly criticising the president or withdrawing their support. Even in a separation of powers system, the support of all coalition parties is important to ensuring the passage of the president's legislative agenda. Indeed, the very fact that these rules have not been broken in more than twenty years provides some indication that the political sanctions would be costly, encouraging presidents to comply with the rules.

A third practice is more contested and there is less agreement about whether to call it a rule at all. This practice concerns the role of the parties in executive recruitment. Unlike the coalition governments common in European parliamentary systems, where parties negotiate the distribution of cabinet portfolios but then party leaders rather than the prime minister select 'their' ministers, in Chile, the power to select rests both formally and informally with the president. Yet, that does not mean that the parties play no role at all in executive recruitment. Instead, their role is less clear, and appears to shift dramatically depending on who is president. Existing studies of cabinet formation (especially Dávila 2011; Fernández and Rivera 2013), along with my own interviews with former ministers, party leaders, presidential advisers and political experts, concur that the first three post-transition presidents – Patricio Aylwin, Eduardo Frei and Ricardo Lagos – consulted with party leaders when selecting individuals for executive posts, but that Michelle Bachelet (2006–2010, re-elected in 2014) and Sebastián Piñera (2010–2014) did not. What is perhaps more clear and uncontested is that all presidents communicate, often in face-to-face meetings, with party leaders. But what actually goes on in those meetings is not well known. A notable feature of both Bachelet's and Piñera's cabinets, however, is that the parties' wishes seem to have been ignored, at least initially. Both presidents constructed initial cabinets that were remarkable for the absence of party elites with lengthy political trajectories. Piñera deviated the most from past practices by appointing a majority of ministers to his initial cabinet who were not professional politicians at all, but instead were technocrats and independents.[5]

If categorising a practice as an informal rule requires that there is some sort of third-party enforcement, to what extent can we say that taking parties' wishes into account when appointing ministers is indeed an informal rule? This question is difficult to answer. On the one hand, Bachelet and Piñera, the two presidents who reportedly went the furthest in flouting party wishes, quickly encountered difficulties in managing their coalitions. Basically, the sanction both leaders experienced was widespread dissatisfaction in the parties of their coalitions. Notably, both leaders responded by shuffling their cabinets in ways that conformed more closely to past practice. In other words, they brought into cabinet the more traditional party heavyweights. As one political expert put it, Bachelet's 'government began badly, with a lot of conflict, a lot of tension, and Bachelet ended up modifying her decisions . . . appointing people to cabinet who were more representative of the parties, people who had greater trajectories, with more political capital'.[6] A former minister explained that when political crises hit, more traditional party elites were brought into cabinet, replacing the newcomers. Piñera did the same: after appointing a record number of independents, he eventually appointed people with more traditional trajectories in the two parties making up his coalition.[7] He did so because, like Bachelet, 'he also began to have problems [with the parties] and many cabinet shuffles later, he was appointing people that he respected, but who were also people with more weight in their respective parties'.[8] The fact that both leaders ultimately felt compelled to reverse course and appoint more traditional party heavyweights implies that ensuring the party leaders feel represented in cabinet can be considered an informal rule.

How are these informal rules gendered? The informal rules for executive recruitment are clearly gendered in their effect, which is that men enjoy greater opportunities to be appointed to executive posts than do women (see Table 6.1). Even though the formal rule is that presidents can select whomever they wish, thc informal rules constrain presidents because there are so many moving parts to balance (Siavelis 2014). As a result, the eligibility pool of possible ministers becomes very small, and even presidents committed to gender equality, like Michelle Bachelet, have a difficult time keeping that promise. Although Bachelet managed to appoint an initial gender parity cabinet in 2006, and selected a large number of women as intendants and governors, party leaders were not happy with some of the ministers she appointed. As a result, an early cabinet shuffle removed some of the female ministers from the prominent posts (like SEGPRES and defence), and for much of her term, no women at all held posts in the political committee (Franceschet and Thomas 2015). Tellingly, upon announcing her cabinet after her 2014 re-election, Bachelet said that she would have liked her cabinet to be gender equal but 'it is not that way'. Instead of gender parity, Bachelet's initial cabinet in 2014 included women in 39 percent of posts. Sadly, women's presence in the executive branch worsened over the first two years of Bachelet's term. By May 2015, after shuffling cabinet (and sub-secretaries, in keeping with the informal rule of transversalism), women held only 30 percent of cabinet posts and 35 percent of sub-secretary posts. Worse, by 13 July 2015 Bachelet removed two of the remaining three female intendants. This left just one out of fifteen regional governments in female hands, the lowest figure since 1990, when all of the regional governments were led by men.[9]

Although women today enjoy greater opportunities to enter cabinet than they did two decades ago, they clearly do not enjoy equal access to the posts that afford the greatest degree of political and policy influence. Men's

Table 6.1   Women's cabinet representation* (1990–2014)

President (Year Initial Cabinet Appointed)	Aylwin (1990)	Frei (1994)	Lagos (2000)	Bachelet (2006)	Piñera (2010)	Bachelet (2014)
Total ministers	18	19	16	20	22	23
Men	17	16	11	10	15	14
Women	1	3	5	10	7	9
Male percentage	94.4	84.2	68.7	50	68.2	60.9
Female percentage	5.5	15.8	31.3	50	31.8	39.1

*These figures reflect women's inclusion in *initial* cabinets. The only exception is President Aylwin's cabinet, where the initial cabinet had no women at all, but when Sernam was created (in 1991), its director had cabinet rank. The first director was Soledad Alvear.

dominance is particularly stark when it comes to the four spots in the political committee. Between 1990 and 2013, forty-four individuals occupied the four posts and just five of them were women (11%). All of them were appointed after 2006.[10] Michelle Bachelet was the first president to appoint a woman, Paulina Veloso, to the political committee.[11] It is also telling that of the five women who have served in the political committee, four of them held what is perhaps the least important post in that committee, namely the government's spokesperson (SEGOB). No woman has ever held the two most powerful posts, which are the finance minister or interior minister.[12] According to a political observer, even though Bachelet appointed women to half of the posts in her first cabinet, it was the men who exercised real power throughout her government.[13]

In sum, recruitment to executive offices in Chile, particularly to cabinet and other high-ranking posts like sub-secretary, is governed primarily by informal rules. The first and strongest rule is that presidents must distribute posts proportionally across the coalition parties. All presidents appear to comply with this rule. The other important rule is that presidents try to ensure that party leaders are relatively content with the ministers the president selects. This rule appears to be somewhat weaker, and presidents Bachelet and Piñera challenged the rule by appointing ministers to their initial cabinets that were not favoured by party leaders. Of course, there is a blurry line between party leaders being critical of the president's choices and party leaders feeling so dissatisfied that they withdraw support and undermine a president's ability to govern. Notably, both Bachelet and Piñera ultimately experienced the sanction of party dissatisfaction and both ultimately responded by replacing newcomers in their cabinets with more traditional party heavyweights.

On its own, the proportionality rule would not necessarily advantage men, but when placed alongside the rule of satisfying party leaders, the difficulties for women are more evident. Satisfying party leaders means selecting individuals from relatively closed networks of party elites so that party leaders feel that their party is well represented in the president's cabinet. Elite party networks can be understood as shifting groups of individuals, most of whom have served as party president, senator, cabinet minister or long-time member of the Chamber of Deputies. Notably, few women figure prominently in elite party networks; only two women have served as presidents of the parties of the centre-left coalition, and few women have occupied other positions that are markers of political status in Chile, like senator and cabinet minister.[14] Between 1990 and 2006, men held 83.9 percent of all cabinet posts (Altman 2008, 264), women's representation in the senate has ranged between 6 and 18 percent since 1989 and the overwhelming majority of party presidents have been men. In 2009, each of Chile's five largest parties was headed by a man, and women comprised between 8 and 22 percent of party executives.[15]

Women's absence from the more powerful posts on the political committee can likewise be explained in light of the criteria for appointment to these posts. Former ministers referenced criteria like 'being influential', 'knowing how to manage things' and being able to deliver the support of groups whose support the president needs, when I asked them what sort of criteria presidents use to select ministers.[16] One of the former ministers went on to say that women's relative absence from politics means that they have not accumulated the political experience and skills to figure prominently in the eligibility pool for cabinet.

Although the rules for cabinet recruitment are informal, there is not much space for political actors to change them. Even Michelle Bachelet, a president with an explicit commitment to gender equality, did not succeed in changing the rules in ways that could break men's greater access to executive offices in general, and in particular, to those posts that confer the greatest degree of political influence.

Executive Functioning

How the executive functions on a day-to-day basis shapes the possibilities for women to access the most important decision-making and agenda-setting arenas. In particular, bureaucrats, ministers and advocates who wish to promote a feminist policy agenda must be able to access those arenas where the policy agenda is determined. Yet as noted earlier, we know little about how Latin American executives function on a day-to-day basis. Unlike parliamentary systems, cabinets in Latin America's presidential systems do not function as collective bodies structured by formal rules, procedures and routine meetings. Instead, in most countries in the region, including Chile, the work of cabinet is organised through thematic inter-ministerial committees, for instance, in committees formed by the economic, social or political ministries (Martínez-Gallardo 2010, 134). This is the case in Chile as well. There is no constitutional requirement for cabinet as a whole to meet, and each president has followed a different style when it comes to convoking meetings of the full cabinet and organising relationships between the cabinet and the president's advisors. A former minister explained that, to a great extent, how the executive branch functions 'is influenced by the personal characteristics of whoever occupies chief executive office', as well as the nature of the political coalition and the broader political context (Arriagada 2012, 13). As such, informality rules rather than informal rules prevail. The absence of rules means that presidents can choose how to organise the work of the executive, and no sanctions would apply to presidents who choose to organise the executive differently than their predecessor(s).

Post-1990 Chilean cabinets have ranged in size from sixteen to twenty-three individuals, and do most of their work through four thematic inter-ministerial committees, the most important of which is the political committee (Dumas, Lafuente and Parrado 2013).[17] This committee consists of the three ministers whose offices are physically located in the presidential palace (La Moneda): Interior, SEGPRES and SEGOB. But the committee also includes the finance minister. The political committee follows the most regularised schedule, with weekly meetings each Monday morning.[18] According to a former minister who served in multiple cabinets, the political committee receives instructions from the president on Sunday, and plans how to put these instructions in place during their Monday morning meetings. On Monday afternoons, the political committee meets with deputies and congressional committee leaders. At the meetings with parliamentarians, ministers outline the legislative plans and discuss any potential challenges that might arise.[19] The political committee also meets regularly with the presidents of the coalition parties and the presidents of the chamber and senate to discuss and plan the legislative agenda (Arriagada 2012, 17; Egaña Baraona and Chateau Herrera 2011, 149).[20]

According to a study by Dumas, Lafuente and Parrado (2013) Chile's 'centre of government', that is, the set of institutions that directly support the president in coordinating, planning and communicating the work of the executive, consists of three mechanisms: (1) the political committee (outlined above); (2) other inter-ministerial sectoral committees, like the social and economic committees; and (3) bilateral relations between ministers and the president, normally with the participation of the budget officer (DIPRES), the SEGPRES minister and the president's top advisers. The authors note that the budget office has become an increasingly important player in the executive. Other scholarly analyses of Chile's executive likewise note a gradual shifting of power and policy influence away from its formal dimensions, namely cabinet, towards an informal group of advisors housed on the second floor of the presidential palace (Fernández and Rivera 2012; Siavelis 2014). But according to interviews with former ministers and presidential advisors, presidents are entirely free to change how these mechanisms work and how their work relates to each other.[21] According to one advisor, 'Presidents can do whatever they want.'

The emergence of what is now called the 'Second Floor' (*Segundo Piso*) is said to have originated at the beginning of President Ricardo Lagos's term (2000–2006), ten years after Chile's transition to democracy. During the first two post-transition governments of Aylwin (1990–1994) and Frei (1994–2000), power and policymaking influence were concentrated in the formal aspects of the executive, namely the cabinet, where each president's closest and most trusted advisors could be found. In Alywin's government, the most influential person next to the president himself was the minister of SEGPRES, who carried out most of the strategic planning, and coordinated the president's policy agenda with congress.[22] But, according to Peter

Siavelis (2014, 7), over time, 'presidents gradually came to rely less on advisers within the formal structures of government (and particularly ministers) and more on informal networks outside the ministries'. According to all accounts, it was President Lagos who created the Second Floor, which Siavelis describes 'as a kind of super cabinet . . . [It] directed policy and [was] charged with overseeing cabinet ministers'. According to a former minister in Bachelet's government, those working in the Second Floor 'are a little bit in the shadows because they never appear on television nor anywhere [public], but they accumulate a certain degree of power because they work closely with the president'.[23] An adviser in Lagos's Second Floor explained that keeping out of the public eye and never speaking to the press was essential to their effectiveness.[24]

At the same time, as the Second Floor was playing a bigger role in the executive, the importance of the finance and interior ministers was also growing and a corresponding decline in the role of the sectoral ministers occurred (Siavelis 2014). The declining role of the sectoral ministries continued, and indeed worsened, in Bachelet's first government, when existing mechanisms for coordination in the executive branch were fragmenting and weakening. Since then, power and influence has become increasingly concentrated in fewer hands: According to Dumas, Lafuente and Parrado (2013, 9), 'Perhaps as a consequence of the Ministry of Finance's hegemony throughout the years 2000–2010, public policy and strategic planning decisions became more and more centered on an increasingly smaller number of interlocutors.' Other scholars note a similar shift, particularly during Bachelet's first government, when strategic planning began to be performed by her advisers in the Second Floor, working more closely than ever with the finance minister. As a result, the succession of ministers in SEGPRES saw their role reduced even more (Egaña Baraona and Chateau Herrera 2011). These shifts in power away from cabinet ministers towards presidential advisors can occur because the organisation of the executive branch is not governed by formal or informal rules. It is informality rather than informal rules that creates a permissive environment for the concentration of power among ever fewer individuals.

How is the shifting balance of power between the informal and formal dimensions of the executive branch gendered? In their discussion of the gendered disposition of the UK core executive, Annesley and Gains explain, 'feminists intent on pursuing gendered policy change need to hold positions that grant access to power or resources' (2010, 918). With the exception of one woman – Michelle Bachelet – reaching the presidency, women are clearly not accessing positions of power or influence in Chile's executive. Indeed, even Bachelet appointed men to the most powerful posts in her cabinet, particularly to the finance and interior ministries. Although many of her advisers in the Second Floor are women (especially in her second government), they are not perceived as powerful or influential. According to many accounts, Bachelet staffed her Second Floor with individuals with whom she has close relationships of trust, rather than people with political skills or influence in the coalition parties. In both of her administrations, the Second Floor has been described as less influential than that of her predecessor, Ricardo Lagos.[25] Of course, criticisms that her Second Floor is weaker are themselves gendered, since they ultimately rest on the fact that Bachelet herself, along with the other women in her personal networks of friendship and trust, are not members of Chile's traditional party elite, and hence, less politically powerful.

Sectoral ministries, such as health or education, where women are more likely to be found, are losing influence in the policy process because they are not part of the centre of government. Likewise, gender-equality policies are more likely to fall under the purview of the sectoral ministries rather than the political ministers. Even though presidents do convoke full cabinet meetings approximately once per month (although sometimes even less frequently), such meetings do not provide opportunities for a fulsome discussion of policy. Instead, full cabinet meetings are occasions during which the president provides direction and information for ministers (Arriagada 2012, 17). According to a former minister, such meetings are 'more about orientation that the president gives the ministers rather than the other way around . . . In general, cabinets are not spaces for profound political reflection'.[26] Thus, even though the director of the former National Women's Service (today the Ministry for Women and Gender Equality) enjoys full ministerial rank, this does not translate into significant opportunity to ensure that a gender perspective informs public policy overall since that minister does not participate in the centre of government.

Because the organisation of the executive branch is not ultimately rule-bound, a president with a commitment to gender equality could effect change without experiencing sanctions for breaking rules. Ultimately, it is informality or the absence of rules that permitted the creation and expansion of the Second Floor and the declining influence of sectoral ministers. However, informality could allow a president committed to gender equality (whether male or female) to ensure that more women are present in the top cabinet posts (especially in finance or interior), and could ensure that those wishing to promote gender-equality policies have regular access to the centre of government. Although Bachelet has not brought other women into the centre of government, she has taken steps to ensure that ministers and policymakers take gender issues more seriously (Thomas 2016). For instance, Bachelet took action to ensure that one of the inter-ministerial committees, namely the Equality Committee, was taken more seriously by ministers and other officials. In particular, the president attended the committee's meetings herself and openly supported the goals of the women's policy agency. According to Thomas, 'The informal practices of ministerial deference to the presidential agenda worked to promote attention to gender equality' (2016, 110). Although a number of feminist policy gains were achieved during Bachelet's term (Waylen 2016), the broader trends in which power shifted away from sectoral ministers to the centre of government continued.

CONCLUSION: FUTURE DIRECTIONS FOR RESEARCH ON GENDER AND EXECUTIVES

The executive branch offers scholars unique opportunities to see how the absence of rules (whether formal or informal) affects the participation of women and men differently. But to fully appreciate the sources of gender inequality and the opportunities for change, researchers need to distinguish informal rules from informality. The main difference between the two is that rules create constraints, since violating rules, even informal rules, involves sanctions. Although the range of sanctions for violating informal rules is vast, leading some political actors to decide to bear the cost of breaking a rule, political actors have even more latitude to effect change when rules are absent. As such, gender scholars should seek to identify more clearly whether patterned behaviour in the absence of formal rules is indeed the result of informal rules, and what the sanctions would be if those rules were violated. Where it is not possible to identify sanctions, then informality is perhaps a more appropriate descriptor. Informality creates a permissive environment for the emergence of practices and networks that perpetuate men's advantages in public life. Old-boys clubs exclude women, so where these kinds of networks act as gatekeepers, or where participation in these networks is the main marker of political influence, then women will continue to be disadvantaged. But the possibilities for challenging these practices are greater when the role of networks is not rule-bound.

   In the case of Chile, we see that Bachelet tried unsuccessfully to change some things that disadvantaged women. She brought more women into cabinet but, in so doing, experienced the sanction of party disapproval, prompting cabinet shuffles that led to a decline in the number of women in top posts. Although presidents are empowered by formal and informal rules to appoint ministers without party interference, party elites can subsequently withhold support from presidents who do not appoint a sufficient number of ministers whose qualifications include membership in elite party networks. Presidents are thus constrained in ways that ultimately perpetuate men's advantages in reaching executive office since few women will have held positions that confer access to that shifting group of notables that characterise elite party networks. On the other hand, more possibilities for change appear to be present when we look at how the executive branch functions. Informality means there are no constraints on presidents to choose different ways to organise the executive branch's work. Since 2000, presidents are making choices that have the effect of concentrating power among a smaller number of individuals and some of them are not members of cabinet at all. Most important, women's presence is scarce in the centre of government. More research is needed, however, on how the executive branch operates, namely the basis on which presidential advisors are selected, how they relate to and share power with the cabinet and what opportunities for change actually exist.

NOTES

1. I conducted twenty-three interviews over the course of three field trips in January 2013, August 2014 and July 2015. Interview respondents include former ministers, party presidents, presidential advisers and ministerial staffers, and political experts and commentators. All interview respondents were guaranteed anonymity. The research is part of a broader project on the executive branch in Chile and Spain funded by an Insight Grant (2013–2017) from the Social Sciences and Humanities Research Council of Canada.

2. Chile's electoral system compels parties to compete as a coalition. As such, coalitions do not emerge after the election, but have effectively been more or less permanent since the return of democracy in 1990. The parties of the centre and left formed the Concertación (Concertation) (now called Nueva Mayoría, or New Majority) and the right parties formed the Alianza (Alliance). The Concertación was made up of four parties, the Socialists (PS), the Party for Democracy (PPD), the Radical Social Democrats (PSRD) and the Christian Democrats (PDC). The newly created Nueva Mayoría coalition grew to include the Communists (PC) and two smaller leftist parties. The Alianza includes just two parties, the moderate National Renovation (RN) and the deeply conservative Independent Democratic Union (UDI).

3. The only limitation on this power is that members of Congress are not eligible to serve in an executive post. Presidents have, nonetheless, appointed congresspersons to cabinet, but in these cases, the individuals involved had to give up their seat in Congress to take up their ministerial post.

4. Although one might loosely translate this term as 'quota' (which would be *cuota* in Spanish) that would be somewhat misleading, especially since quotas are now understood as formal mechanisms (rules) that ensure a minimum proportion of spaces for women. The term *cuoteo* has a very different connotation.

5. N.A. 'Dos rasgos y una rareza' [Two characteristics and an oddity], *El Mercurio*, 10 February 2010.

6. 9 July 2015, Santiago, Chile.

7. Interview with a former staffer, 13 July 2015.

8. Interview with political columnist and former staffer, 10 July 2015.

9. N.A. 'Ajustes sepultan la promesa de paridad de Bachelet' [Adjustments bury Bachelet's promises of parity], *La Tercera*, 19 de Julio 2015.

10. This figure was calculated based on data from Dumas, Lafuente and Parrado (2013).

11. Unfortunately, Veloso was shuffled out of cabinet within her first year. Subsequent cabinet shuffles brought two women to the Ministry Secretariat General of Government (Carolina Tohá and Pilar Armanet) although both held the post for short periods of time.

12. In formal terms, the Interior Minister is the most powerful cabinet post: They are designated the *jefe de gabinete* (cabinet chief) and perform presidential functions when the chief executive is out of the country.

13. Interview, 8 January (1), 2013, Santiago, Chile.

14. Interviews, 15 January 2013; 11 August 2014; 17 July 2015.

15. http://www.iadb.org/es/investigacion-y-datos/geppal/detalles-del-pais,17693. html?country=CHL

16. Interviews, 6 August 2014 and 11 August 2014.

17. The other committees are economic, social and infrastructure (Egaña Baraona & Chateau Herrera 2011).

18. Interviews with former ministers: 8 January 2013; 6 August 2014; and 11 August 2014, Santiago, Chile.

19. Interview 6 August 2014. This schedule was also described by another former minister who served in both Lagos's and Bachelet's governments, 8 January 2013.

20. According to Egaña Baraona and Chateau Herrera (2011, 149) during Bachelet's first government, the Political Committee expanded to include the minister of justice, thereby permitting all four of the coalition parties representation in the centre of government.

21. Interviews, 8 January 2013 and 19 August 2014.

22. Interview with former minister, 6 August 2014, Santiago, Chile.

23. Interview, 11 August 2014, Santiago, Chile.

24. Interview, 19 August 2014, Santiago, Chile.

25. Interviews, 8 January 2013; 6 August 2014; 19 August 2014; 9 July 2015; 10 July 2015, Santiago, Chile.

26. 6 August 2014, Santiago, Chile.

REFERENCES

Altman, David. 2008. Political Recruitment and Candidate Selection in Chile, 1990–2006: The Executive Branch. In Peter M. Siavelis and Scott Morgenstern (eds.). *Pathways to Power: Political Recruitment and Candidate Selection in Latin America*, Pennsylvania Park: The Pennsylvania State University Press. 240–270.

Annesley, Claire and Francesca Gains. 2010. Gender and the Core Executive: Gender, Power, and Change. *Political Studies* 58 (5): 909–929.

Arriagada Herrera, Genaro. 2012. Introducción: !Bienvenidos a la 'Presidenciología [Introduction: Welcome to presidentology!]. In María de los Angeles Fernández and Eugenio Rivera (eds.). *La Trastienda del Gobierno: El Eslabón Peridido en la Modernización del Estado Chileno* [*The backroom of government: The missing link in the modernization of the Chilean state*]. Santiago de Chile: Catalonia. 9–22.

Atchison, Amy. 2015. The Impact of Female Cabinet Ministers on a Female-Friendly Labor Environment. *Journal of Women, Politics, and Policy* 36 (4): 388–414.

Bjarnegård, Elin. 2013. *Gender, Informal Institutions, and Political Recruitment: Explaining Male Dominance in Parliamentary Democracies.* Basingstoke: Palgrave Macmillan.

Chappell, Louise and Georgina Waylen. 2013. Gender and the Hidden Life of Institutions. *Public Administration* 91 (3): 599–615.

Dávila, Mireya. 2011. Governing Together: The Concertación Administrations in Chile, 1990–2009. Ph.D. Dissertation, University of North Carolina, Chappell Hill.

Dogan, Mattei (Ed.) 1989. *Selecting Cabinet Ministers. Pathways to Power: Selecting Rulers in Pluralist Democracies.* Boulder: Westview Press. 1–18.

Dumas, Víctor, Mariano Lafuente and Salvador Parrado. 2013. Strengthening the Centre of Government for Results in Chile. Inter-American Development Bank, Technical Note.

Egaña Baraona, Rodrigo and Jorge Chateau Herrera. 2011. El Centro de Gobierno: Lecciones de la Experiencia Chilena Durante Los Gobiernos de la Concertación (1990–2010) [The centre of government: Lessons from the Chilean experience during the governments of the Concertación]. *Estado, Gobierno, Gestión Política* 17, 137–191.

Escobar-Lemmon, Maria and Michelle Taylor-Robinson (Eds). 2014. *Representation: The Case of Women.* New York: Oxford University Press.

Fernández, María de los Angeles and Eugenio Rivera (Eds.). 2012. *La Trastienda del Gobierno: El Eslabón Peridido en la Modernización del Estado Chileno [The backroom of government: The missing link in the modernization of the Chilean state].* Santiago de Chile: Catalonia.

Fernández, María de los Angeles and Eugenio Rivera. 2013. Instituciones Informales, Coaliciones, y Gabinetes en el Presidencialismo Chileno [Informal institutions, coalitions, and cabinets in Chilean presidencialism]. *Política/Revista de Ciencia Política* 51 (1): 155–184.

Franceschet, Susan and Gwynn Thomas. 2015. Resisting Parity: Gender and Cabinet Appointment in Chile and Spain. *Politics & Gender* 11 (4): 643–664.

Franceschet, Susan and Jennifer M. Piscopo. 2008. Gender Quotas and Women's Substantive Representation: Lessons from Argentina. *Politics & Gender* 4 (3): 393–425.

Franceschet, Susan and Jennifer M. Piscopo. 2014. Sustaining Gendered Practices? Power, Parties, and Elite Political Networks in Argentina. *Comparative Political Studies* 47 (1): 85–110.

Haas, Liesl. 2010. *Feminist Policymaking in Chile.* Pennsylvania Park: The Pennsylvania State University Press.

Helmke, Gretchen and Steven Levitsky (Eds.). 2006. *Informal Institutions and Democracy: Lessons from Latin America.* Baltimore: The Johns Hopkins University Press.

Krook, Mona Lena and Fiona Mackay (Eds). 2011. *Gender, Politics, and Institutions: Towards a Feminist Institutionalism.* Basingstoke: Palgrave Macmillan.

Lowndes, Vivien. 2014. How Are Things Done around Here? Uncovering Institutional Rules and Their Gendered Effects. *Politics & Gender* 10 (4): 685–691.

Lowndes, Vivien and Roberts, Mark. 2013. *Why Institutions Matter. The New Institutionalism and Political Science*. Basingstoke: Palgrave Macmillan.

March, James G. and Johan P. Olsen. 1989. *Rediscovering Institutions: The Organizational Basis of Politics*. New York: The Free Press.

Martinez-Gallardo, Cecilia. 2010. Inside the Cabinet: The Influence of Ministers in the Policy Process. In Carlos Scartascini, Ernesto Stein and Mariano Tommasi (eds.). *How Democracy Works: Political Institutions, Arenas, and Actors in Latin American Policymaking*, Washington, D.C.: Inter-American Development Bank. 120–145.

Shugart Matthew Soberg and John M. Carey. 1992. *Presidents and Assemblies: Constitutional Design and Electoral Dynamics*. Cambridge: Cambridge University Press.

Siavelis, Peter M. 2000. *The President and Congress in Postauthoritarian Chile: Institutional Constraints to Democratic Consolidation*. Pennsylvania Park: The Pennsylvania State University Press.

Siavelis, Peter M. 2006. Accommodating Informal Institutions in Chilean Politics. In Gretchen Helmke and Steven Levitsky (eds.). *Informal Institutions and Democracy in Latin America*, Baltimore: Johns Hopkins University Press. 33–55.

Siavelis, Peter M. 2010. Cabinets, Quotas, Iron Circles and the Second Floor: Formal and Informal Organization of the Executive Branch in Chile. Paper prepared for the Asociación Latinoamericana de Ciencia Política, Buenos Aires, 29–30 July.

Siavelis, Peter M. 2014. The Fault Lines of Coalitional Presidentialism: Cabinets, Quotas, and the Second Floor in Chile. Paper presented at the 23rd World Congress of the International Political Science Association, Montreal, Canada, 19–24 July.

Thelen, Kathleen and Sven Steinmo. 1992. Historical Institutionalism in Comparative Politics. In Sven Steinmo, Kathleen Thelen and Frank Longstreth (eds.). *Structuring Politics: Historical Institutionalism in Comparative Analysis*, New York: Cambridge University Press. 1–32.

Thomas, Gwynn. 2016. Promoting Gender Equality: Michelle Bachelet and Formal and Informal Institutional Change within the Chilean Presidency. In Georgina Waylen (ed.). *Gender, Institutions, and Change in Bachelet's Chile*. New York: Palgrave Macmillan, 95–120.

Waylen, Georgina. 2014. Informal Institutions, Institutional Change, and Gender Equality. *Political Research Quarterly*. 67 (1): 212–223.

Waylen, Georgina (Ed.). 2016. *Gender, Institutions, and Change in Bachelet's Chile*. New York: Palgrave Macmillan.

Chapter 7

Leveraging Informality, Rewriting Formal Rules: The Implementation of Gender Parity in Mexico

Jennifer M. Piscopo

Gender quota laws, which compel political parties to nominate specified per-centages of women for public office, set formal rules in place that challenge men's longstanding political dominance. Yet as research on quota imple-mentation has demonstrated, male dominance is not so easily overturned: from running women in losing districts to manipulating rank-order rules on electoral lists, party elites (who are typically men) deploy numerous informal practices to preserve the choicest candidacies for men (Kenny and Verge 2013; Johnson 2016; Verge and Espírito-Santo 2016; Hinojosa, this volume). These processes of quota subversion, which exploit quota laws' silence on exactly which candidate positions count towards the quota, reveal that male dominance has survived its formal dismantling: states have adopted consti-tutional equal rights clauses, passed equal opportunity laws and plans and legislated affirmative action in politics (Piscopo 2015), but the vast majority of countries under-fill their quota laws. Women and men enjoy the same legal rights and privileges, but the gendered distribution of political power remains largely intact. Male dominance continues as the object and outcome of infor-mal institutions, especially unwritten candidate selection rules. Women's inability to break male power monopolies has become conventional wisdom in political science (Bjarnegård 2013; Kenny 2013; Bjarnegård and Kenny 2016).

At the same time, women's networks – as political actors – have worked tirelessly to ensure that quota laws, as formal institutions, actually achieve their target percentages. Most scholarship has focused on these networks' roles in the first post-quota elections (Baldez 2004; Marx, Borner, and Cami-notti 2007; Krook 2009), though their advocacy has proved crucial to securing later-generation reforms that strengthened quota provisions and even replaced quotas (typically set at 30 or 40 percent) with parity (50 percent). This chapter examines how party women in Mexico formed a 'quota network' to influence electoral officials' rule-writing processes, which resulted in tighter regulations that compelled parties to evenly distribute the top candidacies between men and women. These reforms accelerated Mexico's adoption of parity and positioned state regulators and electoral judges – rather than lawmakers or party leaders – as the best defence against quota subversion. When parity applied for the first time in the 2015 elections, the 'quota network' worked with electoral officials to layer clear written rules onto parity's general provisions. The resultant regulations led to the equitable distribution of female candidates across winning and losing districts at the federal level, and extended parity to executive and legislative positions at the municipal level.

The story of Mexico's quota reforms thus enhances scholars' understanding of the nexus between formal institutions, informal institutions and institutional change. As political scientists have documented, formal institutions that promote gender equality (quotas) have not sufficiently disrupted the informal institutions (recruitment) that concentrate power among men: legal rules change, but informal practices persist, preserving men's monopoly on power (Franceschet and Piscopo 2014; Bjarnegård and Kenny 2016). Yet informal practices can also benefit those on the outside, as excluded groups – in this case, women – can devise their own strategies and tactics for accessing policymakers and winning change. In Mexico, women's 'quota networks' developed set practices that brought them into contact with electoral regulators and electoral judges, and ultimately persuaded these state officials to write stricter candidate selection rules, ones that would make quota and parity laws more numerically effective. Gender equality measures require strong implementation, an outcome that often stems from the informal relationships that female activists develop with each other and with state officials. Quota networks are actors that can leverage informality – meaning 'back channel' avenues and relationships, and the practices that sustain them – to achieve institutional layering – understood here as amendments to the quota rules that improve their numerical effects. Consequently, informal spaces of negotiation and contestation are not universally 'bad' for women: women can use these spaces to deepen gender equality reforms.

To illustrate these claims, I draw on primary source evidence, including court documents, detailed newspaper accounts and thirty-eight interviews conducted over three fieldwork trips to Mexico (December 2013, March 2014 and May 2015). I focus on two periods covering three different instances of reform. After reviewing the theoretical literature and case background, I discuss events between 2009 and 2014, when a network of female activists, known as *Mujeres en Plural* (Women as Multiple), succeeded in closing loopholes and ending the silences found in the earlier-generation quota laws. This process established the groundwork for parity. I then cover the 2014–2015 electoral process, where Mujeres en Plural and electoral authorities worked to write formal rules that would implement the parity law more effectively. Federally, this process entailed devising regulations that interpreted the electoral code's general admonition that parties could not nominate women 'exclusively' to losing districts. At the municipal level, implementing parity meant determining whether the states' electoral codes applied parity vertically (alternation down the list) or horizontally (gender balance across position types). Sixteen Mexican states held municipal elections concurrent with the federal elections, but I focus on the eight cases that garnered the most media attention: Baja California Sur, Guerrero, Querétaro, México, Morelos, Nuevo León, Sonora and Tabasco. Across government levels, quota networks favourably amended the quota rules, revealing that informality can undercut male political dominance, giving women the space to demand and win gender equality reforms.

INSTITUTIONAL CHANGE, POLITICAL PARTIES AND QUOTAS IN LATIN AMERICA

The 'institutional turn' in political science has placed rules at the centre of causal analyses. Since institutions (i.e. constitutions or legislative bodies) shape actors' incentives, strategies and behaviours, those wishing to explain outcomes must first understand how the institutional rules are created, communicated and enforced (Shepsle 1989; March and Olsen 1996). Institutions and their rules can be formal or informal: regularised interactions and predictable outcomes emerge not just from written documents, such as constitutions and statutes, but from unwritten conventions such as clientelism and nepotism (Helmke and Levitsky 2006). Informal institutions can overlap with, interact, challenge, uphold and reshape their formal counterparts. By bringing gender into these analyses, scholars of feminist institutionalism (FI) have highlighted how institutions and their rules interface with the normative goal of gender equality (Mackay, Kenny, and Chappell 2010; Gains and Lowndes 2014; Waylen 2014). FI scholars of political recruitment have detailed the functional adaptation of rules to privilege men and masculinity, arguing that even formal institutions are subverted by informal practices that perpetuate women's exclusion (Lovenduski 1998; Bjarnegård 2013; Kenny 2013; Bjarnegård and Kenny 2016; Franceschet, this volume).

This core insight has shaped researchers' understanding of gender quota implementation. In Latin America, first-generation quota laws required certain percentages of female candidates, leaving open *which* candidacies counted towards the quota (Hinojosa 2012; Piscopo 2015). Sometimes the laws contained explicit loopholes exempting parties from filling the quota in certain conditions, as in the Mexican case (discussed below). More commonly, however, the laws remained silent on distributional questions, allowing parties to continue using modes of candidate selection that favoured men (Hinojosa 2012). These included nominating the required number of women, but running them in losing districts (Langston and Aparicio 2011); filling the quota by counting alternate rather than titleholder candidates (Hinojosa, this volume); manipulating women's ballot ranking to diminish their electoral chances (Johnson 2016; Zamora Chavarría 2009); allocating women few campaign resources (Sacchet 2008) and excluding them from the leadership positions that most commonly guarantee future electoral opportunities (Roza 2010; Franceschet and Piscopo 2014). Women certainly experienced this systematic discrimination before quotas, but quotas' adoption ensured that these informal practices entrenched and evolved, keeping parties as bastions of male dominance.

Because both loopholes and silences allowed parties to under-fill quota targets, struggles over implementation ensued, leading to various rounds of quota law reform (Piscopo 2015). In successive rounds of institutional layering (Mahoney and Thelen 2010, 16–17), Latin American countries amended quota rules. These incremental changes specified *how* parties were to fill quotas: for instance, reforms added rank-order rules to candidates running on closed lists; specified that parties could not count substitute candidates towards the quota; extended affirmative action to party directorates and even established minimum financing requirements for female leadership training (Hinojosa 2012; Piscopo 2015). Between 1991 and 2015, eleven Latin American countries reformed their quota laws at least once; eight more than once and seven countries advanced beyond quotas and adopted parity.[1] All Latin American nations save Guatemala and Venezuela currently have either a quota or parity law.

The layering of new quota rules onto old quota rules occurred largely thanks to the concerted efforts of female activists. Cross-party networks of political women played key roles in securing quota laws' initial passage in the 1990s and early 2000s (Baldez 2004; Marx, Borner and Caminotti 2007; Krook 2009). These networks remained active and vigilant in the first post-quota elections, bringing lawsuits before the national electoral authorities when parties outright ignored the law or placed female candidates in the least viable list positions (Jones 1996; Zamora Chavarría 2009). They used media to aggressively shame party leaders, calling them 'dinosaurs' (Baldez 2004). Electoral judges and lawmakers then found themselves trapped by negative publicity, on the one side, and their own constitutional, statutory and jurisprudential commitments to gender equality (women's rights treaties and gender equality laws) on the other (Piscopo 2015). Party leaders lacked the legal basis upon which to block quota reforms in congress, and quota advocates won multiple victories.

Yet party leaders anticipate continuing to exploit the laws' loopholes and silences in practice. As an official in Mexico's national women's institute explained, 'The parties continue to believe they can do one thing in congress, and another thing in the party.'[2] Party leaders instruct their members to vote 'yes' in the plenary because they must, but – in a layering process of their own – continue to adapt their informal candidate recruitment procedures to privilege men. However, few case studies have examined the interplay between legal reforms, informal party practices and women's networks in the most recent generations of quota reforms. These later-generation reforms are notable both for their accomplishments (the elimination of longstanding practices such as sending women to losing districts) and venues (their adoption and implementation in the regulatory, rather than the legislative, arena). Many studies mention that Latin America's electoral management bodies have upheld the quotas' constitutionality and written clearer rules (Crocker 2011; Piscopo 2015), but no studies have explicitly examined *how* state officials became allies in overturning male dominance.

Answering this question requires uncovering the role of women's networks in later generation reforms, which in turn raises definitional questions about networks themselves. One approach characterises networks as informal institutions: they are sustained by patterned interactions and regularised rules of engagement, and members may sanction those participants who deviate from shared understandings about strategies or messages. Yet networks' very informality makes sanctioning difficult to observe. Only detailed ethnographies – rather than the elite interviews employed in my study – could capture how networks establish membership criteria, police behaviour and eject participants. Since informal institutions cannot exist without sanctions (Helmke and Levitsky 2004, 727; Chappell and Galea, this volume), networks appear better conceptualised not as institutions, but as 'gendered actors working with the rules' (Gains and Lowndes 2014; Chappell and Mackay, this volume). This approach foregrounds networks' agency and manoeuvrability: networks contest the distribution of power and possibilities for change by interpreting and adapting the rules (Gains and Lowndes 2014, 528–529). 'Quota networks' coalesce as politicians and party members – who are usually women – look to change the rules governing formal institutions (quotas), in order to circumvent the informal recruitment practices that perpetuate male dominance. Elite interviews can reveal networks' strategies, partnerships and messages, as well as their influence and achievements. Networks' reliance on informality does not mean that quota networks are institutions, but that they are actors leveraging informal spaces, relationships and practices to press their demands, and to negotiate and achieve their objectives.

ELECTORAL REFORMS, DEMOCRATISATION
AND GENDER QUOTAS

In Mexico, democratisation occurred via the ballot box (Schedler 2005). The long-time hegemonic Partido Revolucionario Institucional (Institutional Revolutionary Party, known by its Spanish acronym PRI) lost its iron grip on municipalities and states in the 1980s, its super-majority in congress in 1994, its majority in 1997 and the presidency in 2000. The challengers – the Partido Acción Nacional (National Action Party, or PAN) and the Party of the Democratic Revolution (Partido de la Revolución Democrática or PRD) – remain key players today, and Mexico has been characterised as a three-party system since democratisation.[3] The PAN and PRD anchor the ideological spectrum on the left and right, respectively, and the internally heterogeneous PRI occupies the middle.

At the federal level, the parties compete for a 500-seat Chamber of Deputies and a 128-seat Senate. The Chamber of Deputies renews every three years, with 300 deputies selected from single-member districts (SMDs) and 200 deputies selected from five multi-state districts employing closed-list proportional representation (PR). The Senate renews every six years, using closed-list PR, with thirty-two members chosen from a single nationwide district and ninety-six members chosen from statewide districts. ('States' includes the autonomous federal district of Mexico City, which behaves like a state in federal elections.[4]) Prior to the December 2013 constitutional reform, Mexico prohibited independent candidacies as well as immediate re-election to the same post in a municipal government, state legislature or federal chamber.[5] The December 2013 reform – which included parity – was the latest in a series of sweeping electoral reforms that date back to 1987.

A hallmark of these reforms was the creation of independent agencies to run elections. As multiparty competition deepened, the parties could not trust each other, but they could agree to transfer control to independent regulators. The 1987 reform created an electoral court to resolve inter- and intra-party disputes, and the 1990 reform created the Federal Electoral Institute (Instituto Federal Electoral, or IFE) to manage elections. Each successive reform ceded more authority to IFE, and the 1996 reform strengthened the court, known since then as the Electoral Tribunal of the Federal Judiciary (Tribunal Electoral del Poder Judicial de la Federación, or TEPJF). Mexico's desire for 'international democratic credibility' bound all political parties into ensuring IFE's and the TEPJF's autonomy and efficacy (Eisenstadt 1999, 98), features which consolidated over the 1990s and 2000s (Eisenstadt 2003; Estévez, Magar and Rosas 2008; Reyes 2012). Elections in Mexico became, and remain, highly regulated affairs. IFE initiates the electoral season by issuing regulatory decrees, written rules that interpret the federal electoral code and delimit party behaviour; IFE confirms and registers political parties' candidates, monitors parties' campaign behaviours (including expenditures), sanctions violations and manages all technical aspects of the elections, from training poll workers to counting ballots. The TEPJF hears any legal disputes, including disagreements with IFE's regulations or sanctions. Today, IFE officials (the top leaders are called "counsellors") and TEPJF judges are highly respected electoral authorities, with national and international credibility.

Democratisation via electoral reform and the ballot box also had gendered effects. Politically active women reported that the onset of genuine competition raised the value of legislative posts, which diminished their chances to receive candidate nominations (Piscopo 2016). Female party members and female legislators formed cross-party working groups in the 1990s, in which they shared best practices for advancing female candidates within their parties (Bruhn 2003; Ortiz Ortega and Scherer Castillo 2014). Rather than negotiate standalone legislation, they sought to include quotas in the broader electoral reform packages. Congresswomen unsuccessfully sought quotas' inclusion in the 1993 reform. In the 1996 reform, they secured a recommendation that parties nominate 30 percent women. IFE demanded that parties fill the 30 percent recommendation in the 2000 elections, but provided no specific guidelines as to how: parties thus clustered women's names in the bottom (unelectable) positions on the PR lists, nominated women to unwinnable plurality districts and named them as alternates rather than primary candidates. As shown in Table 7.1, the proportion of women elected to congress in 1994, 1997 and 2000 remained below 20 percent.

Congresswomen elected in 2000 entered into a cross-party pact to introduce mandatory quotas into that session's anticipated electoral reform (Ortiz Ortega and Scherer Castillo 2014). Female legislators from the PRD, PRI and PAN lobbied congressional leaders, receiving a boost when the Mexican Supreme Court ruled that a state-level quota was constitutional (Baldez 2004; Piscopo 2016). The 2002 electoral reform thus included a mandatory 30 percent quota

Table 7.1   Women in the Mexican Congress (1988–2015)

Election Year	Percent Chamber	Percent Senate
1988	11.8	15.6
1991	8.8	3.1
1994	14.1	10.2
1997	17.4	15.6
2000	16.0	18.0
2003	24.0	
2006	23.4	18.5
2009	28.0	
2012	37.0	32.8
2015	42.4	

Note: The Mexican Senate began renewing every six years in 2000.

Source: Medina Espino (2010); INE (2015).

for both the house and senate, with a one-in-three-names placement mandate for the PR lists and a prohibition against counting alternate candidates towards the quota. Yet, the 2002 electoral code contained an explicit loophole that would haunt quota advocates for the next decade: parties were exempt from meeting the quota in the SMD districts, *if* they chose SMD candidates via 'direct vote'. This provision meant that parties rapidly adopted primaries, or simply claimed their internal selection procedures *were* primaries (Baldez 2007, 81). IFE regulators were willing to enforce the quota, but unwilling to investigate parties' candidate selection procedures: their written rules enforced the electoral code, but added no provisions or amendments – such as setting standards for primaries – that curtailed parties' ability to claim an exemption. IFE thus accepted parties' claims at face-value, granting numerous quota exemptions (Piscopo 2016). This *carte-blanche* resulted in disappointingly few women elected in 2003 and 2006 (less than 25 percent).

Congresswomen elected in 2006 thus looked to strengthen the quota law (Ortiz Ortega and Scherer Castillo 2014; Piscopo 2016). They sought parity, but settled for raising the quota from 30 to 40 percent, with a placement mandate for the PR lists of two female names for every five, in an alternating manner. They could not eliminate the primary exemption, but did succeed in changing the language from 'direct vote' to 'democratic process'; in theory, this change would compel parties to actually hold primaries. As before, these changes formed part of a broader electoral reform package, passed in 2008. Yet IFE remained steadfast in its unwillingness to write rules delimiting what constituted a 'democratic process' (Piscopo 2016), and the percentage of women elected to the lower house in 2009 rose only by 5 percentage points, to 28 percent.

The first generation of Mexico's quota law thus saw cross-party networks of women working within Congress to secure statutory reforms, and electoral officials in the IFE leaving the quota law's loopholes and silences intact (Piscopo 2016). Regulators were allies but not advocates. With electoral reforms still unfolding in Congress, electoral officials walked a fine line: they needed to prove their independence by enforcing the electoral rules, but they could not be so assertive that the parties would weaken their authority in the next reform (Eisenstadt 2002; Estévez, Magar and Rosas 2008). Only once electoral engineering in Congress slowed in the late 2000s could IFE and the TEPJF assert more control over parties' internal lives.

CLOSING LOOPHOLES AND WINNING PARITY: 2009–2014

The 2009 elections failed to elect 40 percent of women because the 2008 electoral code and the subsequent regulatory decrees did not change parties' distribution of the choicest candidacies to men. First, IFE again placed no parameters on what candidate selection procedures counted as meriting the exemption.[6] Second, parties could still send female candidates to losing SMD districts. Third, the law and the regulations remained silent about same-sex candidate-alternate pairs; women only needed to comprise 40 percent of all alternates. This particular gap resulted in scandal: following the 2009 elections, sixteen female legislators-elect from multiple parties resigned their seats so their male alternates could enter congress. The practice of so-called Juanitas yielding their seats had occurred in previous elections as well, but their appearance after a high-profile quota reform generated widespread outrage from congresswomen and media commentators (Piscopo 2016; Hinojosa, this volume).

Immediately, prominent female party leaders, female legislators and feminist activists – including private consultants, academics and journalists – came together to 'see what could be done'.[7] These participants named themselves 'Mujeres en Plural' to preserve the spirit of multipartism that had long characterised quota advocacy in Mexico. Mujeres en Plural decided to demand 'total parity' in the congress, including an elimination of the primary exemption and a stipulation of same-sex candidate pairings.[8] Yet congress balked. Female legislators pushed a more modest measure mandating same-sex candidate pairs through the lower house in April 2011, but it died in the senate. Mujeres en Plural realised that the parties lacked the 'political will' to make further changes.[9] As one member recalled, 'Looking for legal [statutory] solutions was no longer possible.'[10] The political parties would devolve power no further. The momentum for broader electoral reform also had disappeared, as parties viewed the 2008 reforms as successful (Serra 2012).

Mujeres en Plural turned to IFE, hoping the electoral regulators would write stronger rules for the upcoming 2011–2012 federal electoral process. To engage with electoral officials, Mujeres en Plural relied on two guiding principles: discretion and collectivity. The network met in private, in members' homes and only when a critical mass could attend.[11] There would be no official leaders; women would become associated with Mujeres en Plural by appearing at IFE headquarters, but no meeting between Mujeres en Plural and IFE counsellors occurred unless several network members could attend.[12] This strategy framed the issue as about women, not individual careers or personalities.[13] Nonetheless, Mujeres en Plural found IFE counsellors sympathetic, but unmovable. Mujeres en Plural argued that exempting parties from the quota because they used a 'democratic process' implied that parties also selected candidates using *un*democratic processes – which contradicts the parties' constitutional purpose (Ortiz Ortega and Scherer Castillo 2014, 112–4). IFE disagreed, but suggested that Mujeres en Plural try their argument before the TEPJF.[14]

The TEPJF was the appropriate avenue through which to impugn IFE's regulations, but cases before the tribunal typically centred on a specific entity – an individual or a political party – that had experienced harm. No precedent existed for petitioning on behalf of a class (in this case women), but Mujeres en Plural went ahead, presenting a case signed by high-ranking leaders of the PRD, PRI and other small parties.[15] They argued that because Article 1 of the Mexican Constitution gave international human rights treaties – including the 1979 Convention on the Elimination of all Forms of Discrimination against Women – the weight of constitutional law, the gender-equality principles contained in these statutes required first-order protections. After filing, Mujeres en Plural used the same strategies as they had with IFE counsellors: groups of at least five or six networks members met with every judge, always foregrounding the collective nature of their claims.[16] The strategy proved effective, with one judge recalling, 'We were very moved by this collection of women'.[17]

In what now enjoys renown as a historic decision in Mexico, the TEPJF ruled in favour of Mujeres en Plural on 30 November 2011.[18] The TEPJF agreed that gender equality principles meant respecting the quota 'without exception', thus striking the primary exemption *and* the permissibility of mixed-sex candidate pairings.[19]

The ruling came midway through the 2011–2012 federal election process, but IFE counsellors had received the court order they needed. IFE issued new regulations for candidate registries, requiring strict compliance with the 40 percent quota for nominations in PR and SMD districts. The revised rules made party leaders thoroughly furious.[20] As a counsellor recalled, 'They [party leaders] came to us saying 'well, what are we are going to do'? And we just looked at them, and said, 'well, you comply'. . . . And so they began to play chicken with us'.[21] When the March 2012 deadline for registering candidates arrived, only one party – a small, new competitor – submitted SMD candidate lists composed of 40 percent women.[22] IFE gave the parties forty-eight hours to revise their nominations, else they would lose the chance to compete in a number of SMDs equal to those which were owed to female candidates.[23] An IFE counsellor recalled these as 'frightening days . . . there was no precedent for this. . . . the possibility that we would refuse the candidate registries had never happened before'.[24] Fortunately, the parties blinked, submitting revised candidate registries that assigned women to 40 percent of the SMDs (INE 2015).

Mujeres en Plural's petition, the historic sentence and the candidate registration standoff changed how electoral authorities understood women's political rights and, consequently, the rules they would write to ensure quota implementation. All IFE and TEPJF interviewees identified the 2011–2012 electoral process as critical for placing gender equality at the centre of their institution's identity and mission. An IFE counsellor explained that the TEPJF's ruling 'gave us the courage to move forward', referring to the institution's about-face on candidate registry rules.[25] Another IFE counsellor explained that, once the TEPJF ruled, IFE needed to maintain public trust – especially given that women comprise half of the public.[26] TEPJF judge María del Carmen Alanis Figueroa reflected, 'This had been women's fight for years: first, to win the right to vote, then to obtain formal equality before law; then the quotas, and now the confrontation with IFE [over the primary exemption] that evidently would throw all these gains in the trash . . . I learned that the quota cannot make exceptions.'[27] Another TEPJF judge identified the 'historic decision' as shaping a new self-image for the TEPJF, one that would defend women's rights.[28] Indeed, the TEPJF followed its historic decision with a series of additional rulings, also in response to cases brought by Mujeres en Plural, which affirmed full alternation (zippering) of men's and women's names on the PR lists.[29] Together, these rulings made the statutory adoption of parity a foregone conclusion.

ASSIGNING WOMEN TO WINNING DISTRICTS IN 2015

In strengthening the quota's formal rules, IFE and the TEPJF positioned themselves as defenders of gender equality. Both institutions derived their powers from electoral reforms that party leaders passed in congress. The institutions' earlier reluctance to scrutinise internal party practices stemmed from their fear that party leaders would retaliate and curtail their power. Yet once public opinion and constitutional jurisprudence tipped in favour of women's fair access to the best candidacies, the IFE and the TEPJF could move against the parties, since any vengeful attempts by the parties-in-congress to delimit the regulators' power would raise suspicion. Mujeres en Plural leveraged informality to gain access to the IFE and the TEPJF, and state officials acted for principled and self-interested reasons. This fruitful coincidence of the quota network's goals and electoral officials' ambitions continued during the 2014–2015 elections, the first to implement Mexico's new parity regime.

In December 2013, the Mexican Congress revised the constitution to eliminate no re-election, to allow for independent candidacies and to require parity for election to the federal and state congresses. Controversy emerged not over the constitutional reform, but over the redaction of the new electoral code in February 2014. No debate occurred over including parity with alternation (zippering) on the PR lists, mandating same-sex candidate pairings and allowing no exemptions, because the TEPJF already set these rules. Tensions rose over what the TEPJF had *not* decided: the distribution of candidates across the lower-house SMD districts. In 2012, parties had to nominate 40 percent women to the SMDs, but they still concentrated them in losing districts

(Piscopo 2016, 506). Women from the PRI, PAN and PRD thus proposed dividing the SMDs into three categories – safe, competitive and losing – and requiring that parties nominate 50 percent men and 50 percent women in each category.[30] Yet party leaders would not surrender control over the distribution of winning districts: exasperated, one senate leader asked his female colleague, 'What more do you women want?'[31] The final electoral code contained only a general statement: parties could not assign women 'exclusively' to districts where they received the lowest proportion of votes in the previous election.[32]

Just like 'direct vote' and 'democratic process' during the quota era, the interpretation of the electoral code's 'exclusively' provision would fall to regulators. The 2013–2014 reforms rechristened IFE as INE (the Instituto Nacional Electoral), perhaps befitting its new regulatory zeal. First, INE issued regulations on candidate selection that contained thirteen gender equality action items, including a requirement that parties articulate candidate selection procedures that contained 'neither arbitrariness nor subjectivity'.[33] Political parties had to submit their candidate selection procedures to INE for ratification. These formal regulations served two purposes: INE could head-off potential disputes by working with party leaders before the candidate selection phase, and parties that violated these procedures could be impugned before the TEPJF.[34]

Second, INE's regulations for the candidate registries warned parties that the distribution of women and men across SMD districts would receive close scrutiny during the candidate certification process. Privately, INE counsellors determined that they would use the three-tier method the congresswomen had proposed. INE counsellors explained that this approach – a formal commitment to close scrutiny combined with an informal three-tier analysis – balanced the letter and the spirit of the law. INE feared they could not legally sanction parties for disproportionately sending women to losing districts: technically, so long as at least one woman was assigned to a competitive or safe district, parties were in compliance with the electoral code. Yet the word 'exclusively' also gestured towards a more fair distribution of male and female candidates.[35] Thus, INE 'placed the spirit of the law in the method of evaluation'.[36] INE could not deny the registry if the party failed the three-tier test, but they could shame that party publicly, issuing statements and showing the data to the press.[37]

INE officials, in partnership with Mujeres en Plural, thus formed a 'gender observatory' for the 2015 elections. Congresswomen who lost the battle over the electoral code had continued pressing party leaders: for instance, the PRD's Secretary for Gender Equality demanded that party leaders appoint women evenly across districts the party had won, could win and had never won.[38] Mujeres en Plural reached out to INE officials, who were eager to talk: both activists and regulators worried that parties would ignore their exhortations and concentrate women in losing districts. When the moment for registering candidates arrived, the observatory publicised the distribution of female and male candidates across district types, 'with special attention to the twenty most safe [seats], and the twenty least competitive'.[39] The desire to avoid negative publicity largely drove the parties' voluntary compliance with the three-tier rule (INE 2015), ultimately leaving little for the observatory to protest. As a Mujeres en Plural leader reflected, 'The day of the registry, all the parties pronounced themselves to be in favour of parity, because it's politically correct.'[40] Her colleague also noted the increased effectiveness of public shaming in the 2014–2015 electoral process, which raised the political costs for parties contemplating a reversion to their old ways.[41]

Formal rules written to govern party behaviour in the 2014–2015 federal electoral process thus incorporated more monitoring, scrutiny and publicity of candidate selection procedures than ever before. When imposed over the electoral code's general admonition about not concentrating women exclusively in losing SMD districts, these formal rules severely reduced parties' ability to employ informal practices that distributed the choicest candidacies to men. Tellingly, Mujeres en Plural and INE officials used informality – messages passed through networks, threats of negative publicity – to achieve these formal changes.

FROM VERTICAL TO HORIZONTAL PARITY: FEDERALISING MUNICIPAL ELECTIONS

The 2015 federal elections occurred concurrently with subnational elections in the federal district of Mexico City and sixteen states (Baja California Sur, Campeche, Chiapas, Colima, Guanajuato, Guerrero, Jalisco, México, Michoacán, Morelos, Nuevo León, Querétaro, San Luis Potosí, Sonora, Tabasco and the Yucatán).[42] Together, these seventeen subnational entities elected 641 deputies to the state congresses and 1,009 officials to the municipal governments, known as *ayuntamientos*.[43] Prior to the 2014–2015 election process, all states were required to 'harmonize' their state constitutions and state electoral codes to comply with the federal constitution's extension of parity to the state congresses. Since state congresses are also elected using mixed-member systems, states too mandated same-sex candidate pairings for SMD and PR districts and the zippering of men's and women's names on PR lists. Variation entered at the municipal level, where states determine the electoral rules used to elect the ayuntamientos. The Mexican Constitution had referred only to parity in the federal and state congresses, but during the harmonisation process, all states with elections in 2015 added parity in the ayuntamientos to their constitutions and electoral codes (save México, Nuevo León and Sonora, which only placed municipal parity in their electoral codes).

Yet these provisions said nothing about how municipal-level parity would interface with the unique institutional and electoral structure of Mexico's municipalities. Ayuntamientos are governed by a *cabildo* (a collegial, deliberative body), comprising an *alcalde* (a municipal president), a *síndico* (a position that combines the duties of a comptroller with those of an in-house counsel) and *regidores* (commissioners with voice and vote). Regidores blend legislative and executive power, in that they – alongside the alcalde – both make and execute policy. The number of regidores and the discretionary powers of the cabildo depend on the size of the municipality, which states determine according to varying criteria. Some states elect cabildos using a single unified ticket: alcaldes, síndicos and regidores appear on one list, which is then chosen via plurality rules. In other states, proportional rules will apply to a single list where the alcalde is ranked first, followed by the síndico and then the regidores, or proportional rules will apply to a list of regidores, while alcaldes and síndicos are chosen via plurality rule (running either separately or on a unified two-person ticket).[44] When state electoral codes said 'parity with alternation' for the state congresses and the ayuntamientos, this provision included the various permutations of lists and multi-person tickets used to elect the cabildos.[45]

The question then became whether alternation would apply vertically (down the lists) or horizontally (across positions types): would state-level regulators require that parties evenly distribute women among the alcalde and síndico positions? Mujeres en Plural already had begun pushing horizontal parity in the executive branch. For example, when Beatriz Mojica Morga (PRD) sought her party's nomination for the governorship of Guerrero, state party leaders moved to block her candidacy – even though she led the polls. In response, several of the party's federal congresswomen, also leaders of Mujeres en Plural, issued a press release: 'The PRD must respect parity: Yesterday Silvano Aureoles [a man] was named the party's candidate as governor for Michoacán, it is fair that now Beatriz Mojica is named a candidate.'[46] Mexico's parity law does not affect gubernatorial races, but female activists used its logic to insist that parties distribute gubernatorial nominations evenly between men and women. At the municipal level, this logic could go further: the unique single-ticket electoral system for executive and legislative posts, in combination with state constitutions' and electoral codes' general provision about 'parity with alternation', provided a unique opportunity for groundbreaking formal rule changes.

Mirroring the regulatory structure at the federal level, state electoral institutions (*institutos electorales estatales* or IEEs) write the rules for state or municipal elections. Challenges to these regulations are heard first by state electoral tribunals (*tribunales electorales estatales* or TEEs). Disputants may appeal TEE decisions to the TEPJF, beginning with the five regional chambers and ending with the principal Mexico City chamber. If the dispute involves federal constitutional matters, litigants can bypass the TEE and proceed directly to the TEPJF regional chamber. In issuing their initial regulations for the 2014–2015 state and municipal elections, all IEEs except Morelos followed IFE's old strategy: they simply repeated the text of the states' electoral codes, requiring parties to respect parity in the municipalities, with alternation for lists.[47]

Unsurprisingly, when parties submitted their candidate registries to the IEEs for approval, few women were nominated to the alcalde post. In states presenting cabildo candidates on a single ticket, men received the first position, with alternation thereafter, which complied with parity but concentrated women in the second position, that of síndico. The PRI in Guerrero, for instance, nominated women as municipal presidents in just six of eighty-one municipalities.[48] In Sonora, twenty-one women received alcalde nominations – compared to 132 men.[49] Since the rank-order places alcaldes first, síndicos second and regidores third and onward, male candidates also disproportionately received the first regidor nomination (the third list position).[50]

Mujeres en Plural in fact anticipated this outcome.[51] In each state, with the leadership and support of Mujeres en Plural, local women formed parity observatories, such as the Observatory for Gender Parity and Women's Political Rights in Querétaro, the Parity Observatory in Sonora, the Chiapas Network for Effective Parity and the Network for Women's Political Advancement in Guerrero. As at the federal level, state-level networks included women from different political parties, as well as journalists, leaders of civil society organisations, academics and representatives from the state-level women's policy institutes.[52] These networks *did* proactively press the IEEs to issue regulations that went beyond simply restating the electoral code, but only in Morelos did regulators require gender balance across alcalde and síndico nominations. All other state IEEs remained silent about fair candidate distributions, and validated candidate registries that contained few women as alcaldes. Building on strategies developed at the federal level, the state-level observatories prepared to contest women's exclusion before the TEEs and the TEPJF.

CHANGING FORMAL RULES TO IMPLEMENT HORIZONTAL PARITY

The subnational level reveals again how informal partnerships among politically active women, and between quota networks and state regulators, can layer new rules onto existing quota statutes. In Morelos, IEE rules required that parties nominate 50 percent women and 50 percent men for each municipal position. The PRD, the PAN, the PRI and a smaller fourth party impugned these regulations before the TEE. The court rejected the parties' claims that the IEE had inappropriately assumed legislative authority by writing rules beyond the electoral code. Rather, the TEE affirmed that, because the state constitution made general reference to parity, 'it is evident that the candidacies for municipal president and síndico follow this same principle'.[53] Party leaders protested, and the quota network pushed back. For example, PRD women called a press conference in which they characterised the state party president's ongoing resistance as 'showing the PRD to be a retrograde entity, distant from modern society, and fighting against representative democracy and pluralistic equality'.[54]

Unmoved, the parties appealed to the regional TEPJF, claiming they 'had no women to nominate'.[55] Women from Morelos then visited the TEPJF judges, bringing copies of their resumes and other documents to demonstrate that they indeed had the qualifications and the votes.[56] In this first horizontal parity case to come before the TEPF, the court ruled for the women and against the parties. One judge based his decision on the comma's placement in the constitution's parity clause, which reads that political parties must 'write rules that guarantee gender parity, in candidacies for federal and state legislatures'. The comma, he argued, made the gender parity guarantee independent from the government levels.[57] Another argument recognised the unique institutional design of the cabildos, which merge executive and legislative roles.[58] Further, the electoral system at the municipal level meant that the *absence* of horizontal parity would violate gender equality principles: as magistrate Salvador Nava Gomar explained, 'You cannot condition the gender of the síndico on the gender of the municipal president'.[59] This last consideration proved especially important, as parties' practice of ranking men first and women second meant most alcaldes would be men, and most síndicos women. The TEPJF ruling forced parties to substitute female candidates for male candidates, until 16 of Morelos's 33 municipalities had female nominees as alcaldes.

Elsewhere, the battle for horizontal parity unfolded with women – not parties – seeking rule changes from the tribunals. In Baja California Sur, for example, IEE president Rebeca Barrera Amador had sought to include horizontal parity in the electoral regulations, insisting the rule would comply with international treaties stipulating gender equality and the political parties' own statutes (which must include parity principles as a matter of law). However, she lacked support from her fellow electoral counsellors, as party leaders protested – as they had in Morelos – that such regulation would constitute the IEE's inappropriate seizing of legislative powers.[60] Like their counterparts at the federal level, female activists rebuffed by the IEE then approached the courts. Baja California Sur elects its five ayuntamientos using one unified ticket, and the IEE registered candidate slates from the PRI and the PAN in which no women appeared in the top position. The complete exclusion of women allowed the parity observatory to proceed directly to the regional TEPJF, claiming that the IEE had violated women's constitutional rights.[61] Ruling in their favour, the court forced the PAN and the PRI to replace at least two male nominees for alcaldes with two women.

Quota networks forced similar candidate substitutions in other states. Female petitioners brought suit before the TEEs or TEPJF in Guerrero, México, Nuevo León, Querétaro, Sonora and Tabasco. In Guerrero, female petitioners moved forward even before the IEE confirmed the candidate registries. The IEE had mandated only vertical parity for regidor lists, and members of the Network for Women's Political Advancement (representing approximately 480 women in the state), with technical support from Mujeres en Plural, impugned these regulations before the TEE. Ruling in favour of horizontal parity, the Guerrero TEE gave the IEE forty-eight hours to rewrite its regulations and stipulate that women receive the alcalde nomination in forty of the state's eighty-one ayuntamientos.[62] This adjustment in turn disrupted the already-unfolding candidate selection processes within the political parties, who became forced to redistribute nominations before registering their candidates with the IEE.[63]

The timing of the substitutions, however, soon proved an issue. In Baja California Sur, Guerrero, Morelos, Querétaro and Tabasco, judicial processes began in late February and were resolved in March and early April – about six weeks to three months before the 7 June elections. In México, Nuevo León and Sonora, however, the cases reached the regional TEPJFs in mid-April – much closer to the election date. This delay caused the regional tribunals to *uphold* the IEE regulations, arguing that the electoral process was too advanced to allow candidate substitutions.[64] In the last days of April, the federal TEPJF agreed: they affirmed the constitutionality of horizontal parity (as they had for each and every case they received), but postponed its imposition in México, Sonora and Nuevo León until the 2018 elections. In a four-two vote, the judges determined that candidate substitutions could not occur with only five weeks left before the election.

The TEPJF's reversal surprised many. The two dissenting judges, María del Carmen Alanis Figueroa and Manuel González Oropeza, argued that no actual situation – such as the advancement of an electoral campaign – should contravene a constitutional principle, noting that the candidate registry was amendable up until election day.[65] Aided by the public dissents of Alanis and González, Mujeres en Plural launched a negative publicity campaign. Mujeres en Plural issued a press release, expressing their profound disappointment.[66] A federal INE counsellor, Javier Santiago Castillo, wrote an op-ed in a leading newspaper that described the TEPJF's decision as 'incredible' and 'inconsistent'.[67] This pressure quickly compelled the TEPJF to follow up with a 'jurisprudential thesis' that established the constitutionality of horizontal parity, mandating its application to all *future* municipal elections.

Thus, women applying pressure through informal networks lost the battle in México, Sonora and Nuevo León, but won the war. As a Mujeres en Plural leader explained, the decision to litigate female candidates' access to municipal positions was coordinated and planned as soon as the federal electoral reform passed without parity in the ayuntamientos.[68] A TEPJF judge observed that Mujeres en Plural's petitions were deliberately tailored to address the distribution of candidacies in the ayuntamientos (and did not, for example, address the distribution of list-header positions in the PR lists for the state and federal congresses).[69] She also noted that, whenever the women visited the magistrates, 'They arrive[d] in a network, in a group'.[70] Following the jurisprudential thesis that installed horizontal parity in the ayuntamientos, Mujeres en Plural issued a press release attributing this victory to women's ability to directly access and interface with the electoral courts.[71] Informal collaboration, strategising and messaging again altered the formal quota rules, expanding women's access to the choicest candidate nominations at the municipal level.

CONCLUSION

The implementation of parity in Mexico tells an important story about gendered actors working within formal and informal institutions. As Gains and Lowndes (2014) explain, actors' interpretations and adaptations of the institutional rules depend on perceptions about the appropriate distribution of power and the possibilities for change. In Mexico, Mujeres en Plural saw that the formal rules governing the distribution of women across the choicest candidacies *could* evolve, but that layering new rules onto existing quota statutes would require regulatory and judicial action. In turn, officials in the electoral institutions and courts proved accommodating because intervening more firmly in parties' candidate selection procedures served their own goals: in positioning themselves as defenders of women's political rights, INE and the TEPJF bolstered their reputations as guarantors of equity and fairness, using this political capital to further secure their own autonomy vis-à-vis the parties-in-congress. Together, these quota networks use formal rules to foreclose upon informal practices that previously perpetuated male dominance over the choicest electoral opportunities.

The Mexican case thus underscores how networks, as political actors, can bring about institutional layering: together, female activists and electoral officials added formal rules that closed the loopholes and ended the silences surrounding *how* parties must fill quota and parity laws. This process highlights the role that informality – the back channel avenues and practices of negotiation and contestation – plays not just in the adoption of gender equity policies, but in their implementation (see also Nazneen, this volume). Indeed, an astonishing feature of the 2015 federal and municipal elections has been the degree to which female politicians and activists have entered the public sphere, using coordination, publicity and litigation to shame and punish the very same party leaders on whom they depend for candidate nominations. The regulatory arena has empowered female actors, but at what long-term costs within the parties? Future work might return to examining gendered institutional practices at the party level, asking about the political fates of those who lead observatories, join Mujeres en Plural, petition judges and collaborate with electoral regulators.

NOTES

1. The Venezuelan electoral institute has enforced parity in candidate registrations since 2005. Since this regulation has no statutory basis, I do not count Venezuela as having a quota law.
2. Interview, national women's institute official, 7 May 2015.
3. Evidence of party system fragmentation in the 2015 elections may change this assessment.
4. In 2016, Mexico City converted from a federal district to a state.
5. Independent candidacies began in 2015. Legislators elected in 2018 will be the first to stand for re-election.
6. Interviews, IFE official, 11 December 2013; IFE counsellor, 8 May 2015.
7. Interview, former congresswoman, 8 May 2015.
8. Interview, former congresswoman, 8 May 2015.
9. Interview, female activist, 12 May 2015.
10. Interview, female activist, 12 December 2013.
11. Interviews, female activist, 12 December 2013; female senator, 8 May 2015.
12. Interviews, female activist, 12 December 2013; political consultant, 16 December 2013; female senator, 8 May 2015.
13. Interview, senator, 11 May 2015.
14. Interview, IFE counsellor, 8 May 2015.
15. Interview, TEPJF judge, 7 May 2015.
16. Interviews, female activist, 12 December 2013; female senator, 7 May 2015.
17. Interview, electoral judge, 7 May 2015.
18. Sentence 12642–2011.
19. Sentence 12624–2011.
20. Interview, IFE counsellor, 14 May 2015.
21. Interview, IFE counsellor, 8 May 2015.

22. Interview, IFE official, 11 December 2013.

23. Interview, IFE counsellor, 14 May 2015.

24. Interview, IFE counsellor, 14 May 2015.

25. Interview, IFE counsellor, 8 May 2015.

26. Interview, IFE counsellor, 14 May 2015.

27. Quoted in a document drafted by Mujeres en Plural; received during interview with female activist, 12 December 2013.

28. Interview, TEPJF judge, Mexico City, 7 May 2015.

29. Interview, TEPJF judge, Mexico City, 7 May 2015.

30. Interviews, national women's institute official, 7 May 2015; female senator, 7 May 2015.

31. Interview, official from the national women's institute, 7 May 2015.

32. General Law on Political Parties (*Ley General de Partidos Políticos*), Article 3, Number 5.

33. Interview, INE official, 12 May 2015.

34. Interview, INE official, 12 May 2015.

35. Interviews, INE counsellors, 4 May, 11 May and 12 May 2015.

36. Interview, INE official, 12 May 2015.

37. Interview, INE counsellor, 11 May 2015.

38. Interview, congresswoman, 6 May 2015.

39. Interview, INE official, 8 May 2015.

40. Interview, former congresswoman, 8 May 2015.

41. Interview, senator, 11 May 2015.

42. Due to unique circumstances, Chiapas held its elections on 19 July, rather than 5 June.

43. "Elecciones 2015 serán las más complejas en la historia: INE [The 2015 elections will be the most complex in history: INE says]." *Excelsior*, 1 April 2015.

44. Some states may also elect some portion of the regidores using plurality rules.

45. Of the states with elections in 2015, only Chiapas placed conditions on the alternation rule in its electoral code, requiring that women appear as list-headers when there is an odd number of districts.

46. 'Piden a PRD respetar delantera de Beatriz Mojica en encuesta para Guerrero [The PRD is asked to respect Beatriz Mojica's lead in polls in Guerrero].' *La Jornada,* 9 February 2015. Mojica was eventually nominated, but lost the election.

47. The Nuevo León IEE stipulated that parties could not concentrate female candidates for the ayuntamientos in losing districts. The parties contested this regulation, but the regional TEPJF upheld it. ('Trife da la razón a CEE sobre paridad de género [The state electoral institute gives the state electoral commission its reasoning on gender parity].' *Milenio,* 28 February 2015.)

48. 'Paridad de género obliga al PRI Guerrero cambiar lista de candidatos [Gender parity obliges the PRI in Guerrero to change the list of candidates].' *Notimex*, 11 April 2015.

49. Alanis Figueroa and González Oropeza, Voto Particular, SG-JDC-11138/2015.

50. 'Impugna ONG resolución del IEPC que no respeta paridad en las candidaturas [A civil society organization challenges the state electoral institute's decision

for failing to respect gender parity in candidacies].' *La Jornada Guerrero* 17 March 2015.

51. Interview, senator, 8 May 2015. See also 'Mujeres de Sonora crean Observatorio de Paridad para proceso electoral 2015 [Women in Sonora create a Parity Observatory for the 2015 electoral process].' *El Occidental*, 24 March 2015.

52. 'Constituyen mujeres el observatorio electoral [Women form an electoral observatory].' *Diario de Morelos*, 12 February 2015; 'Mujeres de Sonora crean Observatorio de Paridad para proceso electoral 2015 [Women in Sonora create a Parity Observatory for the 2015 electoral process].' *El Occidental*, 24 March 2015.

53. Tribunal Electoral Estatal de Morelos, Expediente [Ruling]: TEE/RAP/012–2015–1Y, 14 February 2015, page 37.

54. 'Mujeres perredistas piden respetar equidad en Morelos [Women from the PRD in Morelos ask that gender parity be respected]'. *El Universal,* 17 February 2015.

55. Interview, TEPJF judge, 4 May 2015.

56. Interview, TEPJF judge, 4 May 2015.

57. Interview, TEPJF judge, 7 May 2015.

58. Interview, TEPJF judge, 7 May 2015.

59. 'Confirman obligación de partidos paridad de género en elecciones en Morelos [The obligation for gender parity in the elections in Morelos is confirmed].' *Siempre!* 15 March 2015.

60. 'Baja California Sur incluye paridad para ayuntaminetos [Baja California Sur includes parity in the municipalities]'. *Ciudadania Express,* 1 April 2015; 'Paridad 'sí', pero para la próxima.' *La Crónica*, 18 March 2015.

61. 'Baja California Sur incluye paridad para ayuntaminetos [Baja California Sur includes parity in the municipalities]'. *Ciudadania Express*, 1 April 2015.

62. 'Más mujeres en el poder, a 60 años de ejercer el voto [More women in power, sixty years after the right to vote]'. *Express Zacatecas*, 3 July 2015.

63. 'Principio de paridad de género causa crisis interna en el PRD Guerrero [The principle of gender parity causes an internal crisis for the PRI in Guerrero]'. *Proceso*, 30 March 2015.

64. 'Declara TEPJF improcedente paridad de género en Edomex [The Federal Electoral Tribunal declares gender parity unfair in the State of Mexico]'. *Proceso*, 17 April 2015; 'Nuevo León, Sonora, y Edomex no tendrán paridad horizontal esta elección [Nuevo Leon, Sonora, and the State of Mexico will not have horizontal parity in this election]'. *Excélsior*, 29 April 2015; 'Paridad no estará en elecciones para alcaldías, decide TEPJF [Parity will not be in place for elections of the municipal presidents, the Federal Electoral Tribunal decides]'. *Milenio*, 9 April 2015.

65. Alanis Figueroa and González Oropeza, Voto Particular, SG-JDC-11138/2015.

66. Press Release, Mujeres en Plural, Mexico City, 5 May 2015.

67. 'Paridad de género e inconstancia [Gender parity and inconsistency]'. *La Crónica,* 5 May 2015.

68. 'Baja California Sur incluye paridad para ayuntaminetos [Baja California Sur will include parity in the municipalities]'. *Ciudadania Express,* 1 April 2015.

69. Interview, TEPJF judge, 4 May 2015.

70. Interview, TEPJF judge, 4 May 2015.

71. Press Release, Mujeres en Plural, Mexico City, 5 May 2015.

REFERENCES

Baldez, Lisa. 2004. 'Elected Bodies: The Gender Quota Law for Legislative Candidates in Mexico'. *Legislative Studies Quarterly* 24 (2): 231–58.

Baldez, Lisa. 2007. 'Primaries v. Quotas: Gender and Candidate Nominations in Mexico, 2003'. *Latin American Politics and Society* 49 (3): 69–96.

Bjarnegård, Elin. 2013. *Gender, Informal Institutions, and Political Recruitment: Explaining Male Dominance in Parliamentary Representation.* New York: Palgrave Macmillan.

Bjarnegård, Elin and Meryl Kenny. 2016. 'Comparing Candidate Selection: A Feminist Institutionalist Approach'. *Government & Opposition* 51 (3): 370–92.

Bruhn, Kathleen. 2003. 'Whores and Lesbians: Political Activism, Party Strategies, and Gender Quotas in Mexico'. *Electoral Studies* 22 (1): 101–19.

Crocker, Adriana, ed. 2011. *Diffusion of Gender Quotas in Latin America and Beyond.* New York: Peter Lang.

Eisenstadt, Todd A. 1999. 'Off the Streets and into the Courtrooms: Resolving Postelectoral Conflicts in Mexico'. In *The Self-Restraining State,* edited by Andres Schedler, 83–104. Boulder: Lynne Rienner Publishers.

Eisenstadt, Todd A. 2002. 'Measuring Electoral Court Failure in Democratizing Mexico'. *International Political Science Review* 23 (91): 47–68.

Eisenstadt, Todd A. 2003. 'Thinking Outside the (Ballot) Box: Informal Electoral Institutions and Mexico's Political Opening'. *Latin American Politics and Society* 45 (1): 25–54.

Estévez, Federico, Eric Magar and Guillermo Rosas. 2008. 'Partisanship in Nonpartisan Electoral Agencies and Democratic Compliance: Evidence from Mexico's Electoral Institute'. *Electoral Studies* 27 (2): 257–71.

Franceschet, Susan and Jennifer M. Piscopo. 2014. 'Sustaining Gendered Practices? Power and Elite Networks in Argentina'. *Comparative Political Studies* 47 (1): 85–110.

Gains, Francesca and Vivien Lowndes. 2014. 'How Is Institutional Formation Gendered, and Does It Make a Difference?' *Politics & Gender* 10 (4): 524–48.

Helmke, Gretchen and Stephen Levistky, eds. 2006. *Informal Institutions and Democracy: Lessons from Latin America.* Baltimore: The Johns Hopkins University Press.

Hinojosa, Magda. 2012. *Selecting Women, Electing Women.* Philadelphia: Temple University Press.

INE. 2015. 'Impacto del registro paritario de candidaturas en el Proceso Electoral Federal 2014–2015 [Impact of the registration of candidates under gender parity in the Federal Electoral Process of 2014–2015]'. Mexico City: INE.

Johnson, Niki. 2016. 'Keeping Men In, Shutting Women Out: Gender Biases in Candidate Selection Processes in Uruguay'. *Government & Opposition* 51 (3): 393–415.

Jones, Mark P. 1996. 'Increasing Women's Representation via Gender Quotas: The Argentine Ley de Cupos'. *Women & Politics* 16 (4): 75–98.

Kenny, Meryl. 2013. *Gender and Political Recruitment: Theorizing Institutional Change.* New York: Palgrave Macmillan.

Kenny, Meryl and Tània Verge. 2013. 'Decentralization, Political Parties, and Women's Representation: Evidence from Spain and Britain'. *Publius: The Journal of Federalism* 43 (1): 109–28.

Krook, Mona Lena. 2009. *Quotas for Women in Politics: Gender and Candidate Selection Reform Worldwide*. New York: Oxford University Press.

Langston, Joy and Javier Aparicio. 2011. 'Gender Quotas Are Not Enough: How Background Experience and Campaigning Affect Electoral Outcomes'. Working Paper Number 234. Mexico City: Centro de Investigación y Docencia Económicas.

Lovenduski, Joni. 1998. 'Gendering Research in Political Science'. *Annual Review of Political Science* 1 (1): 333–56.

Mackay, Fiona, Meryl Kenny and Louise Chappell. 2012. 'New Institutionalism through a Gender Lens: Towards a Feminist Institutionalism?' *International Political Science Review* 31 (5): 573–88.

Mahoney, James and Kathleen Thelen, eds. 2010. *Explaining Institutional Change: Ambiguity, Agency, and Power*. New York: Cambridge University Press.

March, James G. and Johann P. Olsen. 1996. 'Institutional Perspectives on Political Institutions'. *Governance: An International Journal of Policy and Administration* 9 (3): 247–64.

Marx, Jutta, Jutta Borner and Mariana Caminotti. 2007. *Las legisladoras: Cupos de género y política en Argentina y Brasil* [Female legislators: Gender quotas and politics in Argentina and Brazil]. Buenos Aires: Siglo XXI.

Medina Espino, A. 2010. 'La participación política de las mujeres. De las cuotas de género a la paridad'. México, DF: CEAMEG.

Ortiz Ortega, Andrea and Clara Scherer Castillo. 2014. *Contigo aprendí: una lección de democracia gracias a la sentencia 12624* [With you I have learned: a lesson in democracy thanks to Sentence 12624]. Mexico City: Tribunal Electoral del Poder Judicial de la Federación.

Piscopo, Jennifer M. 2015. 'States as Gender Equality Activists: The Evolution of Quota Laws in Latin America'. *Latin American Politics and Society* 57 (3): 27–49.

Piscopo, Jennifer M. 2016. 'When Informality Advantages Women: Quota Networks, Electoral Rules, and Candidate Selection in Mexico'. *Government & Opposition* 51 (3): 487–512.

Reyes, Juan M. 2012. 'El tribunal de los militantes: el control judicial de los conflictos intrapartidistas en México'. *América Latina Hoy* 62: 131–53.

Roza, Vivian. 2010. 'Gatekeepers to Power: Party-Level Influences on Women's Political Participation in Latin America'. PhD dissertation. Washington, DC: Georgetown University.

Sacchet, Teresa. 2008. 'Beyond Numbers: The Impact of Gender Quotas in Latin America'. *International Feminist Journal of Politics* 10 (3): 369–86.

Schedler, Andreas. 2005. 'From Electoral Authoritarianism to Democratic Consolidation'. In *Mexico's Democracy at Work,* edited by Russell Crandall, Guadalupe Paz and Riordan Roett, 9–38. Boulder: Lynne Rienner Publishers.

Serra, Gilles. 2012. 'The Risk of Partyarchy and Democratic Backsliding: Mexico's 2007 Electoral Reform'. *Taiwan Journal of Democracy* 8 (1): 31–56.

Shepsle, Kenneth A. 1989. 'Studying Institutions: Some Lessons from the Rational Choice Approach'. *Journal of Theoretical Politics* 1 (2): 131–47.

Verge, Tània and Ana Espírito-Santo. 2016. 'Interactions between Party and Legislative Quotas: Candidate Selection and Quota Compliance in Portugal and Spain'. *Government & Opposition* 51 (93): 416–39.

Waylen, Georgina. 2014. 'Informal Institutions, Institutional Change, and Gender Equality'. *Political Research Quarterly* 67 (1): 212–23.

Zamora Chavarría, Eugenia María. 2009. 'Derechos políticos de la mujer en Costa Rica: 1986–2006' [Political rights of women in Costa Rica: 1986–2006]. *Derecho Electoral [Journal of the Supreme Electoral Tribunal]* 7: 1–44.

Chapter 8

Negotiating Gender Equity in a Clientelist State: The Role of Informal Networks in Bangladesh

Sohela Nazneen

How and why do political actors adopt gender-equitable policies in clientelist and patronage-based political contexts where promotion of gender equity policies does not generate any immediate political or material gains? How do pro-women policy coalitions influence this political process, where women as a group have limited access to resources, information, political actors and policy-making processes – all of which make them unattractive as a collective to the power-holders? Answering these questions requires not only an understanding of the formal political and policy-making rules and processes, but also an unpacking of how the informal rules, norms and practices operate and how pro-women policy actors navigate these informal norms and practices. 'Informal rules, norms and practices' significantly influence what kind of institutional and policy changes are possible and the extent to which the policy reforms are successfully implemented (Waylen 2014). These rules, norms and practices are often less visible. Actors, both inside and outside the particular institutions, take these rules for granted. This chapter investigates how informal rules, norms and practices shaped gender-equity negotiations around a specific piece of legal reform in Bangladesh and its implementation. The key actors whose behaviour and actions are explored in the chapter are the following: the executive, particularly the prime minister and the cabinet; the key relevant ministries and their heads – the women's minister, the Ministry of Women and Children's Affairs, the Ministry of Law; the legislative body; and the members of the civil society policy coalition on domestic violence, largely comprised of women's rights organisations. The chapter explores the processes that led to the formulation of a draft law on domestic violence, the negotiations that occurred before a draft was placed for parliament, and why procedural and institutional gaps exist in implementing the law. Through analysing these processes, the chapter does the following. First, it highlights the role personal relations or interpersonal capital and women's informal networking played in subverting the constraints created by the formal procedures. The chapter explores the active role played by the prime minister in containing opposition to the law in the cabinet and in the Parliament, and the role of the women's minister in facilitating the drafting of the law by the civil society coalition. It investigates how interpersonal capital of the members of the policy coalition and informal network were crucial in mediating access to key decision makers and gaining inside information. It also illustrates how informal practices contained opposition to the content of the law. Second, the chapter shows how these informal practices and norms operate when it comes to implementation of a new legal change. The chapter shows that besides capacity and resource gaps, 'layering' as a strategy to bring about change (in this case imposition of a new implementing structure on top of existing one) is limited by the inability of the 'rule makers' to control implementation, non-compliance of the 'rule-takers/implementing personnel' at the local level, inconsistencies within the formal rules, all of which creates space for various informal practices to operate (Capoccia 2016; Streeck and Thelen 2005).

This chapter uses the definition by Helmke and Levitsky (2004, 272) to define informal institutions as 'socially shared rules, usually unwritten, that are created, communicated, and enforced outside of officially sanctioned channels'. Informal rules along with formal ones shape actor's incentives and preference for strategies and constrain their behaviour in particular ways, thus leading to predictable outcomes (ibid). The unwritten nature of the informal rules, norms and practices poses particular difficulties in researching them as these are embedded within the everyday functioning of the institutions and are difficult to identify (Culhane, this volume). Research is particularly challenging when it comes to investigating sanctions for not following informal rules, as these may be difficult to observe empirically and information on this aspect may not be forthcoming from participants (see Piscopo, this volume).

In this chapter, I unpack the role of informal institutions in the following manner. First, I explore how informal norms and practices manifest themselves through the use of personal relations or interpersonal capital and informal networking among political and policy advocacy actors, subverting formal rules. Second, I investigate how informal practices subvert gender-equitable outcomes during implementation processes.

My interpretation of women's informal networking as a mechanism through which informal norms and practices manifest themselves implies that these informal networks are bearers of informal institutions, and *not* institutions or actors. The interpersonal capital of the women political and policy advocacy actors shapes their ability to engage in informal networking activities with different power-holders and access policy spaces. By women's informal networks, I refer to sustained informal interactions by individuals (both women's rights activists and also state officials) and the policy coalition with key decision-makers (in this case the prime minister) to influence policy outcomes. These actors' (individuals and the policy coalition) ability to influence is not necessarily tied to or corresponds with their official position. I use the term *network* also to indicate that these actors have engaged in a regularised pattern of interactions that sustained over a period of time. They primarily relied on leveraging interpersonal capital and informal practices[1] (behaviour not based on written rules and procedures of engagement) to change formal/existing rules or policies.

In clientelist contexts, interpersonal capital and informal networking are key mechanisms through which inside information is shared, access to key decision-makers is mediated and the privilege of the dominant social group is maintained. Feminist institutionalist scholars researching political recruitment have identified how interpersonal capital and informal networks play gatekeeping roles in candidate selection and exclude women (Bjarnegård 2013; Culhane this volume; Franceschet and Piscopo 2014). These scholars explore the gendered nature of interpersonal capital and how men are able to easily access this, compared to women, to build informal political networks that allow men to access clientelist networks and become political power brokers. Mainstream development politics literature also comments on the adverse impact of informal networks and personalised nature of formal institutions on marginalised groups, particularly those groups that have low social and political capital (Casson et al. 2010). Women in the developing countries are included among these marginalised groups. The good governance literature has long viewed informal institutions in a negative light, highlighting how patronage and clientelism subverted governance reforms (Casson et al. 2010; O'Donnell 1996). Existing literature on patronage politics do show that women tend to be adversely affected by corruption and patronage (Bjarnegård 2013; Goetz 2003). Women have less to offer to patrons in terms of material and social resources.

However, the impact of interpersonal capital or informal networks, rules and practices are not universally adverse for women (Benstead 2015; Piscopo this volume). Scholars have argued that informal and formal institutions interact and these interactions can have both positive and negative effects on the performance and functions of the formal institutions. For gender-equitable policy changes advocated by gender entrepreneurs both inside and outside the formal institutions, a key area of concern is that reforms imposed upon existing formal structures will have limited impact as old ways of working would subvert the outcomes intended by the changes (Waylen 2014). Recently, feminist institutionalists have focused on informal rules, networks and practices more closely and how they operate alongside the formal in a gendered manner, and how gender-equitable institutional changes are influenced by the nature of these interactions in different contexts. This chapter offers empirical evidence of how gender-equitable institutional changes are influenced by the interactions between formal and informal institutions. In studying how the formal and informal interact, feminist institutionalist scholars have also debated what an informal institution is and whether informal networks are informal institutions or actors or intermediaries or bearers of informal institutions (Bjarnegård et al. 2016; Chappell and Mackay, this volume). This chapter offers empirical evidence on how women's informal networking operates in the real world and act as mechanisms (or bearers of informal norms and practices) through which formal rules are undermined.

The chapter illustrates how the interpersonal capital and informal networking may at times work to the benefit of the gender equity lobby. It focuses on both the policy adoption process and the gaps in implementing the same policy, and how the informal operates at both these levels. Linking the two processes will add to the existing gendered analysis of institutions where the emphasis has been on the formal, getting the rules, processes and systems 'right'. Most of the research by feminist institutionalists has focused on political recruitment (Bjarnegård 2013; Culhane this volume), recruitment in the executive branch (Franceschet, this volume), parliamentary quota practices (Piscopo and Hinojosa this volume), negotiations of a new constitution etc. (Waylen 2014). Few have explored how the informal rules operate at specific policy-implementation level. This analysis also aims to challenge the emphasis placed in gender mainstreaming and policy literature on getting formal rules and procedures right, by highlighting why getting the design of the formal institutions 'right' may not be enough for promoting and implementing gender-equitable policy changes.

The research was conducted in Bangladesh in 2014–15 as a part of a large comparative research project. The project investigated two successful-[2] gender-positive policy adoption cases across six different countries' contexts using a common analytical framework.[3] Process tracing was used for researching these two policy cases, which involved constructing a timeline that captured the major events that led to the policy change, mapping the key actors involved in policy negotiations (including those who resisted change), interviews with key informants (around twenty for each case), review of previous research and analysis of policy documents, including data collected by the Internal Monitoring and Evaluation Division (IMED) of the Government of Bangladesh, on the effectiveness gaps in implementing the Domestic Violence Act of 2010. Participant observation was used to collect data from workshops organised by the Ministry of Women's Affairs Children's Affairs (MOWCA) of the Government of Bangladesh. These workshops were organised to consult with the civil society coalition on domestic violence and the various state service providers. However, not all relevant documents were found as the state keeps insufficient records. A few of the key informants could not be interviewed due to unavailability. These may mean that the policy adoption story, particularly the informal aspects of the story pertaining to the Domestic Violence Act, has not been captured in full.

Researching informal rules, norms and practices or identifying the boundaries of the informal institutions is difficult. How the informal network operated and interpersonal capital was used during policy adoption and implementation processes presented particular challenges. It required having pre-existing relationships and strong rapport with some of the key informants to access the 'policy elites and insiders' and also for the insiders to trust and open-up with sensitive information. My own positionality as a Bangladeshi academic, whose long attachment and personal relationships with various interviewees, mattered in gaining access and trust. However, this may also mean that the kinds of information that I was privy to was influenced by what the interviewees thought could be disclosed to me given my past (and present) links with various women's movement actors.[4] Second, the information disclosed by the key informants posed specific types of challenges and raised ethical concerns. For some pieces of information disclosed by the interviewees, it was difficult to protect the identity of the interviewee if their particular side of the story was revealed. These stories and insights were not used when presenting the research in public or discussed with other key informants. However, this meant, at times, specific lines of enquiry would be closed. Third, revealing and further investigating particular bits of the policy adoption story meant making public the internal power struggles among the pro-women coalition actors on domestic violence. This would make the policy coalition vulnerable to various future risks, particularly given the changing political context in Bangladesh where the feminist movement was/is facing increasing pressure from the state agencies and the political right. Concealing these internal struggles from other key informants made triangulation of data difficult. Some of the information provided by the state agency officials also needed to be handled carefully, particularly critiques of the top-most executive, as revelation of these carried political risks for the interviewees.

The chapter is structured in the following manner. The next section describes the Bangladesh context. The third section briefly outlines the policy adoption story and the current stage of implementation of the Domestic Violence Act of 2010. The fourth and fifth sections explore how the informal rules, norms and practices influenced negotiations, adoption and implementation of the Domestic Violence Act. Adoption of the Domestic Violence Act is a surprising outcome in a clientelist and patronage-based political context where promotion of gender equity policies does not generate any immediate political or material gains, and requires unpacking. Reflections on what motivated the political actors to make a gender-positive policy change and what the findings mean for furthering our understanding of how gender-equitable change takes place are discussed and conclusions are drawn in the final section.

THE CONTEXT: BANGLADESH

Recently, Bangladesh has been lauded for its success in improving women's condition and promoting gender equity. These successes include a significant reduction in maternal mortality, gender parity in primary and secondary school enrolment and an increase in women's participation in national legislature and local government through gender quotas. The state has also enacted various laws on violence against women since the 1980s (World Bank 2008). The pace with which these changes were achieved since the 1970s is remarkable. Undeniably, the state took innovative and cohesive policy measures in making these changes. What motivated the state and political actors to make these changes in a political context that is clientelist and patronage-based, and the state agencies operate in a highly personalised manner? (Hassan 2013). Unpacking this conundrum and understanding what role the informal rules, networks and practices may have played in promoting gender-equitable change requires a closer look at the Bangladesh context. The following section provides a quick overview of the nature of the relations between the executive, other government agencies and the civil society in Bangladesh. It also illustrates the relations women's movement actors have with the state and political actors.

Bangladesh is a Muslim-majority state with a parliamentary system of government. It gained independence in 1971 through a war of independence against Pakistan, and has gone through alternating periods of military (1975–1990; 2006–2008) and democratic rule (1971–1975; 1991–2006; 2009 to present). After the democratic transition in 1990, the two centrist parties – the Awami League (AL) and the Bangladesh Nationalist Party (BNP) – have dominated the political scene, which created a de facto two-party system. These political parties are informal-centralised parties, where the senior leadership, particularly the heads of the party, have unchallenged authority. This authority is further strengthened by the dynastic nature of party leadership. The AL is headed by Sheikh Hasina, the daughter of the previous leader (who led the struggle for independence), and the BNP by Khaleda Zia, the wife of the founder leader.

Patron–client relationships remain the dominant form of social organisation for structuring relationships between classes. Systemic bureaucratic and political corruption (clientelism), politicised judiciary, ineffective regulatory capacity and political instability have weakened state capacity (Hassan

2013). The three most powerful elite groups in Bangladesh are the politicians, bureaucracy and the military. In recent years the political class has emerged as the most powerful group. The top leadership of the incumbent party, particularly the prime minister, has *de facto* control over the way parliament functions and major policy and allocation decisions. The top political leadership also has significant control over how the law and enforcement agencies operate. The civil society actors – from the professional associations such as doctors', teachers', lawyer's associations to trade unions – are strongly aligned with either the AL or the BNP. The polarisation of the civil society actors into two camps has significantly constrained the power of these groups to promote their interests and demand accountability. The power of the incumbent party is to some extent constrained by the higher judiciary, private media, some rights-based NGOs and Islamist groups. The latter has veto power over certain policy areas, particularly those pertaining to religion, culture and women's rights. Inevitably, the partisan nature of the civil society and the dominance of the executive and the political elites have influenced the strategies used by the pro-women/gender equity actors, their access to formal policy spaces, the issues they can campaign around and how they are able to promote gender equity in the policy and political arena.

The Bangladeshi state and its political leaders have always held a contradictory position in matters related to women's rights and gender equity (Jahan 1995; Kabeer 1994). They have promoted women's economic engagement through various schemes and education, and enacted various laws to protect women. Despite these positive measures, these actors have many times acted to preserve gender-biased religious personal laws and designed and implemented policies to sustain male privilege. The UN Women's Decade (1975–1985) and donor willingness to fund Women in Development (WID) programs played critical roles in motivating these actors to address issues related to women's needs and rights. WID-focused work created scope for targeting women as development agents and also led to the creation of gender mainstreaming machineries, such as the Ministry of Women and Children's Affairs (MOWCA). High level of donor dependency during the decades of 1970s and 1980s created incentives for the military generals in power (1975–1990) to promote gender and development issues. Support for these schemes also strengthened the legitimacy of their regime among donors (White 1992).

After the democratic transition (1990 onwards), women's movement actors (which include women's rights organisations, feminist research and academic organisations, human rights organisations) and pro-women coalitions have become visible in policy and consultative spaces. Women's movement actors had a significant role in the pro-democracy movement during the 1980s and the various consultations during the 1990s (particularly for the preparations for the Beijing Conference in 1995). This entry into the policy spaces allowed women's movement actors to collaborate with the state on various issues. The state was also willing to collaborate with women's movement actors as it needed assistance. While the women's movement actors have made significant policy gains, their association with international donor-funded schemes on gender and development has allowed the critics to label them as 'westernized', promoting agenda that violates cultural and religious norms (Nazneen and Sultan 2014). The other challenge that women's movement actors faced is the rise of the Islamist political groups in politics. The military dictators had removed the principle of secularism from the Constitution, declared Islam as the state religion and removed the ban on religious political parties in the decades of 1970s and 1980s. After the democratic transition, both centrist parties, the AL and the BNP, had courted the Islamist political parties to create tacit or overt alliances to win elections. This emphasis on Islam in public life and political alliances with religious political parties has constrained the space to raise issues that challenge religious norms. It has led to difficulties for women's rights organisations to advocate for changes in matters that are determined by religious personal laws (i.e. marriage, divorce, inheritance, custody).

While the women's movement actors have made their mark in policy-making processes, this has not been the case for women representatives in the Parliament and the local government. Women's representation had increased due to gender quotas (at present fifty reserved seats in the Parliament, where the party selects women to the parliamentary seats; and one-third seats are reserved in each union and *upzila,* the two lowest tiers of the local government). Most of these representatives are perceived as proxy representatives (Chowdhury 1994; Panday 2008), and the reserved seats in Parliament are used for negotiating with coalition parties and distributing patronage by the ruling party (Akter and Nazneen 2014). The women representatives are accountable to the top-party leadership for nominating them, and not to the constituents. The representatives do not come in with a gender mandate. The control exerted by the senior party leadership over party agenda, the weak position of the Parliament and the local government vis-à-vis the executive and the bureaucracy, further constrains the role of the women MPs and local representatives. The women representatives are compelled to toe the party line and face difficulties promoting women's rights agenda and ensuring accountability of the service providers at the local level for implementing gender-equitable changes.

Given the above context, how do gender-equitable policy changes, such as the enactment of a Domestic Violence law, take place? What and who drives the negotiation process for legal reform and its implementation? And what role do informal rules, networks and practices play in this process?

THE DOMESTIC VIOLENCE ACT OF 2010

The Domestic Violence Act was enacted by the Parliament in 2010. Violence against women in Bangladesh is widespread. According to a national survey conducted by the Bangladesh Bureau of Statistics (BBS) in 2011, of the 12,000 women surveyed, about 87 percent of the ever married women experienced violence. The patriarchal structure in Bangladesh constructs women as economic dependents limiting women's access to material and social resources, mobility in the public sphere and interactions with non-related males (Jahan 1995). About 66 percent of the girls are married by the age of sixteen (Save the Children Fund 2016), and marriages tend to be outside of one's natal village. Early marriage, economic dependency, limited mobility and social capital, and being based outside of one's village, make it difficult for women to leave an abusive marriage and seek recourse from in laws or the community, where the woman is an outsider.

A law that specifically addresses domestic violence has been demanded for a long time by women's movement actors. The process that led directly to the enactment of the law began in 2002 by women's legal-aid organisations. They researched various provisions and laws of other countries on domestic violence. Assistance was sought from the female lawyers, male judges and international feminist lawyers from neighbouring countries, mainly India and Malaysia to prepare drafts of a proposed law. The evidence gathered by different groups led to the production of three different drafts. In 2007, a decision was made within the movement to come together and form a policy coalition – the Citizen's Initiative against Domestic Violence (CiDV). The policy coalition consisted of twenty-five women's rights, human rights and legal-aid organisations. In 2007, a military-backed technocratic regime was in power, which created opportunities for the coalition to engage with the executive and the state agencies without the fear of being politically aligned with a party. CiDV's work ran into difficulties in 2008, when controversy over a proposed clause on women's control over acquired assets led to wide scale protests by the Islamist groups and the technocratic government was reluctant to move forward with any agenda pertaining to women's rights.

In 2009, the AL won a two-thirds majority and came into power. The Ministry of Women and Children's Affairs (MOWCA) was headed by a long-term women's movement activist. This created an opening for CiDV. The new minister suggested that MOWCA's donor funded Multi-Sectoral Project on Violence Against Women (MSVAW) be used to institutionalise the work of the coalition. This partnership allowed the coalition to finalise the draft law, which was placed to the Ministry of Law for vetting. The draft was forwarded to the cabinet. The close relationship between the minister of women's affairs and the prime minister expedited the cabinet discussion on the law, particularly in tackling queries and criticisms. The cabinet's queries were passed on to CiDV by the minister of women's affairs (a practice outside of formal rules), so that they could help the minister convince the prime minister regarding the necessity of the clauses in question. The prime minister was strongly in favour of enacting the law. The AL government had previously compromised on women's rights issues and Bangladesh was up for review at the Committee on Status of Women (CSW) in New York. The AL government was eager to project itself as a gender-friendly regime. Moreover, in July 2010, the key leaders of the Jamaat E Islami, the opposition coalition partner, went on trial on charges of collaborating with the Pakistani Military during the 1971 war of independence. This reduced the power of the Islamist groups to oppose women's rights issues. It also created the need for the AL government to seek support from secular elements of civil society, including women's movement actors (Nazneen and Hickey 2016).

The strong support of the prime minister for the bill reduced resistance inside both the cabinet and the Parliament. The male members of Parliament (MPs), who may have potentially opposed the law, were lobbied by CiDV members. The bill faced relatively little scrutiny in the Parliament, once it went through the cabinet and was adopted in October 2010. The provisions under the act include the following: protection orders for women, women's right to reside in the marital home, recovery of personal assets and assets acquired during marriage and temporary custody of children. Marital rape was not included in the law. The law only covers blood and marital relationships, and adopted children. Each stage of the negotiation process was marked by a high degree of informality, involving backdoor negotiations, use of personal relationships and informal networks, and other informal practices.

The implementation of the law has been slow. A three-year delay around developing rules of procedure had initially stalled the implementation process. Development of prescribed forms took another year. The coordinating ministry, which is MOWCA, requires co-operation from various other ministries such as Law, Home, Justice, Finance and Social Welfare, which still remains absent. Moreover, it was envisioned that the implementing officer would be the MOWCA officer at the local level, who would liaise with the court, police, hospitals and local CSOs. Six years after the enactment, MOWCA officers still lack adequate training and resources. The catchment areas for services are yet to be clearly demarcated and the list of service-providing organisations in each area was only drawn up in 2014. The training of all MOWCA officers, police officers and judges is yet to be complete. An evaluation found that about half of the MOWCA officers interviewed had not received training and of the police officers interviewed in five districts only 10 percent of the officers knew about the Domestic Violence Act (BNWLA

2013). The number of one-stop crisis centres and shelters is inadequate, six and nine respectively, to cover sixty-four districts (MOWCA website). Adequate monitoring mechanisms are yet to be developed to track implementation by the state.

The gaps in implementation reveal not only weak state capacity but also the gap between actors who championed policy-adoption process (i.e. rule makers) and actors who would implement the policy (i.e. rule enforcers; Waylen 2014). Cappocia (2016), in his discussion on endogenous institutional changes and non-compliance at the bottom, points out that this gap between rule makers and rule enforcers results from: the cognitive limits of the rule makers and their inability to control implementation. The implementation is also hindered by implementing officers who are unwilling to accept the new formal rules and procedures (non-compliance) and the ambiguity and inconsistencies within formal rules (Streeck and Thelen 2009) that allow for the informal practices to operate. These are discussed at length in later sections.

Enactment of the Law and the Role of Personal Relations and Informal Networks

The policy story of how the Domestic Violence Act of 2010 was enacted reveals that the law-making process did not follow the conventional route taken in a parliamentary democracy. The policy coalition did not start by lobbying the members of parliament, including the female members of parliament. The Parliament and the MPs had a limited role. CiDV members did meet the female MPs a few times; the meetings were arranged through the MOWCA secretary. They had also briefed the female MPs about the draft law towards the tail end of the process. The law itself was ritualistically discussed in the Parliament. It was tabled on the last day of the fifth session, and was adopted within two weeks of the Sixth session and signed by the president within a week after it was adopted.[5] The initial draft of the law was not prepared by the Ministry of Law but the Ministry of Women's and Children's Affairs (MOWCA) and CiDV members. The Prime Minister's Office (PMO), which keeps a close lid on the proceedings of the cabinet, had shared information about the discussions on this piece of law with CiDV members, bypassing the formal practice. Why were these formal rules and practices subverted by the policy coalition (CiDV), MOWCA and the PMO? And what role did personal relations or interpersonal capital play in it?

Although Bangladesh is a parliamentary democracy with a Westminster-style government, the prime minister herself and the PMO wield vast agenda-setting powers that are beyond the usual remit of these offices in a parliamentary form of government. This agenda-setting power is partly due to the historical legacy of having a presidential form of government for fifteen years (1975–1991), where the president wielded considerable power and the government was heavily centralised. Dynastic politics (and the lack of any alternative political leaders), a de-facto two party system, partyarchy (where the party dominates all forms of political process and politicises society along party lines (Coppedge 1993)) and the lack of internal democracy with the parties have centralised power in the hands of the top-party leadership. The prime minister and the executive are the strongest arms of the government with vast agenda-setting power. The prime minister exerts considerable control over legislature and the members of Parliament through formal and informal rules and practices.[6] Given this context, the behaviour of the policy coalition and also the PMO in bypassing the legislature is hardly surprising.

Franceschet (this volume) shows how, in Chile, the president is able to shift power and influence from executive branches' formal dimensions, particularly the cabinet, to a small group of advisors, since the organisation of the executive branch is not governed by clear formal rules, but what she terms as *informality*. Franceschet argues that the role played by individual advisors with whom the head of the executive has a trusted relationship provides access to the centre of the executive branch, and participation in these networks are the main markers of political influence. Women's access to these networks is key in influencing the possibilities for women being able to promote a gender-equity agenda at the top executive level. These factors play a key role in the Bangladesh case also.

Personal relations and the informal networks between the 'core executive'[7] (Elgie 2011) and the 'policy coalition' were key for the policy coalition to gain access to powerful actors, particularly the PMO and the prime minister herself, and also for navigating the complex processes related to introducing a legal reform agenda. The key actors in enacting the Domestic Violence Act of 2010 were: (a) the policy coalition – CiDV; (b) the Ministry of Women's and Children's Affairs (MOWCA); (c) the minister of women's affairs, Shirin Sharmeen Chowdhury; (d) the prime minister, Sheikh Hasina; (e) the cabinet; (f) Ministry of Law and (f) the Parliament. The relationships between the policy coalition, the women's minister and the prime minister were crucial in moving the agenda forward on domestic violence.

The policy coalition's lead organisations were composed of members who were classmates at university and friends of the prime minister or the women's minister. The women's minister herself was a women's rights activist and a member of two of the leading organisations of the policy coalition. The women's minister was a trusted ally of the prime minister and a member of the closed inner-circle within the cabinet. The close nature of the relationship between the prime minister and the women's minister was based on the relationship both their fathers had. The women's minister had remained a loyal friend and supporter during the 2007–2008 army-backed technocratic regime, when Shiekh Hasina was facing corruption and other charges and many of the political leaders of the AL had abandoned her.[8]

These relationships and informal connections provided unprecedented access to the ministers and the PMO. It also allowed the policy coalition to gain insider knowledge, particularly about the leanings of the prime minister herself and the proceedings within the cabinet. This access also allowed both the coalition and the women's minister to tackle possible resistance to the draft law by the cabinet members and the Ministry of Law, and assist the prime minister in diffusing any resistance by these groups and the Members of Parliament.

In their interviews, the CiDV members repeatedly stressed that the proactive role of the women's minister and the prime minister, and their informal links with CiDV, had allowed CiDV to succeed in pursuing its agenda. One interviewee, a classmate of the prime minister, said that their personal connections had allowed them to sustain the pressure on the prime minister, creating a sense of personal obligation and responsibility to see the legislation through. It also allowed the coalition members to highlight informally how the image of the prime minister and the regime may benefit from passing this new law, both nationally and internationally. One CiDV interviewee made the following statement:

> . . . X had gone to the university with the Prime Minister – they have a '*tumi – tumi*' relationship (the informal 'you') – and sometimes they meet socially. She is not the only one . . . You do not always meet to talk shop [discuss domestic violence act] – but you can raise it in these occasions and they have done so. They have reminded her that this was an election pledge . . . that we [women's movement actors and their allies] are hoping that she will come through, and how both nationally and internationally this will contribute to her legacy . . . She [PM] was also able to ask for clarifications and advise on matters informally a few times . . . and she trusted these friends. (Interview, Supreme Court Advocate and CiDV member)

The close relationship the coalition members had with the women's minister, and the relationship the women's minister had with the prime minister, also allowed for very frank discussions about the possible pitfalls and pockets of resistance, and strategies that were needed to be undertaken by each of these actors to tackle these. The following observations were made by the CiDV members:

> Shirin Sharmeen Chowdhury (the women's minister) was one of us . . . She was also a lawyer so it was easier to explain things . . . The minister took a personal interest and was willing to place the Ministry's resources at our disposal . . . She lobbied to get MOWCA in charge of drafting the law, and not the Ministry

of Law. MOWCA being in charge allowed us to preserve and polish the draft we had developed. They [Ministry of Law] lacked the capacity . . . I think her close relationship with Sheikh Hasina (the PM) helped in getting MOWCA in charge . . . She tipped us off about any queries that may be placed on the draft, even if it was during late hours, she had our cell phone numbers . . . and we researched that issue . . . contacting us or for us to contact her was not difficult. (Interview, former BNWLA employee CiDV member)

When the act was presented at the Cabinet, Shirin (the Women's Minister) had asked for a special briefing [from the coalition]. She had a list of points that had been raised. Shiekh Hasina (the PM) had called her and privately asked her to find answers to these queries. She [the PM] said that she wanted minimum debate in the Cabinet and was keen to see this through but needed to minimize resistance . . . This was of course unusual, and not the norm that we have access to what the Cabinet may ask, but bypassing this worked for our benefit. (Interview, BLAST employee and CiDV member)

These personal interactions were not limited to exerting informal pressure on the key actors or passing on insider's knowledge so that the process could be facilitated; it played a key role in diffusing resistance during the different stages of drafting. In drafting the law, MOWCA had a lead role along with the Bangladesh Law Commission and the Ministry of Law. The women's minister's personal interest in the matter, close relationship with CiDV and also the alignment of CiDV's work with the ministry's policy priority and the regime's interests all led to the institutionalisation of CiDV's role under the MSVAW project implemented by MOWCA. The Domestic Violence Act became deliverable for the donor-funded project, which gave the women's minister leverage in policy discussion with the bureaucrats. Institutionalisation through the MSVAW project also led to CiDV's work gaining weight and allowed CiDV to enter into policy spaces. CiDV was able to amend the draft it had developed and rework it.

As stated earlier, MOWCA had been chosen as the ministry for drafting the law and not the Ministry of Law, which was a deviation from the formal practice, this created tensions between the two ministries. The Ministry of Law saw this as an encroachment by MOWCA on its territory. While the expertise of the female lawyers who were members of CiDV was acknowledged by the Ministry of Law, the officials working at this Ministry felt that the CiDV members lacked knowledge about the processes and functioning of the government. They also had very different ideas about who/what the law should cover (i.e. definition of the family – only blood, martial, and adoptive children not cohabiting couples or gay relationships), and what women should be entitled to under the law, and what kinds of violence can be addressed (i.e. not marital rape). There were several rounds of revisions and discussions on these issues with the Ministry of Law. The women's minister personally got involved in these discussions and was adamant that the draft forwarded by MOWCA would not be changed by the Ministry of Law. One CiDV member made the following statement,

> The Law Ministry kicked up a fuss over our definition of the family in the draft as we had an expanded definition to include different types of relationships [including cohabiting and gay couples], and they felt that this would needlessly draw criticism from the political right and tarnish the image of the government . . . but Shirin [the Women's Minister] was very tough . . . she insisted that our draft should not be tinkered with. . . . (Interview, Supreme Court Lawyer and CiDV member)

In terms of resources, personnel and position within the government MOWCA is a weaker ministry but it was able to withstand the pressure from the Ministry of Law, because the women's minister was a part of the inner circle of power and the prime minister was willing to back the women's minister's decisions. The support of the prime minister and the PMO played a critical role once the draft law was placed in the cabinet for discussion. One of the employees of the PMO pointed out that 'the Prime Minister explicitly stated that she wanted the law to be placed before the parliament as soon as possible and that the law should be in the books before the next round of elections'. This clear signalling of the PM's intentions in a context, where power is highly centralised, minimised discussions on the draft. As highlighted in earlier discussions, the prime minister also provided the women's minister with a list of queries which may lead to possible contentions and asked her to be prepared to brief the cabinet. These queries were then passed on to the CiDV members, who briefed the women's minister. After the bill was placed in the Parliament, the PMO sent clear signals to the legislative body that the bill had prime minister's support and should be passed without delay. This expedited the process. The prime minister informally let the key male MPs from the AL know they should reign in any untoward discussions on the bill (interviews, donor organisation worker and CiDV members). She also identified and asked some of the female MPs to speak on behalf of the draft bill publicly and in the Parliament (interview, Female MP 1). Given Bangladesh's context where the legislative is a weak institution rarely able to withstand executive pressure, the Parliament went through the formal motions of adopting a new law, but did not hold extensive debates or scrutinise the draft. The bill was tabled and sent to the Standing Committee on the last day of the fifth session, and it was adopted within two weeks into the sixth session on 5 October 2010, and signed by the president within a week of adoption.

Role of Informal Practices in Implementation

As discussed earlier, the implementation of the law has been slow partly due to lack of a coherent organisational structure to deliver on various provisions. Various informal norms and practices have also subverted the implementation process and the substantive aim of the law. There were delays in developing the rules of procedure and prescribed forms for filing complaints, demarcating catchment areas and developing lists of service-providing organisations, building new shelters, and training the police, judges and MOWCA officers on the law. It was envisioned that the new law would operate alongside the existing laws addressing violence against women. Observers from the field pointed out that on many occasions the law is not used, but cases are filed under the previous laws (Interview, Magistrate 1; Interview, BLAST lawyer; observations made by MOWCA officers at the CiDV-MOWCA workshop). The state agencies that were assigned to deliver services to the victims of violence were: the police, the judiciary, social welfare and medical personnel and the MOWCA officers. The role of the MOWCA officer at the district level was envisioned as the enforcer and the focal point for liaising with these various services. This was added to the existing duties of the MOWCA officer's role as a wel-fare officer. This not only increased the workload of the officers without adequate compensation or resources, but they were also insufficiently trained. For the MOWCA officers, to succeed in their new roles, they needed to be effectively integrated within the existing administrative structures and also for the gender mainstreaming mechanisms (i.e. local gender desk) within the administration to function effectively. This was missing. 'Layering' (Capoccia2016; Schickler 2001; Waylen 2014) gender mainstreaming mechanisms on top of existing structures as a strategy has had mixed results in the past in Bangladesh, and in the case of implementing domestic vio-lence law, it was not very effective.

Gender scholars and feminist institutionalists have long pointed out that the institutions themselves have 'gendered dispositions' (Annesley and Gains 2010) and that the actors within the institutions are gendered (Lowndes 2014). The police, lower judiciary and the medical service providers (who deal with the women who have experienced domestic abuse) are largely male-dominated professions and institutions in Bangladesh. The institutional culture and how the officers employed in these organisations understand their positions within these professions are gendered. They generally have a paternalistic attitude towards women (Sultan, n.d.; various interviews, CiDV members). Most of these actors behave as 'blockers' (Waylen 2014) in implementing the law. Women who lodge complaints of domestic abuse are largely persuaded by these actors to pursue mediation and reconciliation, instead of following the various procedures and provisions set in the law. This partly stems from the practical realities of women's lives in Bangladesh, where they are economically dependent on the husband. It also stems from the paternalistic view to protect women from the loss of economic and social security. In addition, the predominant view within the police and the lower judiciary is that the domestic violence cases tend to destroy the 'family which is the core unit of the society' (observations made by Magistrates of their colleagues at the MOWCA-CiDV meeting; interviews, BLAST lawyers 1, 2 and 3 – all CiDV members). These views influence how the various options and provisions of the law are implemented by the officers. The CiDV members who work in legal-aid organisations cited numerous examples where they had difficulties in filing complaints, secure assistance for enforcing protection orders and ensuring that the women were not thrown out of the marital homes. In addition, the personalised nature of the bureaucracy at times subverts or facilitates implementation of the provisions of the law. The following case narrated by a CiDV member and a BLAST[9] lawyer highlights how personal connections are used to gain access to service providers and how informal practices operate within the system:

My client was an educated woman who held a job. She was physically and verbally abused by her husband and in laws, which started four-five months after her marriage. In the end, she was thrown out of the house and all her certificates, official documents and jewelry and other material possessions were kept by the in laws. She had married against her family's wishes so she had nowhere to go. We had gone to file a complaint and secure a court order for the 'right to reside' and also to reclaim her possessions. The judge was sympathetic but did not know much about the new law. He wanted to see papers. I have argued in his court before and he knew my organization, so he did not dismiss us outright. We finally got these together and secured the court orders ... When we went to the police, the police officers were dragging their feet as she [client] was not being abused at the time ... They were not convinced why she should have the right to reside in the martial home, as it was not owned by her ... My senior knew the local police's superior officer, was in touch [with local officers], so we finally got the police on our side ... We went and got the certificates and other official documents, but we were unable reclaim anything else. The husband's family had hidden the material things and informed the local political leader, a high up, once we arrived. His [local leader] goons were there ... and police had some discussions with them. .... Later the police said we should leave without anything else and that they would be unable to protect the girl if she exercised her right to reside ... Very quickly the husband initiated divorce proceedings so that the girl could not return ... So you see, there are loopholes in the law, but also there are so many hidden things that affect how the law is implemented, we did not anticipate this when we were drafting the provisions ...'.[10]

What the preceding story illustrates is that the 'rule enforcers or takers' are not the 'rule makers' who pushed for legal change, and that a disconnect remains within the two groups that hinders the implementation process. Non-compliance with the new changes results from the rule makers' limited ability to control the implementation processes, inconsistencies within the law and how rule enforcers interpret their responsibility in upholding women's rights. It also reveals the different ways the informal norms and practices operate during implementation, and acts as a double-edged sword. Personal relations were useful for engaging the police and getting them to take action; however, the personal relations that the husband's family had with the local leader also constrained the actions of the police. The actors, certainly the police, were gendered, their personal views influencing their initial reluctance to enforce the right to residence. The informal power structure, in this case the local political leader weighing in, subverted the operation of formal rules, in this case the police enforcing the court order.

CONCLUSION

So what does the Bangladesh story tell us about the informal rules, networks and practices? It shows how the informal norms, practices and rules operate alongside the formal rules and procedures. The creation of new formal rules, a law on domestic violence, involved actors (policy coalition, ministers) engaging in informal practices and subverting existing formal rules. In this case, the feminist policy coalition used informal norms and practices to advance the gender-equity agenda (domestic violence law). For the policy adoption process, the following aspects of informal institutions, particularly the personal relationships, interpersonal capital and informal networks between key actors and the policy coalition and subversion of formal rules related to law making, positively influenced gender-equitable outcome (i.e. the law itself). The case also illustrates that the creation of new formal rules, in this case a piece of legislation that promotes gender equity, does not automatically replace the informal norms and practices that influence how state agencies operate in a gender-biased manner and the gender-biased behaviour of the state officials who are part of these agencies. The case illustrates that the interactions between the formal and informal rules and practices may not readily lead to gender-equitable outcomes when it comes to the implementation of gender-equitable policy changes.

Second, the research methods used to gather data for this particular case reveal the importance of the personal relationship and informal networks. Researching the informal networks in policy-making and practice requires investigating and unpacking sensitive issues. This requires good rapport and previous relationships with the policy elites and insiders, which means that these relationships needed to established and invested in before the actions by various insiders can be analysed. The positionality of the researcher becomes a significant factor in determining access and also shaping how much is revealed by the policy insiders. The Bangladesh case also highlights the difficulties that researchers face when revelation of specific pieces of sensitive information may create different types of risks for policy insiders, and the challenges it raises about triangulation of data. These are areas that need to be discussed further by researchers exploring the informal.

Third, the findings in terms of policy implementation, both for gender activists promoting changes and insiders within state agencies promoting gender equity, raise some uncomfortable questions. In this particular case, the policy coalition was able to subvert the formal rules and practices to their benefit in a political context where dynastic politics and monopolistic partyarchal control had centralised power in the hands of the political elite. This centralisation of power is a double-edged sword. While it expedited the adoption process of this specific piece of legislation in the long run, it contributes to constraining the development of formal rule-based processes and accountability of various state agencies. It also raises questions about what strategies women's movement actors may use effectively to promote an agenda that does not align clearly with the interests of the regime. This is an area that needs to be furthered explored in the research on the informal institutions.

NOTES

1 It should be noted that the use of the term *practice* is intentional to signal that the nature of interaction between the actors is based on widely understood and established patterns of behaviour circumvention which has adverse implications for actors seeking access to power-holders. However, the line between informal rule and practice is blurred, and questions can be raised about when informal practices become codified into informal rules since both of these are unwritten.

2. Success is defined in terms of gender-positive policies being adopted not in terms of implementation of the policies.

3. Effective States and Inclusive Development (ESID) Research Center.

4. Women's movement actors include women's rights organisations, human rights NGOs, feminist research organisations and academic networks.

5. Parliament records.

6. Floor crossing (i.e. voting against the party which nominated a person) is formally prohibited.

7. Cabinet, co-ordinating institutions, network of advisers.

8. This is not to argue that the gender of the prime minister made a key difference. The family connection and personal loyalty created the bond of trust, which the prime minister has with a few other key advisors also.

9. Bangladesh Legal Aid Services Trust.

10. In Bangladesh, Muslim men have a unilateral right to divorce; they do not have to show grounds and can divorce after sending three notices within three months.

REFERENCES

Akter, Marufa and Sohela Nazneen. 2014. Inclusive Democracy: Engendering Political Parties, in *The State of Governance Report: Bangladesh 2013*, Bangladesh: BRAC Institute of Governance and Development, BRAC University.

Annesley, Claire and Francesca Gains. 2010. Gender and Core Executive: Gender, Power, and Changes. *Political Studies* 58(5), 909–929.

BBS. 2011. *Violence against Women in Bangladesh 2011*, Dhaka: BBS.

Benstead, Lindsay J. 2015. Why Quotas Are Needed to Improve Women's Access to Services in Clientelistic Regimes. *Governance* 29(2), 185–205.

Bjarnegård, Elin. 2013. *Gender, Informal Institutions, and Political Recruitment: Explaining Male Dominance in Parliamentary Representation*, New York: Macmillan.

Bjarnegård, Elin, Meryl Kenny and Tania Verge. 2016. *Conceptualizing Informal Networks within Feminist Institutionalism*, Paper prepared for the 24th World Congress of Political Science, IPSA, Pozan, 23–26 July 2016.

BNWLA. 2013. *Ending Impunity: Monitoring Report for the Implementation of the Domestic Violence Act (Prevention and Protection) Act 2010*, Dhaka: BNWLA.

Capoccia, Giovanni. 2016. When Do Institutions Bite? Historical Institutionalism and the Politics of Institutional Change. *Comparative Political Studies* 49(8),1–33.

Casson, Mark C., Marina D. Guista and Uma S. Kambhampati. 2010. Formal and Informal Institutions and Development. *World Development* 38(1),137–141.

Chowdhury, Najma. 1994. Bangladesh: Gender Issues and Politics in a Patriarchy, in Barbara Nelson and Najma Chowdhury (eds.), *Women in Politics Worldwide*, Yale: Yale University Press.

Coppedge, Michael. 1993. *Strong Parties and Lame Ducks,* California: Stanford University Press.

Elgie, Robert. 2011. Core Executive Studies Two Decades. *Public Administration* 89(1), 64–77.

Franceschet, Susan and Jennifer M. Piscopo. 2014. Sustaining Gendered Practices? Power and Elite Network in Argentina. *Comparative Political Studies* 47(1), 85–110.

Gains, Francesca and Vivien Lowndes. 2015. How Is Gender Implicated in Institutional Design and Change? Paper presented at Informal Institutions Workshop, Manchester, 10 September 2015.

Goetz, Anne Marie. 2003. The Problem with Patronage, in Anne Marie Goetz and Shireen Hassim (eds.), *No Short Cuts to Power: African Women in Politics and Policy Making*, London: Zed Books.

Hassan, Mirza. 2013. Political Settlement Dynamics in a Limited Access Order: The Case of Bangladesh, *ESID Working Paper 23*, University of Manchester, UK.

Helmke, Gretchen and Steven Levitsky. 2004. Informal Institutions and Comparative Politics. *Perspectives in Politics* 2(4), 725–740.

Jahan, Roushan. 1995. Men in Purdah and Women in Public: Rokeya's Dreams and Women's Struggles in Bangladesh, in Amrita Basu (ed.), *The Challenges of Local Feminisms: Women's Movement in Global Perspective*, Boulder: Westview Press.

Kabeer, Naila.1994. *Reversed Realities: Gender Hierarchies in Development Thought*, Verso: London.

Lowndes, Vivien. 2014. How Are Things Done around Here?: Uncovering Institutional Rules and Their Gendered Effects. *Politics and Gender* 10(4), 681–691.

Nazneen, Sohela and Sam Hickey. 2016. Political Settlements and Gender: What Drives Women's Political Inclusion and Gender Equity Initiatives? *ESID Comparative Synthesis Paper*, University of Manchester (mimeo).

Nazneen, Sohela and Sultan Maheen. eds. 2014. *Voicing Demands: Feminist Activism in Transitional Contexts*, London: Zed Books.

O'Donnell, Guillermo. 1996. Illusions and Consolidations. *Journal of Democracy* 7(2), 34–51.

Panday, Pranab Kumar. 2008. Representation without Participation: Quotas for Women in Bangladesh. *International Political Science Review* 29(4), 489–512.

Save the Children Fund (SCF). 2016. *A Study on the Effectiveness of Social Protection Policy on Child Marriage in Bangladesh,* Bangladesh: Save the Children.

Schieckler, Eric. 2001. *Disjointed Pluralism,* Princeton: Princeton University Press.

Streeck, Wolfgang and Kathleen Thelen. eds. 2005. *Beyond Continuity*, Oxford: Oxford University Press.

Sultan, Maheen. (n.d.) *Gender Equality and Women's Empowerment in Public Administration: Bangladesh Case Study*, Dhaka, Bangladesh: UNDP.

Waylen, Georgina. 2014. A Seat at the Table—Is It Enough? Gender, Multiparty Negotiation and Institutional Design in South Africa and Northern Ireland. *Politics and Gender* 10 (4), 495–223.

White, Sarah C. 1992. *Arguing with the Crocodile: Gender and Class in a Bangladeshi Village,* London: Zed Books 495–552.

World Bank. 2008. *From Whispers to Voices: Gender and Social Transformation in Bangladesh*, Dhaka: World Bank.

Chapter 9

An 'Alternate' Story of Formal Rules and Informal Institutions: Quota Laws and Candidate Selection in Latin America

Magda Hinojosa

If candidate recruitment and selection is the secret garden of politics (as Gallagher and Marsh 1988 suggested), then the process of recruitment and selection of political alternates is an invisible – yet ubiquitous – tree in that hard-to-find garden. Political alternate positions are used in countries across the globe, including Argentina, Burkina Faso, Croatia, Iceland, Romania and Uruguay, among many others,[1] and yet there is almost no academic work examining these positions.[2] In these systems, parties nominate alternates alongside titleholders. If the titleholder cannot serve (i.e. due to illness, travel, appointment to an ambassadorial post), the alternate steps in. This chapter examines the manipulation of these alternate positions in response to the adoption of gender quotas and argues that informal institutions emerge to undermine the new formal rules imposed by quotas.

Formal institutions are 'rules and procedures that are created, communicated, and enforced through channels widely accepted as official' such as 'state-enforced rules (constitutions, laws, regulations)' (Helmke and Levitsky 2004, 727). Alternates – also known as substitutes and often referred to in this chapter by the Spanish word suplente(s) – have long been codified in constitutions; formal rules dictate not only the conditions under which alternates may substitute for their titleholders (and the processes by which titleholders must request leaves of absence), but the legislative roles that alternates are allowed to assume both when substituting for titleholders and when not serving in office, and how they will be remunerated for their legislative work. Despite the existence of these formal rules, political alternate positions are poorly understood, and the informal norms that exist alongside this formal institution have been ignored.

In contrast, the much newer formal institutions created by gender quota legislation have received considerable academic attention, as have the myriad accompanying informal practices which have sprung up to thwart gender quotas. Academics have noted that there is 'ample evidence of informal party practices of quota subversion, ranging from running women in "no-hope" seats where they have little chance of winning, to practices of local patronage and the privileging of "favorite sons", and, even, in some cases, committing electoral fraud in order to sidestep formal gender equality reforms' (Bjarnegård and Kenny 2015, 752; Culhane this volume).

How can alternate positions be manipulated in order to subvert quotas? First, parties can place women as alternates rather than as titleholders and count this form of representation towards quota goals. Second, parties can nominate women to titleholder positions and then ask them to step down after either the certification of candidacies or the election in favour of their male alternates. Third, parties can ask women to run simultaneously for two political offices knowing that if a woman wins both seats she will be legally obligated to cede one to her alternate. These three informal means of undermining gender quotas contravene the spirit of the quotas while staying on the right side of the law.

The first and second of these are examples of informal institutions. Informal institutions are 'socially shared rules, usually unwritten, that are created, communicated, and enforced outside of officially sanctioned channels' (Helmke and Levitsky 2004, 727). It has become routine behaviour in a number of Latin American countries to utilise these alternate positions to avoid meeting quota obligations. The rules here are unwritten, but the vast application of these practices – which is evidenced in no small part by legislation created specifically to address these nefarious practices (Hinojosa and Piscopo 2013) – indicates that they have been broadly communicated. The sanctioning with these informal institutions is applied not to those who have failed to subvert quotas in this way but to those who refuse to go along with a party's plans to do so. Failure to do so would bring party disapproval. In list PR systems where candidate lists are controlled by political parties, such party disapproval comes with significant political costs.

The final practice of having women run for seats in both legislative chambers to meet the quota requirement is an act of subterfuge, like the other two forms described above, given that electoral rules prohibit women from assuming both seats. However, this is not yet an example of an informal institution, since a pattern of behaviour must occur over some time in order to become institutionalised. As I mention in the conclusion to this chapter, these informal practices might never become institutionalised since the Uruguayan quota applies only to the 2014 elections.

Informal institutions, such as these, emerge for a number of reasons; often these originate when actors are unable to achieve a formal institutional change or when their goals are 'not considered publicly acceptable' (Helmke and Levitsky 2004, 730). The informal practices that alter the use of suplente positions in order to debilitate gender quotas are examples of accommodating informal institutions: 'These informal institutions create incentives to behave in ways that alter the substantive effects of formal rules, but without directly violating them; they contradict the spirit, but not the letter, of the formal rules' (Helmke and Levitsky 2004, 729). The purpose of these accommodating informal institutions is sabotage: 'Accommodating informal institutions are often created by actors who dislike outcomes generated by the formal rules but are unable to change or openly violate those rules. As such, they often help to reconcile these actors' interests with the existing formal institutional arrangements' (Helmke and Levitsky 2004, 729).[3] Accommodating informal institutions, then, can emerge to torpedo formal institutions. Because these institutions are created for the purpose of sabotage and because flagrantly violating the formal institution is unacceptable, identifying these accommodating informal institutions is challenging.

This chapter examines the rise of informal institutions across Latin America that serve to undermine gender quotas via the misuse of political alternate positions, and presents an opportunity to examine how the adoption of a new formal institution leads to the creation of these accommodating informal institutions by examining the Uruguayan case in detail.[4] In order to make this argument, I draw on over fifteen interviews carried out during research trips to Uruguay in June 2015 and July 2016. I interviewed current female parliamentarians, a minister of the Electoral Court and former members of parliament who drafted the gender quota legislation that was passed in 2009 and applied in the 2014 elections. I also make use of a dataset cataloguing all articles from 2001 to 2014 appearing in Uruguay's three largest newspapers about the gender quota (and earlier legislative attempts to pass a quota law) (Hinojosa, Fridkin, and Kittilson 2014). In addition, I utilise rich newspaper accounts from across Latin America that document the role of political alternates.

The chapter proceeds in this manner: first, it presents information on political alternates and how these positions can affect women's political representation. Then, it discusses these alternate positions in the context of the use of gender quotas. I, then, turn to the case of Uruguay to flesh out how the implementation of the gender quota motivates the creation of an informal practice intended to disable the gender quota via the crafty use of the political alternate positions. I argue that these informal practices are the first evidence of the creation of an accommodating informal institution.

WHY STUDY POLITICAL ALTERNATES?

Studying political alternates is an indispensable part of academic analyses of political recruitment and candidate selection. First, it is important to study alternates because alternates routinely end up in positions of power. Second, the lack of academic work into political alternates means we know little about the selection methods used to choose political alternates. This lack of understanding about selection processes translates into a lack of knowledge about the types of individuals that we find occupying these positions. Third, we need to study the recruitment and selection of alternates (relative to the recruitment and selection processes for titleholders) in order to understand how these individuals might act while in office.

Alternates substitute for titleholders in the legislature when the titleholder must be absent. These absences can be short term, due to illness or travel, or they can be long term, due to death or the desire to accept an appointed post or acquire a different elected position.[5] While national rules vary regarding when alternates must be called, they appear to be frequently in use. In Brazil, more than 25 percent of politicians in the 49th session of congress were elected as alternates not titleholders (Finan 2004). A report on the Colombian legislature stated that 41 percent of senators and 46 percent of deputies had called their suplentes to step in for them at some point in the previous two years (El Tiempo 2015). Over the course of three years, Uruguayan deputies and senators received a combined total of 10,318 days of leave; suplentes covered each of these absences (El Observador 2/21/2013). The amount of time that alternates hold office can vary dramatically. While some suplentes substitute for a single day due to legislator illness, others take over permanently when their titleholder resigns their post for a different political office. In the Uruguayan case, staggered elections mean that previously elected legislators will first take leave to run in departmental elections and then permanently vacate their posts within months of being elected to take new positions. In these cases, alternates may end up serving nearly an entire term in office.

We know little about the selection methods used to choose political alternates. But, these selection methods matter. They determine the types of individuals that we get into these positions. The anecdotal evidence available indicates that alternates are selected using different methods than those used to select titleholders. For example, in Mexico, alternates for subnational positions are often handpicked by the titleholders leading to a situation whereby alternates are often relatives of the titleholders (Vidal Correa 2014). These situations in which titleholders wield the power of selection certainly affect the individuals that are chosen for these positions and the incentives for those individuals. Due to the lack of academic studies on political alternates, we have limited knowledge about these positions; researchers often treat 'candidate selection as an undifferentiated process, when in many countries in Latin America and beyond, candidate nomination processes include both primary and substitute candidates' (Vidal Correa 2014, 321).

The lack of information about political alternates means that we know next to nothing about their motivations and, hence, how they might behave in office. We neither know what drives them or whom they are accountable to. Are they accountable to a titleholder who handpicked them for the position? Are they accountable to national leaders who selected them? Pizarro notes that the political aims of the substitute member of Congress may differ from those of the elected parliamentarian (Pizarro 2006, 85). Anecdotal evidence from Colombia indicates that suplentes there do not feel accountable to their titleholders, as news reports indicate that these substitutes have voted in favour of projects that their titleholders had rejected (El Tiempo 2015).

Political alternate positions take a variety of forms. For example, in Mexico, a single alternate serves alongside a titleholder. In the Ecuadorian case, each titleholder has both a first alternate and a second alternate. The system in Uruguay is more complex, as will be explained later, with four different ways to select alternates. One commonly used form in Uruguay requires that each titleholder be listed on the ballot alongside three alternates (Johnson 2015; multiple interviews).

There is also little consistency with regards to remuneration for these posts. Payment varies considerably. For example, in the Nicaraguan case suplentes receive a salary of approximately US $700/month regardless of whether they are called in to substitute. This sum represents about 1/6 of what the titleholder earns per month. Additionally, alternates receive a stipend for each substitution. Moreover, these suplentes gain invaluable privileges in addition to the financial compensation that they receive: (1) they have legal immunity, and (2) they can submit legislative proposals (Hinojosa and Vijil Gurdián 2012). In Uruguay, suplentes are much better paid for their service, receiving Uruguayan $5,500/ day (approximately US $220) for their service (El Observador 2/21/2013).

Alternate positions are poorly understood and generally disliked by the public. Newspapers routinely highlight concerns about the financial waste in employing suplentes. There were real concerns in Colombia that the titleholders and alternates were rotating in the post in order to game the system; by doing so, both the titleholders and their alternates would receive salaries. Ultimately, these concerns led to the dissolution of the Colombian system of substitutions. Alternates there no longer step in temporarily for officeholders; substitutions are allowed only when the titleholder will be permanently unable to carry out his or her duties. In addition to concerns about the cost of continuing with the system of alternates, some have argued that alternates are not accountable to voters. A news article from Colombia explained that recent legislation concerning presidential re-election was ultimately decided by two alternates who cast the deciding votes (El Tiempo 2015). These alternates voted contrary to the wishes of their titleholders. Moreover, some have noted that the alternate position 'allows persons who were not popularly elected to use their time in Congress to improve their political pull in certain provinces by proposing legislative projects' (Bejarano 2001, 232 as cited in Pizarro 2006).

THE EFFECTS OF ALTERNATE POSITIONS ON
WOMEN'S REPRESENTATION

A handful of scholars of Latin American women's representation have considered the relationship between women's political representation and the
existence of alternate positions (Bruhn 2003; Baldez 2007; Saint-Germain
and Chavez Metoyer 2008; Hinojosa and Vijil Gurdián 2012; Vidal Correa 2014). Previous work identified four possible ways in which political
alternate positions affect female political representation (Hinojosa and Vijil
Gurdián 2012). First, alternate positions can serve as 'apprenticeship' and
ultimately benefit female political representation by providing women with
further political experience that will make them more attractive candidates in
future elections. Second, female political representation can be advantaged by
'substitution', whereby women are strategically nominated as suplentes for
titleholders that are likely to step down from their positions. Parties can select
female alternates for positions likely to be vacated[6] in an effort to increase
women's representation; Beckwith terms this 'sneaking women into office'
and claims that it can be a way for national leaders to 'avoid (if they cannot
win) confrontation with local party leadership over the direct nomination of
female candidates for safe seats' but still get women into office (Beckwith
1989, 4–5). Titleholders leave their elected seats quite regularly in Latin
America to take appointed positions (Morgenstern and Nacif 2002; Saint-
Germain and Chavez Metoyer 2008). Third, the political representation of
women can be enfeebled via 'circumvention'; in these situations, political
parties use the alternate positions to minimally meet their quota requirements.
These acts of circumvention have forced the re-writing of gender quota legislation. Fourth, political parties may use the suplente positions to make up
for women's underrepresentation in titleholder seats; that is parties will place
more women as alternates to compensate for their inadequate representation in titleholder positions. This form of 'compensation' ultimately stymies
women's access to power.

The conventional wisdom has been that suplente positions prevent women
from acquiring positions of power or that awarding alternate spots is a 'way
of seeming to value the election of women without advancing women as
serious candidates on the primary list' (Saint-Germain and Chavez Metoyer
2008, 91). In other words, these suplente posts are largely seen as allowing
for either 'circumvention' or 'compensation' rather than encouraging either
'apprenticeship' or 'substitution' to take place. However, alternate positions
have been instrumental in bringing women into political office across Latin
America. For example, the female alternate for the mayor of the Costa Rican
capital ascended into that position when the titleholder opted to seek the
presidency (Taylor-Robinson et al. 2015). Female suplentes are often able to

take over for their titleholders in congress, increasing women's representation in these legislative bodies. This was the case in Ecuador where women's presence in the legislature increased 25 percent due to substitutions (Pacari 2002). In their study of the use of these positions in Nicaragua prior to the adoption of a gender quota, Hinojosa and Vijil Gurdián found that the use of suplentes was not undermining women's political representation (2012). The introduction of gender quotas can, however, alter the ways in which these alternate positions are utilised by political parties, as some political actors may attempt to use the suplente posts to sabotage quotas.

GENDER QUOTAS: FORMAL INSTITUTIONS CHANGING CANDIDATE SELECTION PROCEDURES

Quotas are 'measures passed by national parliaments requiring that all parties nominate a certain percentage of women' (Krook and O'Brien 2010, 260). More than fifty countries across the globe currently use gender quotas as part of a stated effort to increase women's political representation (Krook 2009). Gender quotas are commonplace across Latin America. Presently, only Guatemala and Venezuela fail to use gender quotas for national legislative elections.[7] These gender quotas are an attempt to alter candidate selection processes; by requiring political parties to increase the proportion of female candidates that they nominate, these quotas force political parties to revise old practices of recruitment and selection (Hinojosa 2012).

The implementation of quotas has not been static. In response to violations of both the letter of the gender quota law and its spirit, quota regulations have routinely undergone alterations (Hinojosa and Piscopo 2013). The dynamic processes that we have witnessed over the last twenty-five years aim to prevent political parties from exploiting loopholes. One such set of changes has attempted to target the misuse of political alternate positions. Further, I discuss three ways in which alternate positions have been used to undermine quota laws.

First, parties can meet gender quotas by nominating women to alternate posts. The conventional wisdom has long held that parties across Latin America will attempt to meet their quota obligations by running women as alternates rather than as titleholders. In the case of Mexico, parties routinely met the 1996 quota recommendation by placing women as alternates rather than as titleholders (Reynoso and D'Angelo 2006; Baldez 2007). Moreover, political parties relied on these alternate spots to meet their own internal party quotas, which like the 1996 quota recommendation, lacked enforcement mechanisms (Baldez 2007). The misuse of the suplente positions was common knowledge among political insiders. Vidal Correa (2014) analysed women's subnational representation in the Mexican states and determined that where state quota rules did not require that parties nominate women as titleholders rather than alternates, parties relegated women to alternate positions and gave them a smaller percentage of titleholder candidacies. This practice is not confined to Mexico. The use of this practice was also noted in Venezuela and Bolivia (Albaine 2009; Hinojosa and Piscopo 2013). So commonplace was the application of the quota to alternate posts rather than to titleholder positions that numerous countries wrote or revised their gender quotas to explicitly forbid this practice. For example, the Ecuadorean quota of 2000 called for both 30 percent of titleholder and alternate candidates to be women. The law also clearly specified the number of women that needed to be included in both titleholder and alternate lists in order to meet the quota, to avoid a situation where parties rounded down when faced with situations in which required percentages did not translate into a set number of seats (Pacari 2002).

Second, parties can nominate women to titleholder positions but ask them to step down at a later date in favour of their male alternates. The best known example comes from Mexico. Because Mexican political parties had been known to use alternate positions to meet quotas, the 2002 gender quota set out specific guidelines to avoid this practice and ensure that the quota could only be met by placing women as candidates for titleholder spots. Ultimately, even these specifications were not enough to prevent political parties from creatively undermining the gender quota via the use of political alternate positions. The case of the so-called Juanitas was seen as evidence of a 'previous accord' that would allow parties to 'get around the gender quota' (Huerta García et al. 2006; Piscopo, this volume).[8] Shortly after the 2009 legislative elections, sixteen women (who became known as the Juanitas) renounced their seats to their male alternates. These renunciations were widely seen as evidence that political parties were cheating the quota, that is that women had been asked to run only in name and that previous agreements had been in place for them to give up their seats to their male suplentes (NOTIMEX 2010; Martoccia and Camacho 2011). These Juanitas may have earned a memorable moniker, but they were certainly not the first women in Mexico to have been asked to run as titleholders but renounce their seats to their male alternates after the election (Interview, 22 May 2003).[9] And this practice was not unique to Mexico. A similar situation occurred in the Dominican Republic. Women there were dropped from lists only after these had been certified by the electoral tribunal. Political parties claimed that women had ultimately decided not to compete (Bueno 2007 cited in Roza 2010, 190).

The case of the Juanitas ultimately led to a revision of the gender quota (Hinojosa and Piscopo 2013; Piscopo, this volume). In November 2011, the Federal Electoral Judicial Court decreed that candidates to titleholder positions and the suplentes running alongside them would need to be of the same sex (but see the excellent discussion of the efforts by women to end this practice in Piscopo, this volume). This law meant that if a woman renounced her seat, another woman would step in to take her place. More recently, the term Juanitas has been extended in Mexico to include women who are being asked to serve only in name; these are frequently the female relatives (often wives) of known politicians. The media reported such cases in the Mexican states of Tabasco and Querétaro (AM de Querétaro 2015; Excelsior 2016). In a number of instances, the wives of men who were 'dropped' from the lists due to the need to fulfil gender quotas ended up as candidates. These Juanitas are not being asked to renounce their seats; rather, the presumption is that they will allow men (often their husbands) to exercise power.[10] This phenomenon has been reported in other contexts; Franceschet and Piscopo say Argentine parties have applied quotas by turning to these women, which are often referred to as *mujeres de*, although these scholars note that it is impossible to determine exactly how often this happens (Franceschet and Piscopo 2008, 406).

Third, parties can ask women to run simultaneously for two political offices knowing that if a woman wins both seats she will be legally obligated to cede one of those seats to her alternate. This is the practice that we see unfold in the Uruguayan elections of 2014, when the gender quota is first applied. The Uruguayan case allows us to see the emergence of an informal practice, which has yet to become routinised, as a reaction to a new formal institution. I detail this phenomenon in the section that follows.

THE URUGUAYAN GENDER QUOTA

The Uruguayan gender quota law (Law no. 18,476) was first applied for legislative positions in the 26 October 2014 elections. The Uruguayan quota was expected to increase women's representation in the legislature. The law included a placement mandate, requiring that women must be represented in every third spot throughout the entire list or in the first fifteen positions on the list. The placement mandate prevented women from being relegated to unelectable spots on their lists. The quota law also could not be met by placing women as alternates rather than as titleholders. Importantly, the quota law had carefully articulated sanctions. Lists failing to comply with the quota would be rejected.

Women's consistently low representation[11] in the Uruguayan parliament had led to repeated demands for a gender quota beginning in the late 1980s. An initial effort to pass a gender quota law was unsuccessful, but a recommendation[12] for greater gender equality was successful (Archenti and Johnson

2006, 141). A quota law was finally passed in 2009, but the new law included an 'expiration date' which meant that to be applied for more than one election it would need to be readopted (Johnson and Moreni 2009).

The application of the gender quota in Uruguay is complicated by the convoluted electoral system that characterises the small country. While Uruguay uses a closed list proportional system to elect representatives,[13] 'each party presents an important variety of closed and blocked lists that compete among themselves within the party. Intra-party competition softens the rigidity of closed and blocked lists and transforms the Uruguayan system into a kind of intra-partisan preferential vote' (Altman and Chasquetti 2005, 240). Parties run multiple lists since each faction within a party proposes its own list. Political super stars appear on multiple lists since these 'figures of national prestige' attract votes (Altman and Chasquetti 2005, 244; Chasquetti 2008).

URUGUAY'S FORMAL RULES AND THE CREATION OF AN INFORMAL INSTITUTION

Know the rules well, so you can break them effectively.

– Dalai Lama

The Uruguayan quota was far from a resounding success. Because Uruguayan law allows individuals to simultaneously run for a seat in the Senate and a seat in the Chamber of Representatives, the number of seats that would be awarded to women was initially unclear following the elections. For the 2014 elections, there were three women that were simultaneously elected to the Senate and the Chamber of Representatives; these women would each need to give up one of their elected positions. In the weeks following the elections, political parties decided which seats individuals would take; ultimately, eighteen female representatives took office as did eight female senators. While this meant that women's representation doubled in the Senate (increasing from 13.3 percent to 26.7 percent), the results were less dramatic in the lower house, where women's representation increased from 15.2 percent to 18.2 percent.

The Uruguayan quota's lukewarm results can be attributed to: (1) simultaneous candidacies for seats in both legislative chambers, which meant that doubly successful women would need to cede seats to their alternates, and (2) minimal compliance combined with low district magnitude; women rarely emerged victorious from smaller districts where only one or two people from a list would gain office because women rarely held the top spot or the number two position on the list. Women were much more likely to be represented in the third spot on the list as part of a minimal application of the placement requirements of the quota. According to one party elite, when making nomination decisions the attitude was that 'all of the women should be put in the third spot' which she saw as evidence that the party would simply 'comply with the law because there is no other choice' (Interview, 5 June 2015). Due to this minimal application, the quota proved most successful in the large district of Montevideo, but considerably less noteworthy in smaller districts. These two explanations illustrate that candidate selection processes matter even when a quota is in use. First, party leaders were cognisant of the potential results of nominating the same women in electable spots for both the Senate and the Chamber of Representatives; as one architect of the gender quota stated, 'they aren't going to clone them' (10 June 2015). It was certainly no surprise that placing women in two electable spots would mean that these women would have to give up one of their elected positions. Second, and similarly, party leaders were well aware of how unelectable women would be if placed in the third spot in smaller districts.

Prior to the application of the quota, it appeared that the alternate positions would not be used to undermine the gender quota in Uruguay as they had elsewhere. After all, the quota legislation expressly called for the application of the gender quota for both the titleholder and alternate lists. However, ultimately, the suplente positions did create a loophole that would allow political parties to subvert the goals of the gender quota. Alternate positions in Uruguay are complicated. Uruguayan law stipulates that four different suplente systems can be used. The most straightforward of these is referred to as the respective system. Here each titleholder is accompanied by three alternates; that is rather than running in pairs as is done in the Mexican case, they are running in groups of four. These alternates may only substitute for their own titleholder. The ordinal system, in contrast, lists a single column of alternates, who may substitute for any of the titleholders but are called in for substitutions based on their ranking on this list of alternates. In the preferential system, there is no separate list for alternates. Instead, individuals on the electoral list who are not elected then become alternates. The mixed system borrows from both the respective system and the preferential system: if the substitution is temporary, then one of the alternates assigned to the titleholder will step in; however, if the substitution is permanent, then, as in the preferential system, the alternate will be the next person on the titleholder list who did not win election (Johnson 2015: 3 fn 6; Interview: 7 July 2016). Law 18,476 appeared to have been written to prevent the abuse of the suplente system in the application of the quota, since it not only clearly stipulated that it would need to be applied to candidates appearing on both titleholder lists and alternate lists, but also specifically discussed how the law would apply under the various suplente systems in place. For example, the legislation explained that suplente candidates chosen via the preferential system would be treated like candidates in the respective system. Earlier versions of the quota legislation initially attempted stricter guidelines regarding alternate composition, but ultimately these were not included in the final quota that was approved (Interview, 5 June 2015).

The arcane rules that dictate the political alternate systems in Uruguay present opportunities for those that can understand (and manipulate) these procedures. Even among Uruguayan politicians, there is real confusion regarding alternate positions. The extraordinarily complex system is a cause for consternation among elected officials who had trouble recalling what type of system their own party was using, what type of system other parties were using and what options were available (multiple interviews). The complexity of the system forces us to consider when parties will use one type of system over one of the other three options. The decision to select one type of alternate system over another has important implications.

The case of Mónica Xavier, president of the Frente Amplio, highlights the ways in which the choice of these suplente systems matters. The Frente Amplio ran Xavier on numerous lists, including the second spot on the Senate list. Unsurprisingly, Xavier was elected in this very electable position. However, as president of her party she was barred from holding public office. Xavier had insisted that she would run on the condition that she be substituted by a woman. Because the Socialist Party had opted to use the mixed system for suplentes, different substitutes would step in depending on whether her absence was temporary or permanent (El Observador 11/14/2014). The formal rules therefore determined that 'for a woman to take her spot she had to renounce her post'; alternatively, if she failed to renounce her post and instead opted to take a leave of absence then her first alternate, a man, would step in. Xavier ultimately was allowed by her party to maintain both posts until after the May departmental elections and in August 2015 announced her resignation as head of the Frente Amplio in order to maintain her position within the Senate (Portal del Sur 2015). Had she wanted to maintain her position as president of her party and resume her position in the Senate after finishing her presidential term, she would have been forced to only temporarily vacate her seat. Doing so would have meant that her suplente would be a man. The type of substitution system in use has important effects for women's representation, as the case of Xavier illustrates.

In Uruguay, alternate positions improved women's representation prior to the application of a gender quota, but have had a different effect once a quota is in use. Johnson (2015) carefully documents how the alternate positions have either increased or decreased female political representation in the Uruguayan case. For example, she notes that in 1990, 2000 and again in 2010 women resigned their seats to male suplentes (total of five women). In 2013, the same situation occurred because Mónica Xavier was elected president of her party and was forced to resign her senate seat. But, Johnson points out, in the last twenty-five years, twelve female suplentes have ultimately taken up the titleholder positions when their (overwhelmingly male) titleholders had to permanently leave their posts (Johnson 2015, 6). According to Johnson, women's representation increased in the three legislatures between 2000 and 2015 due to permanent substitutions, but declined in the 2015–2020 legislature. It is important to note that while Uruguay passed a gender quota law in 2009, it was not applied for legislative elections until 2014. In other words, the 2015–2020 legislature – the first in which women's representation dropped due to the use of alternate positions – is also the first elected using a gender quota.

The fact that only in the current legislative session has women's representation declined as a result of substitutions could certainly be viewed as coincidental. However, I argue that this is the result of informal norms created to subvert the gender quota. The Instituto Nacional de Mujeres (National Institute for Women) came out with a message shortly after the October election stating it is 'important that the female candidates elected to the Senate not renounce their seats, which would then be occupied by their male suplentes, since this would go against the spirit of the quota law'. It was no secret that simultaneous candidacies and the resulting resignation of women in favour of their alternates were a means of evading the quota. The Instituto Nacional de Mujeres called these practices *'trampas'*, which translates as tricks or cheating (*La República* 11/9/2014).[14]

The informal practice of quota subversion beginning to take form in the Uruguayan case is an example of an embryonic accommodating informal institution. The misuse of the alternate positions in order to meet gender quota requirements was a reaction to formal rules that were disliked by a number of political actors. While it was not uncommon for individuals to appear as candidates for titleholders on lists for both the Chamber of Deputies and for the Senate, these simultaneous candidacies were used as a 'guarantee' that the candidate would be elected to one position. For the most recent elections, however, female candidates were placed in electable positions on both lists which led to perceptions that these simultaneous candidacies were a means of cheating the quota (Johnson et al. 2015, 72).

A few cases illustrate the use of the simultaneous candidacy and its results. In each of these examples, the women who were placed as candidates in both chambers were well aware that they would have to give up one of the two seats (multiple interviews) and were seen as having 'gamed the quota' (Interview, 8 June 2015). Verónica Alonso, of the Partido Nacional, was located in the top spot on her list for the Chamber of Representatives and simultaneously appeared on the third spot for a Senate seat. Both of these were electable spots and Alonso was ultimately elected to both offices requiring that she give up one of her seats. She ceded her seat in the Chamber of Representatives (*El Observador* 11/14/2014). The case of the Colorado Party's Martha Montaner is quite different. While she too ran for both a Senate seat (occupying the third spot) and a seat in the Chamber of Representatives (taking the top spot), she turned her seat in the Chamber over to another woman: her sister (*El Observador* 11/14/2014).

The most problematic case was that of Graciela Bianchi. Bianchi, who hails from the Partido Nacional, appeared in the third spot on both lists and ultimately gave up her position in the Senate to her male alternate. Regardless of which seat she renounced she would ultimately be giving her position to a man – in clear defiance of the intent of the gender quota –, but ultimately her decision to give up the more prestigious post made others think that she was pressured by her party to make this decision (*El Observador* 11/14/2014). As one prominent female politician explained: 'No one thought that this wasn't a previous accord, but surely if you ask the party about this they will deny it time and time again' (Interview, 10 June 2015). Bianchi certainly denied it, claiming that she had made her own decision and stating: 'I waited until the electoral process was over and the new government's line-up was known . . . to make this decision' and later tweeting 'Why do some women find it so hard to accept that there are some women who make their own choices?' (*PanAm Post* 2015).

Shortly after the 2014 election results were released, the newspaper *El País* noted that 'one thing is clear: the gender quota law affected the number of women elected to the Senate. Whether they take their seats or not will depend on each of them and whether or not their seats are filled by a woman will be determined by the corresponding alternate' (*El País* 10/29/2014). What this news account missed was that the determination of which seat a woman would take was done in consultation with her party – and many would say that the decision was exclusive to the party – and that the decisions regarding the corresponding alternate had been made months earlier by party leaders who could choose among various substitute systems and assign individuals to alternate positions. In other words, the newspaper failed to recognise the power structure underlying candidate recruitment and selection decisions.

This informal practice of subversion, which relied on the misuse of alternate systems in order to evade gender quota requirements in Uruguay, may not have an opportunity to become routine. If these practices are not curbed via explicit prohibitions in the new gender quota, they are certainly likely to be institutionalised. When asked if the parties were likely to continue to run women in both chambers to avoid meeting their quota obligations, a female political elite responded, 'But of course!' (Interview, 3 July 2016). The Uruguayan case allowed us to witness the emergence of an accommodating informal institution as a reaction to the implementation of a new formal institution, but the gender quota was written to be applied only once. The fact that the Uruguayan quota could only be applied in the 2014 legislative elections means that this wily practice may not become institutionalised. Nonetheless, the Uruguayan case provides us a view into the dynamic process by which informal rules can matter to the functioning of formal ones, or: 'why the introduction of new formal rules does not always result in the outcomes intended and desired by institutional designers in different contexts' (Chappell and Waylen 2013, 600).[15]

CONCLUSION

The purpose of the law is not to increase the number of women on lists; the purpose of the law is to increase the number of women in Parliament.

– Senator Daniela Payseé (*El Observador* 11/14/2014)

The Uruguayan case indicates that even where quota laws are written to avoid the misuse of alternate positions, political parties will find ways to avoid meeting their quota obligations. In Uruguay, the fact that individuals could run simultaneously for a seat in the Senate and a seat in the lower house created a situation in which parties could meet the quota by placing a woman on lists for both chambers. If a woman won seats in both legislative bodies, she would be forced to resign one of those posts and this would mean ceding her seat to her (often male) suplente. The adoption of this informal practice violates the spirit of the gender quota law though it does not violate the letter of the law.

What can be done to eliminate the development of this informal institution? In the case of an accommodating informal institution like this one, changing the formal institutions is necessary to dispose of these informal rules. Because of its one-off application, the Uruguayan quota will not be applied again unless a new measure is adopted. The formal rules in place could be altered like the Mexican law used to address the problem of the Juanitas. The number of suplente systems available to parties complicates this process dramatically, but changing the rules regarding alternate positions could dramatically simplify efforts to avoid Uruguayan Juanitas. This would require limiting the number of alternate options available to political parties and likely forcing the use of only the respective option. The respective option would then need to be amended to guarantee that the three suplentes listed alongside titleholders were of the same sex as the titleholder. Another formal rule change that would prevent the misuse of the alternate system would prohibit parties from proposing simultaneous candidates; preventing individuals from running simultaneously for both legislative chambers would negate the need for substitutions due to double wins. Changing either the formal institution of the political alternate (by doing away with a choice of systems) or barring simultaneous candidacies seems far-fetched at this point since this would go 'against the Uruguayan legislative tradition' (Interview, 3 July 2016); proponents of the gender quota both inside and outside of parliament are instead working on proposals that prevent cheating the quota without attacking these other formal rules (multiple interviews).

Understanding candidate recruitment and selection procedures is an arduous process because so much of candidate recruitment and selection takes place behind closed doors. It is, of course, exactly because so much of the recruitment and selection process takes place behind those closed doors that makes it susceptible to the use of informal practices that can undermine women's political representation and undercut formal rules designed to increase it.

NOTES

1. The countries that use these alternate positions are: Argentina, Bolivia, Brazil, the Dominican Republic, El Salvador, Guatemala, Honduras, Mexico, Nicaragua, Panama, Paraguay, Suriname and Uruguay in the Americas. Andorra, Angola, Austria, Belgium, Benin, Burkina Faso, Cape Verde, Comoros, Croatia, the Czech Republic, France, Gabon, Iceland, Mauritania, Mozambique, Norway, Romania, Senegal, Slovakia, Spain and Sweden also have alternate positions (IPU 2010). These alternate positions exist in a wide variety of electoral systems. Political alternate positions are commonplace in proportional representation systems, but also are in use in first past the post systems (Comoros and Gabon) and in mixed systems (Bolivia, Mexico, Niger and Panama).

2. Political alternate positions are usually relegated to one or two lines of text or a single footnote. Two English-language publications exist on these alternate positions and women's representation: Beckwith (1989) on the French and Italian cases and Hinojosa and Vijil Gurdián (2012) on the Nicaraguan case. Neither of these works examines alternate positions in a context of mandated gender quotas. There is some new work in Spanish, however, which has begun to explore these questions. See, for example, Vidal Correa (2014).

3. Examining this type of informal institution presents significant methodological challenges given that the political actors involved in the use of this informal institution have a vested interest in denying the nature of their actions and the intent behind their actions.

4. The examples used in this chapter all come from Latin American cases. The extremely limited academic work on political alternates makes it impossible for the author to draw from other cases. Alternate positions are quite common in Latin America: twelve of the nineteen countries use alternates. (Quotas are even more common in Latin America.) The Spanish Constitution of 1812 introduced the alternate position to all of what are now the Spanish-speaking countries of Latin America.

5. In a number of cases, elected politicians who are running for office are required to take a leave of absence. Since most politicians do continue to seek elected office, this provides an opportunity for *suplentes* to step in for an extended period of time.

6. Parties are usually well aware of which individuals on their lists are likely to be tapped for appointed positions in the executive branch or are likely to pursue another elected office sometime during their tenure. Typically, these individuals would occupy some of the top spots on their party's lists.

7. Venezuela applied a gender quota for the 1998 legislative elections. Chile will apply a gender quota for the first time in the November 2017 elections.

8. The little that is known about political alternates and the effect that these positions can have on women's political representation is a result of the infamous case of the Juanitas in Mexico.

9. Interestingly, the first documented 'Juanita' was actually a Juanito! Rafael Acosta Naranja, popularly known by the nickname Juanito, became the candidate for a municipal level post in the city of Iztapalapa with the understanding that he would cede the post to Clara Brugada if he won the position. Brugada had been barred from seeking the position by the federal electoral tribunal due to irregularities in the candidate selection process (Barquet Montané 2012).

10. These new Juanitas appear to be an instance 'where formal rules have been reformed, informal ones can continue to operate to contradict them' (Chappell and Waylen 2013: 607).

11. Women's representation in parliament has been low, and has shown little change over time. In 1999, women comprised 12.1 percent of deputies and 9.7 percent of senators. Ten years later, the percentage of deputies had remained the same, while women's share of senate seats had grown only to 12.9 percent (IPU 2012).

12. Other countries, including Mexico, have first experimented with recommendations before adopting gender quota laws. The 1996 quota recommendation in Mexico was routinely met by placing women in alternate positions rather than in titleholder positions.

13. The Uruguayan Senate is made up of thirty members that are elected from a single nation-wide district, using closed list proportional representation. The Chamber of Representatives is made up of ninety-nine members elected from nineteen subnational units (departments) using closed list proportional representation.

14. Other options for subverting the quota were available. Since lists are traditionally short, it was possible for parties to avoid the placement mandates by combining lists, thereby creating longer lists and leaving women in the bottom spots after meeting the requirement that women appear in electable positions in the top fifteen spots (Kittilson and Schwindt-Bayer 2012). Parties could also dodge the quota by creating many new faction lists (Kittilson and Schwindt-Bayer 2012).

15. The fact that formal rules may not function as they were intended by their designers should encourage researchers to undertake qualitative work – and particularly interviews – to determine both motivations and also reasons for failure.

REFERENCES

Albaine, Laura. 2009. Cuotas de Género y Ciudadanía Política en Bolivia [Gender quotas and political citizenship in Bolivia. Margin: Periodical of social work and social sciences]. *Margen: Periódico de Trabajo Social y Ciencias Sociales* 55: 1–10. http://www.margen.org/suscri/margen55/albaine.pdf.

Altman, David, and Daniel Chasquetti. 2005. Re-Election and Political Career Paths in the Uruguayan Congress, 1985–99. *Journal of Legislative Studies* 11(2): 235–253.

AM de Querétaro. 'Francisco Domínguez, candidato del PAN, a la gubernatura del estado, admitió que varios candidatos a presidencias municipales serán sustituidos por sus esposas [Francisco Dominguez, candidate for the PAN for governorship admits that various candidates to mayoral positions will be substituted by their wives]'. Guillermo Contreras. 15 April 2015. http://amqueretaro.com/queretaro/2015/04/14/en-el-pan-no-hay-juanitas-francisco-dominguez.

Archenti, Nélida, and Niki Johnson. 2006. Engendering the Legislative Agenda with and without the Quota: A Comparative Study of Argentina and Uruguay. *Sociologia, Problemas e Práticas* 52: 133–153.

Baldez, Lisa. 2007. Primaries vs. Quotas: Gender and Candidate Nominations in Mexico, 2003. *Latin American Politics and Society* 49(3): 69–96.

Barquet Montané, Mercedes. 2012. 'De la In/utilidad de la cuota de género. La diputada que no quería ser [Of the (lack of) utility of the gender quota. The female deputy that didn't want to be a deputy]'. *Serie Comentarios a las Sentencias del Tribunal Electoral*, Number 46. Mexico City: Tribunal Electoral del Poder Judicial de la Federación. http://portales.te.gob.mx/genero/sites/default/files/46_in-utilidad_0.pdf.

Beckwith, Karen. 1989. Sneaking Women into Office: Alternative Access to Parliaments in France and Italy. *Women & Politics* 9(3): 1–15.

Bjarnegård, Elin, and Meryl Kenny. 2015. Revealing the 'Secret Garden': The Informal Dimensions of Political Recruitment. *Politics & Gender* 11(4): 748–753.

Bruhn, Kathleen. 2003. Whores and Lesbians: Political Activism, Party Strategies, and Gender Quotas in Mexico. *Electoral Studies* 22: 101–119.

Chappell, Louise, and Georgina Waylen. 2013. Gender and the Hidden Life of Institutions. *Public Administration* 91: 599–615.

Chasquetti, Daniel. 2008. Parlamento y carreras legislativas en Uruguay: Un estudio sobre reglas, partidos y legisladores en las cámaras [Parliament and legislative careers in Uruguay: A study of rules, parties, and legislators in the chambers]. Montevideo: Universidad de la República Oriental del Uruguay.

El Observador. 'Las licencias de los legisladores [The leaves of legislators]'. 21 February 2013. http://www.elobservador.com.uy/las-licencias-los-legisladores-n244155.

El Observador. 'Con el aval de las damas, la cuota femenina fue un fracas [With the support of the ladies, the feminine quota was a bust]'. Martin Viggiano. 14 November 2014. http://www.elobservador.com.uy/con-el-aval-las-damas-la-cuota-femenina-fue-un-fracaso-n292115.

El País. "La cuota impacto en el Senado, pero no en Diputados [The quota made an impact in Senate, but not for deputies]'. 29 October 2014.

El Tiempo. '94 Suplentes en los 2 últimos años [94 Alternates in last 2 years]'. 12 August 2015.

Excelsior. 'PRI usará a *Juanitas* para sustituir candidatos en Tabasco [PRI will use Juanitas for substitutions in Tabasco]'. Fabiola Xicotencatl. 1 May 2016. http://www.excelsior.com.mx/nacional/2015/04/29/1021297.

Finan, Frederico S. 2004. 'Political Patronage and Local Development: A Brazilian Case Study'. Unpublished paper.

Franceschet, Susan, and Jennifer M. Piscopo. 2008. Gender Quotas and Substantive Representation: Lessons from Argentina. *Politics & Gender* 4(3): 393–425.

Gallagher, Michael, and Michael Marsh, eds. 1988. *Candidate Selection in Comparative Perspective: The Secret Garden of Politics*. Beverly Hills: Sage Publications.

Helmke, Gretchen and Levitsky, Steven, 2004. Informal Institutions and Comparative Politics: A Research Agenda. *Perspectives on Politics* 2(4): 725–740.

Hinojosa, Magda. 2012. *Selecting Women, Electing Women: Political Representation and Candidate Selection in Latin America*. Philadelphia: Temple University Press.

Hinojosa, Magda, and Ana Vijil Gurdián. 2012. An Alternate Path to Power? Women's Political Representation in Nicaragua. *Latin American Politics & Society* 54(4): 61–88.

Hinojosa, Magda, and Jennifer Piscopo. 2013. 'Promoting Women's Right to Be Elected: Twenty Five Years of Quotas in Latin America'. In *Cuotas de género: visión comparada* [Gender quotas: A comparative view], edited by José Alejandro Luna Ramos. Mexico City: Electoral Tribunal of the Federal Judicial Power of Mexico.

Hinojosa, Magda, Kim Fridkin and Miki Caul Kittilson. 2014. 'Does Women's Political Presence Matter? Examining Descriptive, Substantive, and Symbolic Representation with a Natural Experiment'. USAID Grant.

Huerta García, Magdalena and Eric Magars Meurs, eds. 2006. *Mujeres Legisladoras en México: avances, obstáculos, consecuencias y propuestas* [Female legislators in Mexico: Advances, obstacles, consequences, and proposals]. Mexico City: Instituto Nacional de las Mujeres.

Inter-Parliamentary Union (IPU). 2010. *PARLINE Database: Search Results by Electoral System*. IPU: http://www.ipu.org/parline-e/mod-electoral.asp.

Inter-Parliamentary Union (IPU). 2012. 'Women in National Parliaments: World Classification'. http://www.ipu.org/wmn-e/classif.htm.

Johnson, Niki. 2015. 'Women's political representation in Uruguay: No critical mass but effective critical acts". Paper presented at the Women's Representation in Latin America Conference. Houston: Rice University. 9–11 April 2015.

Johnson, Niki, and Alejandra Moreni. 2009. 'Representación política de las mujeres y la cuota en Uruguay [Political representation of women and the quota in Uruguay]'. In *Primer Encuentro Nacional de Mujeres Convencionales* [First meeting of traditional women]. Uruguay: Montevideo. http://www.parlamento.gub.uy/externos/parlamenta/.

Johnson, Niki, Gabriel Delacosta, Cecilia Rocha and Marcela Schenck. 2015. *Renovación, paridad: horizontes aún lejanos para la representación política de las mujeres en las elecciones uruguayas 2014* [Renovation, parity: Still distant horizons for the political representation of women in the Uruguayan elections of 2014]. Montevideo: Universidad de la República.

Kittilson, Miki Caul, and Leslie Schwindt-Bayer. 2012. *The Gendered Effects of Electoral Institutions: Political Engagement and Participation*. New York: Oxford University Press.

Krook, Mona Lena. 2009. *Quotas for Women in Politics: Gender and Candidate Selection Reform Worldwide*. New York: Oxford University Press.

Krook, Mona Lena, and Diana Z. O'Brien. 2010. The Politics of Group Representation: Quotas for Women and Minorities Worldwide. *Comparative Politics* 42(3): 253–272.

La República. 2014. 'La cuota no dio los resultados esperados [The quota did not give the expected results]'. http://www.republica.com.uy/la-cuota-no-dio-los-result ados-esperados/487816/.

Martoccia, Hugo, and Carlos Camacho. 2011. 'Qr: Impiden a Diputada Dejar Cargo a Suplente [Qr: Preventing a female deputy from leaving her Alternate post]'. *La Jornada.* http://www.jornada.unam.mx/2011/06/24/estados/034n2est.

Morgenstern, Scott, and Benito Nacif. 2002. *Legislative Politics in Latin America.* Cambridge; New York: Cambridge University Press.

NOTIMEX. 'Suplentes De Juanitas Rinden Protesta'. *El Universal,* 2010.

Pacari, Nina. 2002. 'La participación política de la mujer en el Congreso ecutoriano. Una tarea pendiente [The political participation of women in the Ecuadorian Congress. A pending task]'. In International IDEA *Mujeres en el Parlamento. Más allá de los números.* Stockholm: IDEA.

PanAm Post: News and Analysis in the Americas. 'Loophole in Uruguay's Gender Quota Provokes Feminist Backlash'. Belén Marty. https://panampost.com/ belen-marty/2015/01/29/loophole-in-uruguays-gender-quota-provokes-feminist-backlash/.

Pizarro Leongómez, Eduardo. 2006. 'Giants with Feet of Clay: Political Parties in Colombia'. In *The Crisis of Democratic Representation in the Andes,* edited by Mainwaring, Scott et al., 78–99. Stanford: Stanford University Press.

Portal del Sur. 2015. 'Renunció la presidenta del Frente Amplio [The president of Frente Amplio resigned]'. http://portaldelsur.info/2015/08/en-un-plenario-renuncio-la-presidenta-del-frente-amplio/.

Reynoso, Diego, and Natalia D'Angelo. 2006. Las leyes de cuota y su impacto en la elección de mujeres en México [Quota laws and their impact on the election of women in Mexico]. *Política y Gobierno* 13(2): 279–313.

Roza, Vivian. 2010. 'Gatekeepers to Power: Party-Level Influences on Women's Political Participation in Latin America'. PhD Dissertation. Georgetown University.

Saint-Germain, Michelle A., and Cynthia Chavez Metoyer. 2008. *Women Legislators in Central America: Politics, Democracy, and Policy.* Austin: University of Texas Press.

Taylor-Robinson, Michelle M., Elin Bjarnegård, Gerardo Hernández, Bethany Shockly and Pär Zetterberg. 2015. Women in government: An experimental study of attitudes about governing ability. Paper presented at ECPG. Sweden: Uppsala. 11–13 June 2015.

Vidal Correa, Fernanda. 2014. Federalism and Gender Quotas in Mexico: Analysing Proprietario and Suplente Nominations. *Representation* 50(3): 321–335.

Chapter 10

Who, Where and How? Informal Institutions and the Third Generation of Research on Gendered Dynamics in Political Recruitment

Elin Bjarnegård and Meryl Kenny

The gendered dynamics of candidate selection and recruitment are becoming well documented. Research has pointed to the multitude of ways in which women are at a disadvantage at the different stages of the political recruitment process. Rich case studies have provided important empirical insights into 'the secret garden' of political parties that political recruitment has sometimes been likened to. Feminist institutionalism and its focus on informal institutions have provided theoretical tools with which change and continuity and its gendered consequences can be better identified and understood. This chapter takes stock of existing work on gendered dynamics in political recruitment and outlines its major accomplishments, pointing to the structural and party political barriers that constrain female candidates as well as the discriminatory effect of gendered norms which pervade the candidate selection process. It builds on this body of research and points to three new questions that we suggest that researchers in the field, as a next step in research on informal institutions, start asking themselves: who, where and how?

Who? Who are we studying in political recruitment? Research on gender and political recruitment is still analytically preoccupied with women as one group. We argue that we need to add to the picture how the privilege of (certain) men is sustained by some informal institutions. Informal institutions are excluding in nature as they set the rules of the game, including rewards for sticking to the rules and sanctions for breaking them. By focusing on the logic of inclusion and exclusion we can better pinpoint gender bias in selection processes, and their intersection with other axes of (in)equality.

Where? Where are we studying political recruitment? There is a scarcity of comparative research on informal institutions in general and on informality in political recruitment in particular. We suggest that extending explicit comparisons with other contexts, in previous research as well as in new research designs, would help us distinguish between generally applicable and context-specific gendered dynamics.

How? How do we study political recruitment? While the strong focus on formal institutional change is being challenged in recent work in the field, there is still a need to define and pinpoint the interplay between formal and informal institutions and how this works to keep women out and maintain male dominance in politics.

Focusing on these three questions, we make a theoretical case for shifting the terms of the debate on gender and political recruitment, proposing a new research agenda for the field that has informal institutions at its centre. We begin, first, by taking stock of what we call the 'second generation' of research on gender and political recruitment, pointing to the ways in which analysis of the informal has become increasingly important for advancing our understanding of what really matters in the recruitment process. We then move on to propose and specify an analytical framework for the emerging 'third generation' of research on gender, informal institutions and political recruitment. We argue that a more holistic approach to studying political recruitment leaves open the question as to 'what matters' in candidate selection and recruitment – specifically, *who* the key actors are, *where* certain identified dynamics are valid and where they are not, and *how* the interaction between formal and informal institutions helps maintain (or break) male dominance in the political recruitment process (cf. Celis et al. 2008). The advantage of this framework is that it allows for a more problem-driven approach to researching political recruitment and informal institutions – one in which the question of 'what matters' in political recruitment is subject to systematic comparative analyses and empirical investigation, rather than determined a priori by researchers.

TAKING STOCK

Parties were long described as the 'missing variable' in the study of women's political participation and representation (cf. Baer 1993) and there were surprisingly few studies that directly examined the role of political parties in shaping women's descriptive representation (see Kenny and Verge 2016 for a review). Indeed, as Rainbow Murray notes, the majority of work in the field of women and politics has focused on 'whether women *should* be present in politics, the extent to which they *are* present, institutional and sociological variables that influence the *likelihood* of their being present and what they do once they succeed in getting elected' (2010, 5; original emphasis). This is not to imply that research in these areas has not raised important questions or yielded significant insights (both theoretical and empirical), but rather to argue that 'the mechanisms of the political party still too rarely fall within the scope of gendered political science' (Bjarnegård 2013, 6) and, in particular, the extent to which those mechanisms are formal or informal.

In focusing on how the study of informal institutions has informed research on political recruitment, this chapter builds upon a relatively small but rapidly growing body of work on gender, political parties and candidate selection (see for example Lovenduski and Norris 1993; Kittilson 2006; Murray 2010; Hinojosa 2012; Bjarnegård 2013; Kenny 2013). In this body of work, the dominant framework for understanding the gendered and institutional dynamics of the recruitment process has been the supply and demand model developed by Pippa Norris and Joni Lovenduski in their groundbreaking (1995) study *Political Recruitment: Gender, Race and Class in the British Parliament* (see also Norris 1993; Norris and Lovenduski 1993). Norris and Lovenduski argue that the outcome of particular parties' selection processes can be understood in terms of the interaction between the *supply* of candidates wishing to stand for political office and the *demands* of party gatekeepers who select the candidates. Below, we outline the main advances in the second generation of research on gender and political recruitment, which has built extensively on this first generation of research.

Discrimination against Women in Political Recruitment

The research on supply and demand, as well as subsequent second-generation research in the area of political recruitment, has largely focused on the supply of and demand for *women*. It has devoted less attention to explicitly understanding the informal institutions that continue to reinforce and reproduce male dominance. A major accomplishment, however, is that we now know a lot about overt and indirect discrimination against women in political recruitment (see Kenny 2014a for a more comprehensive review).

Much of this work has focused on obstacles to the recruitment of women at the individual level – for example, on the resources and motivations of prospective candidates, as well as on the attitudes of party gatekeepers. Notably, Norris and Lovenduski conclude that while the candidate selection in Britain favours white, well-educated male professionals, this bias largely reflects the pool of eligible applicants for political office, suggesting that if more women came forward, more would be selected (1995, 248). A similar emphasis on supply-side dynamics and female candidates can be found in the United States, where the gate-keeping powers of parties are weaker than in parliamentary democracies. In this context, a notable study by Jennifer Lawless and Richard Fox (2005, 2010) found that women were substantially less likely than men to consider running for office or to put themselves forward as candidates.

Yet, these findings sit somewhat at odds with both previous and later works on political recruitment, which are generally sceptical of supply-side explanations for women's descriptive under-representation (see Kenny 2013). Indeed, the overwhelming consensus in much of this 'second-generation' scholarship is that party demand is a key barrier to the selection of women candidates. For example, while there may be a gender gap in political ambition, evidence from the United States suggests that the most important factor for increasing women's likelihood of standing for office is party recruitment, with women much less likely than men to be 'tapped on the shoulder' to run (see, for example, Niven 2006; Sanbonmatsu 2006; Dittmar 2015). Meanwhile, ongoing work on British political parties has repeatedly found that the key factor explaining low levels of women's political representation in the House of Commons is a lack of demand on the part of candidate selectors and that incidences of direct and indirect discrimination have been widespread in all of the parties (see, for example, Shepherd-Robinson and Lovenduski 2002; Lovenduski 2005; Evans 2011). Much of this work has, at least implicitly, identified the discriminatory effect of informal norms and practices that pervade the candidate selection process, ranging from gendered assumptions regarding women's traditional roles all the way to explicit sexual harassment.

Building on this work, other studies point to the need to go beyond discrimination at the individual selector level, arguing that 'lack of supply is partly a function of subtly gendered demand' (Murray 2010, 46; see also Verge 2015). For instance, seemingly gender neutral selection rules can have unintended gendered consequences. One example of such an approach can be seen in Murray's (2010) study of candidate selection in France. In her examination of party selection criteria, Murray finds that while none of these criteria are overtly gendered, many of the qualities sought by party selectors were more prevalent in men than women, resulting in a lower supply of female candidates. For example, women were less likely than men to be well known within the party (e.g. holding prominent positions at the local level), they were less likely to be active within the party and they had reduced access to leadership positions (Murray 2010, 64–67). Other studies find that party elites typically list stereotypically masculine characteristics when asked to describe a 'good leader' or a 'good candidate' (Niven 1998; Tremblay and Pelletier 2001). These research findings highlight the pervasive ways in which gendered norms and practices shape the institutions of political recruitment and the demands of candidate selectors, suggesting that elites may be more likely to select male candidates, even as women enter politics in higher numbers (Krook 2010a). However, while institutions are sometimes, and increasingly, acknowledged in this literature, the full explanatory potential of a feminist institutionalist framework has not yet been used. We thus have ample evidence that aspiring women candidates face significant obstacles in the recruitment process, but these obstacles have often not been conceptualised as sets of formal and informal rules. We also know too little about whether this is primarily a sexist exclusion of women or an instrumental inclusion of insiders.

Putting Parties in Context

The obstacles that women face vary greatly across political parties as does the extent to which parties' decisions are steered by formal or informal rules. A lot has happened in this area in the past few years, however. Political parties' role as the most important gatekeepers for women's increased political representation has been increasingly acknowledged and a growing body of research about political parties as gendered organisations is emerging. This work emphasises that political parties do not operate within a vacuum; rather, supply and demand plays out within a wider framework of party recruitment processes, which are shaped and structured by the broader political system (cf. Norris and Lovenduski 1995; Norris 1997). Notable here is the work of Mona Lena Krook (2009, 2010a, 2010b) who argues that more attention should be given to *institutional configurations* – that is, how the systemic, practical and normative institutions of political recruitment fit together in reinforcing and conflicting ways to determine patterns of women's descriptive representation. Indeed, most studies of political recruitment do acknowledge the role of multiple institutions in shaping representative outcomes, albeit often implicitly. Norris and Lovenduski (1995, 194), for example, advocate the necessity of understanding the political recruitment process 'in a comprehensive model, rather than relying upon simple deterministic and monocausal explanations' for selection outcomes. Political recruitment is therefore impacted by the national context and political culture in which it takes place, by the particular political and electoral system and by organisational particularities of the political party, as well as by localised and informal practices. Informal practices have been highlighted as being central to the understanding of political parties as gendered organisations, but, as above, these practices have not always been discussed within a framework of informal institutions. Situating informal practices within a wider framework of informal institutions renders them comparable.

However, in seeking to unpack how supply-side and demand-side factors, as well as the different levels of the political recruitment process, interact with each other, much of the work in the field has continued to focus on single party or country case studies. These types of studies have provided detailed and fine-grained analyses of gendered party environments, while also offering useful insights into behavioural differences between parties operating under similar circumstances. Norris and Lovenduski's (1995) pioneering study, for example, used both survey data and interviews to compare the recruitment procedures of the British Labour Party with those of the Conservative Party. Freidenvall (2006) compared the nomination procedures of three Swedish political parties in two constituencies in order to shed light on how the increased representation of women came about, while Murray (2010) investigated how six French parties reacted differently to the introduction of legislative gender quotas. Bjarnegård (2013) looked at how persistent male dominance was maintained in two political parties in Thailand, while Kenny (2013) compared the representation of women across four different parties in Scotland, and Verge and de la Fuente (2014) examined gendered party practices across five parties in Catalonia. Largely missing from this literature are comparisons of political recruitment across parties _and_ countries. The advancement of the study of informal institutions, however, has brought the research field to a point where such comparisons are not only desirable, but also possible.

The Institutional and Informal 'Turn' in Political Recruitment

As highlighted above, the focus in 'second-generation' political recruitment scholarship has shifted from documenting women's and men's political activities within parties to evaluating the institutional conditions under which women can achieve concrete gains (Kittilson 2013; Bjarnegård and Kenny 2015, 2016). Much of this work is inspired by and increasingly draws upon the perspective of 'feminist institutionalism', an emerging variant of new institutional theory which seeks to 'include women as actors in political processes, to "gender" institutionalism and to move the research agenda towards questions about the interplay between gender and the operation and effect of political institutions' (Mackay, Kenny and Chappell 2010, 574). The central tenet of feminist institutionalism is that political institutions are gendered – in other words, feminist institutionalist approaches share a foundational concern in both 'the _gendered character_ and the _gendering effects_' of political institutions (Mackay 2011, 181; emphasis added). This body of work increasingly understands political recruitment as a process that is guided by both formal and informal rules. When a certain configuration of informal rules go together to form a coherent logic, they constitute an informal institution. Informal institutions are upheld by actors and the networks the actors form part of. The actors abide to a set of formal and informal rules, and it is only by starting from the practices that actually take place we can assess whether they have their origin in formal or informal rules.

Gender is understood here as a constitutive element of social relations based upon perceived (socially constructed and culturally variable) differences between women and men, and as a primary way of signifying (and naturalising) relationships of power and hierarchy (Mackay, Kenny and Chappell 2010, 580; see also Scott 1986; Hawkesworth 2005). To say that the institutions of political recruitment are gendered, then, means that constructions of masculinity and femininity are intertwined in the daily culture or 'logic' of the recruitment process, shaping 'ways of valuing things, ways of behaving and ways of being' (Duerst-Lahti and Kelly 1995, 20). In line with recent developments in feminist and new institutional theory, gender and political recruitment scholars have also increasingly challenged conceptions of institutions as being primarily formal (cf. Helmke and Levitsky 2006; Azari and Smith 2012; Chappell and Waylen 2013). There is, consequently, an increasing number of empirical contributions that specifically focus on informal institutions and the gendered aspects of party recruitment (see for example Kittilson 2006; Cheng and Tavits 2011; Hinojosa 2012; Bjarnegård 2013; Kenny 2013; Kenny and Verge 2016). It should be noted, however, that informal practices have always been acknowledged in the literature on gender and political recruitment – scholars have long pointed out that the formal rules of the recruitment process often have little bearing on party practice (Norris and Lovenduski 1995; Norris 1997). In practice, however, as highlighted previously, both the specific influence of informal institutions and the interplay between the formal and informal rules of recruitment have often been under-theorised and underplayed in empirical studies (see Bjarnegård and Kenny 2015).

More recent studies have taken a closer look at the informal networks that often play a crucial role in selection outcomes (networks which are usually dominated by men). As Verge (2015) highlights, the lack of family-friendly arrangements in the ways parties organise their schedules for party meetings and activities often discriminates against women, while simultaneously facilitating informal (male) networking (see also Verge and de la Fuente 2014). In many countries, access to informal networks is a prerequisite for becoming a candidate – what matters, if you want to get a seat, is who you know. In Chile, for example, Susan Franceschet (2001) finds that women lack access to the informal financial support networks that male politicians enjoy, which are crucial for campaign financing and for obtaining winnable seats. Franceschet and Piscopo (2014, 89) find similar patterns in Argentina, where women enjoy less access to clientelistic resources than men and are therefore less likely to become 'political power brokers' in top-level party politics. And Bjarnegård and Zetterberg (2016) demonstrate that while bureaucratised political parties in Latin America are better at implementing national quota laws, yielding a higher number of women candidates, they do not produce more elected women, as the women candidates are not put in electable slots (Bjarnegård and Zetterberg 2015). The informal 'rules of the game', therefore, have gendered consequences, as women are far less likely to be in strategic positions with access to the resources needed to build and maintain these networks, make political careers and gain electoral power (Bjarnegård and Kenny 2015). We can thus clearly identify an institutionalist and informal turn in the study of gender and political recruitment.

Feminist institutionalism has become a useful theoretical framework for understanding the informal institutions that influence the logic of political recruitment and why and how this logic puts women in unfavourable positions. Several of the chapters on political recruitment in this volume are clear examples of this (see for example Franceschet, Hinojosa, Culhane, Verge and Claveria in this volume). This line of research has now reached an advanced stage, where it is easier to identify next steps and new challenges. Hinojosa's chapter in this volume, for instance, underscores how informal institutions, such as rules regarding alternate positions, emerge to undermine formal quota rules. Chapters also demonstrate how informal relationships and networks may work in the favour of women, in order to enact formal policy change (Nazneen this volume) or to ensure efficient implementation (Piscopo this volume). Increasingly, the strategies of male actors to stay in power, and male privilege, are also problematised (see Verge and Claveria and Culhane this volume). These are all examples of a new discernible move towards a third generation of research on gender and political recruitment, where the informal is studied in interplay with the formal, where it is recognised that outcomes may vary and where the scope of actors and strategies studied is broadened. Taken together, these insights also give us a better understanding of commonalities and differences across very different contexts. We will proceed to outline the most important issues that emerge as the research field moves towards the third generation of research on gender and political recruitment.

TOWARDS THE THIRD GENERATION

As we have seen, the second-generation research in the growing body of literature on gender and political recruitment demonstrates the main advances in this field. It also serves as a basis for taking this field of research into a new, third, generation of increasingly sophisticated and advanced research, the emergence of which is discernible in many of the contributions to this volume (see also Kenny and Verge 2015, 2016). The more advanced understanding that we now have of informal institutions is a prerequisite for stepping into a third generation of research on gender and political recruitment. We here aim to make these emergent trends explicit in the form of a research agenda for the future. If we are to capture the complexities of the 'secret garden' of candidate selection and recruitment, there are three questions that we need to ask ourselves as researchers and that will generate new research questions and answers. We suggest that this approach expands the focus of inquiry in recruitment studies, broadening the scope of 'what matters' in political recruitment to a wider set of actors, institutional sites and outcomes. In the following sections, we sketch out a research agenda organised around three key questions: who, where and how?

WHO? WHO ARE WE STUDYING IN POLITICAL RECRUITMENT?

While scholarship on gender and political recruitment has been instrumental in highlighting the disadvantages associated with being a woman in politics, it has been less successful in identifying which informal institutions exclude women and include men. Certain informal institutions are constructed in ways that advantage certain groups over others. This implies that we need to study how informal institutions can reinforce the recruitment of men, but we must also pay closer attention to exclusionary mechanisms that do not solely operate on the basis of gender. Do informal institutions operate to include certain men and certain women?

The explicit study of men has been left out of the study of political recruitment because their presence is seen as obvious. Political parties have been male-dominated institutions since their inception (Lovenduski 2005). As formal institutions, parties are regulated by rules that were usually made by and for men. Informal institutions and practices that have evolved over time often serve the purpose of protecting those already in power while excluding certain groups (Bjarnegård 2013). If we turn our attention to who is privileged in political recruitment, instead of just who is excluded, we will gain new knowledge. It will contribute to a more accurate problem description of why women and other groups are lacking in politics – and the more precise our problem description is, the more likely we are to come up with efficient solutions (c.f. Bacchi 2009). We thus need to find ways in which to interrogate the norm, but also to qualify and specify the norm. There are certain power advantages ascribed to the male sex, regardless of whether these advantages are recognised or desired (Hanmer 1990; Duerst-Lahti 2008), but we also need to pay attention to the obvious fact that all men do not stand a greater chance of being recruited into politics than every woman. There are intersecting identities and qualifications that affect the prospects of men and women (Celis et al. 2015). Taking the study of informal institutions one step further means that we should now assess their intersecting mechanisms for inclusion and exclusion.

Both men and women are affected by gendered expectations coming from themselves as well as from others. The supply of male candidates is kept constantly high because men, to a greater extent than women, are socialised into seeing themselves as potential politicians. Studies of masculinity formation can help us understand the process by which men as a group gain the assets crucial for a political career, like self-confidence, propensity for risk-taking and homosocial capital (e.g. Connell and Messerschmidt 2005; Bjarnegård 2013). Likewise, the expectations of political parties matter on the demand-side. Studies have shown that women are not necessarily discriminated against by voters, but that they fail to be recruited because political party gatekeepers *think* that women will be at a disadvantage in elections (Norris and Lovenduski 1995; Bjarnegård 2013). When described by party gatekeepers, the ideal candidate often has distinctly male attributes, thus leading to a gender bias in recruitment (Kenny 2013; see also Culhane in this volume). It needs to be reiterated that assets for political careers as well as attributes idealised by party gatekeepers can be found among men as well as women. And the fact that there is a male bias certainly does not mean that all or even most men are socialised into being politicians or fit the criteria of the ideal candidate. Rather, an analysis of the informal institutions in which these characteristics gain value can help us delineate the pool of likely aspirants and scrutinise different potential biases. Scrutinising the criteria that political parties employ when recruiting candidates leads to new ways of looking at old problems. For instance, Murray turns the table on gender quotas when she calls for quotas for men in order to scrutinise men's qualifications instead of constantly questioning 'the others', the women. Because men are the norm in politics, their qualifications often go unchallenged (Murray 2014). There are other norms as well, and there may be other unchallenged informal qualifications: class, ethnicity and sexuality also shape privilege and disadvantage in political recruitment.

Studying who is privileged in informal institutions is also crucial for understanding how status quo is maintained in politics. Politics is about getting to power and staying in power. There are numerous strategies for keeping oneself in power, as well as helping others in the same political party to stay in power. These strategies are thus designed to keep certain people out. Focusing on who these strategies include will help us to nail the homosociality that is often key to strong and reliable networks where few women manage to get in (Bjarnegård 2013). The intersectional nature of homosociality still needs to be elaborated on. Research in management and organisation can serve as a starting-point for understanding homosocial recruitment (Ibarra 1992, 1997; Holgersson 2012). Such a focus will also help us identify which men benefit from these advantages and which do not. Research on hegemonic masculinities and intersectionality are important tools with which to refine our understanding of the conditional advantages of being a man in politics (e.g. Connell and Messerschmidt 2005; Celis et al. 2014).

WHERE ARE WE STUDYING POLITICAL RECRUITMENT?

There is a scarcity of comparative research on informal institutions in general and on informal institutions in political recruitment in particular (Bjarnegård and Kenny 2016). We suggest that the definition of informal institutions (rather than informal practices or networks) is crucial for extending explicit comparisons with other contexts, in previous research as well as in new research designs. An increase in the number of comparative designs would help us distinguish between generally applicable and context-specific gendered dynamics of informal institutions.

There are few comparisons of informal institutions. It is even the case that there are very few comparisons of political recruitment processes in different parties and countries – possibly because we have not yet before had the tools to systematically compare the informal institutions that are crucial for understanding the logic of selection. The frameworks for comparison have generally been weak, as the few comparative studies that exist have been in anthologies, without integrated or systematic analyses (see for example Gallagher and Marsh 1988; Lovenduski and Norris 1993; Norris 1997; Siavelis and Morgenstern 2008). The comparative studies of gendered aspects of political recruitment that have included informal aspects are even rarer (for exceptions see Hinojosa 2012; Bjarnegård and Zetterberg 2016). Given the lack of comprehensive and comparative work in this area, scholars have reached different – and sometimes contradictory – conclusions about the factors behind variations in women's political presence, making it difficult to draw broader generalisations (see Krook 2010a).

As already highlighted, political recruitment cannot be understood in isolation from the electoral context and the specific political party in which it takes place. Comparing candidate selection, therefore, implies nesting the analysis of political parties within an analysis of different hierarchical levels (cf. Norris and Lovenduski 1995). Confidently assessing the relevant context in a large number of countries is of course a challenge. But, while small- to medium-N comparisons may be an optimal research strategy, there are a range of strategies and approaches that researchers might use to surmount these comparative challenges – for example, comparing multiple parties within a country over time; situating the findings of individual cases within existing research and regional patterns to pull out similarities and differences;

or revisiting previous studies through common analytical frameworks (see Kenny and Verge 2016 for examples). There are limits, of course, to which we can generalise from these kinds of comparative studies, but they can still help us identify common causal mechanisms (of power, of continuity or change) which could then be explored in future research in other contexts (cf. Pierson 2004).

HOW DO WE STUDY POLITICAL RECRUITMENT?

While the strong focus on formal institutional change is being challenged in recent work in the field, there is still a need to define and pinpoint the interplay between formal and informal institutions, and how they interact to keep women out and maintain male dominance in politics. In researching the gendered dynamics of selection and recruitment, it is therefore crucially important to 'nail the bias' (Kenny 2014b; cf. Lovenduski 2009). It is not enough to simply assert that gender bias exists in institutions; rather, researchers must move beyond the description stage and systematically identify particular gendered institutional processes and mechanisms and their gendered effects (see Mackay, Kenny and Chappell 2010). Recruitment scholars must start, then, by mapping the formal architecture and informal rules, norms and practices of the particular institutions under study while also remaining attentive to the active and ongoing ways in which gender is reinscribed in these institutions (cf. Lovenduski 2011).

How should we proceed with the study of political recruitment, taking into account the need to look also at informal dimensions of the candidate selection process? As has already been pointed out, the increased focus on informality does not imply that formal institutions and rules do not matter. Indeed, there is a large body of research that has pointed to how formal rules can alter established recruitment practices. Depending on how quotas are designed, their impacts on 'ordinary' procedures within the party are likely to differ (e.g. Bjarnegård and Zetterberg 2011). Also, formal rule change tends to have a larger impact on bureaucratised parties who are 'rule-followers'. We cannot expect parties who are primarily driven by informal practices to efficiently respond to formal regulations (e.g. Bjarnegård and Zetterberg 2016). Determining how strong formal rules are, and to what extent they actually guide how recruitment is being done 'on the ground', is therefore one of the first steps towards understanding what leeway the formal framework leaves for informal practices to play a part in candidate selection (see Bjarnegård and Kenny 2015).

We need a dynamic formulation that is able to capture different combinations of formal and informal rules, or 'rules-in-form' and 'rules-in-use'

(Ostrom 1999, 38; see also Mackay 2014; Bjarnegård and Kenny 2015). When practices on the ground, the 'rules-in-use', correspond to formal regulations for political recruitment, these rules can be considered bureaucratised or formally institutionalised. If the formal rules also reflect what the process actually looks like, what criteria are applied and where important decisions are taken, then the study of written regulations will take us a long way towards understanding the process of candidate selection. It is also highly likely, however, that when looking at what takes place on the ground there are different sets of informally institutionalised rules that dictate behaviour. Such rules can also provide selectors with well-established and shared criteria and knowledge about where certain decisions are de facto taken (Freidenberg and Levitsky 2006; Bjarnegård and Zetterberg 2016). We can therefore never assess formal rules only, unless we have also assessed their effect on actual practices, because their impact is entirely dependent on whether they actually guide the process or not.

The concept of gendered institutional configurations that was proposed by Krook (2010b) is useful here. It does not posit formal and informal rules as opposites, but enables us to look for dynamic and changing configurations of different types of rules, with different content that may have different gendered consequences. The identification of such gendered institutional configurations would help us identify and enable us to analyse the institutional factors that shape access to political office. Krook labels the different configurations systemic, practical and normative (Krook 2010b), but we think that the interaction between different rules can take place at different levels simultaneously. The configurations are therefore partly between insufficient formal rules and strong informal institutions. For instance, when formal rules are not actively maintained or enforced, participants in selection processes may be left with considerable leeway to circumvent and subvert regulations and reforms that clash with their interests – including gender quotas. Indeed, the literature on gender and political recruitment provides ample evidence of informal party practices of quota subversion, ranging from running women on 'no-hope' seats where they have little chance of winning, to practices of local patronage and the privileging of 'favourite sons', and, even, in some cases, committing electoral fraud in order to sidestep formal gender equality reforms (Bjarnegård and Kenny 2015; Hinojosa, this volume; Piscopo, this volume).

This makes the mix of formal and informal elements in the recruitment process an empirical question, one that often requires time-consuming and field-intensive methods such as in-depth interviews and participant observation (cf. Lowndes 2014). Indeed, as Hinojosa notes (in this volume), understanding how candidate selection and recruitment really works is an 'arduous process', because so much of what goes on takes place behind closed doors. However, such an approach is important not only to understand the role informal practices and conventions play in the selection process, but also to investigate whether formal rules and regulations *really do* structure behaviour in practice (Kenny 2013; Lowndes 2014). In short, it is important to study the specific combination of formal and informal elements through which the institutions of political recruitment shape behaviour; how this changes over time; and the extent to which formal and informal elements reinforce one another or exist in tension (Kenny and Lowndes 2011; Kenny 2014b; Bjarnegård and Kenny 2015). It is also possible, however, to include such information in larger data collections. The Latin American political party GEPPAL-dataset (www.iadb.org/es/temas/gobierno/geppal/), for instance, has combined information on formal rules in political parties with survey questions to party officials about how things actually work. Likewise, International IDEA (www.idea.int) has experimented with using survey questions asking party officials at different levels to assess the extent to which certain criteria are employed in the political recruitment process. Such methodological advancement has been made possible because qualitative research has demonstrated that the comparison between formal and informal rules is needed in order to understand what is actually taking place.

The challenge for the third generation is to identify and name different institutional configurations, so that they can be compared across cases on the basis of both their formal and informal content.

CONCLUSION

This chapter has sought to shift the terms of debate in the field of gender and political recruitment by pointing to the importance that an increased focus on informal institutions has had in moving this field forward. Because informal institutions have been identified, studied and discussed, we now have a much better understanding of how political recruitment works, and how and why it excludes certain groups, consciously or unconsciously, based on identities with outsider status. The field is now ready to put this knowledge to use and identify and study informal rules in institutional configurations together with formal frameworks, to compare these institutional configurations across cases and seek to understand what boundaries certain institutional configurations set for different types of groups.

Building on the insights of first-, second- and the emerging third-generation scholarship in the field, we outline a framework for studying political recruitment that centres on three guiding questions for researchers: who, where and how? In doing so, we argue for a problem-driven approach to political recruitment, encouraging researchers to expand their assumptions of *who* we are studying in political recruitment, and *where* and *how* we study it.

Research on informal institutions suggests that they are at play everywhere, and that they may act in favour of or against different political actors at different points in time. In the emerging third generation research, we should therefore no longer exclusively focus on women and how they are disadvantaged by informal institutions, but instead focus on how informality may work to defend the status quo of insiders as well as to advance the position of outsiders. The descriptions of male exclusion of women that are now available should be applied to different identity groups in order to better specify when and how informal institutions work to illegitimately exclude certain identities, and when and how they instead challenge the established and potentially illegitimate strategies that send the message that certain identities are less suitable for the political sphere. We also need to systematically compare the effects of informal institutions in different contexts to expand our knowledge about commonalities and differences in their operation. Finally, we should pay greater attention to how informal institutions interact with formal institutions in different institutional configurations. We suggest that these goals may be reached if researchers start asking the questions *who, where and how*?

In asking these questions, we suggest that researchers will gain a more holistic understanding of the complex and gendered dynamics of the political recruitment process, providing new insights into the critical pathways prior to political office.

REFERENCES

Azari, Julia R., and Jennifer K. Smith. 2012. 'Unwritten Rules: Informal Institutions in Established Democracies', *Perspectives on Politics*, 10 (1), 37–55.

Bacchi, Carol. 2009. *Analysing Policy: What's the Problem Represented to Be?* Pearson: Frenchs Forest.

Baer, Denise. 1993. 'Political Parties: The Missing Variable in Women and Politics Research', *Political Research Quarterly*, 46 (3), 547–576.

Bjarnegård, Elin. 2013. *Gender, Informal Institutions and Political Recruitment: Explaining Male Dominance in Parliamentary Representation*. Basingstoke: Palgrave.

Bjarnegård, Elin and Meryl Kenny. 2015. 'Revealing the "Secret Garden": The Informal Dimensions of Political Recruitment', *Politics & Gender*, 11 (4), 748–753.

Bjarnegård, Elin and Meryl Kenny. 2016. 'Comparing Candidate Selection: A Feminist Institutionalist Approach', *Government & Opposition*, 51 (3), 370–392.

Bjarnegård, Elin, and Pär Zetterberg. 2011. 'Removing Quotas, Maintaining Representation: Overcoming Gender Inequalities in Political Party Recruitment', *Representation*, 47 (2), 187–199.

Bjarnegård, Elin and Pär Zetterberg. 2016. 'Political Parties and Gender Quota Implementation: The Role of Bureaucratized Candidate Selection Procedures', *Comparative Politics,* 48(3), 393–417.

Celis, Karen, Silvia Erzeel and Liza Mügge. 2015. 'Intersectional Puzzles: Understanding Inclusion and Equality in Political Recruitment', *Politics & Gender*, 11(4), 765–770.

Celis, Karen, Sarah Childs, Johanna Kantola and Mona Lena Krook. 2008. 'Rethinking Women's Substantive Representation', *Representation*, 44 (2), 99–110.

Celis, Karen, Silvia Erzeel, Liza Mügge and Alyt Damstra. 2014. 'Quotas and Intersectionality: Ethnicity and Gender in Candidate Selection', *International Political Science Review,* 35 (1), 41–54.

Chappell, Louise and Georgina Waylen. 2013. 'Gender and the Hidden Life of Institutions', *Public Administration*, 91 (3), 599–615.

Cheng, Christine and Margit Tavits. 2011. 'Informal Influences in Selecting Female Political Candidates', *Political Research Quarterly*, 64 (2), 460–471.

Connell, Raewyn and James W. Messerschmidt. 2005. 'Hegemonic Masculinity: Rethinking the Concept', *Gender and Society* 19 (6), 829–859.

Dittmar, Kelly. 2015. 'Encouragement Is Not Enough: Addressing Social and Structural Barriers to Female Candidate Recruitment', *Politics & Gender*, 11 (4), 759–765.

Duerst-Lahti, Georgia. 2008. 'Gender Ideology: Masculinism and Feminalism'. In *Politics, Gender and Concepts. Theory and Methodology*, eds. Gary Goertz and Amy Mazur. Cambridge: Cambridge University Press.

Duerst-Lahti, Georgia and Rita Mae Kelly. 1995. 'On Governance, Leadership, and Gender'. In *Gender, Power, Leadership and Governance,* eds. Georgia Duerst Lahti and Rita Mae Kelly. Ann Arbor: The University of Michigan Press, pp. 11–34.

Evans, Elizabeth. 2011. *Gender and the Liberal Democrats: Representing Women?* Manchester: Manchester University Press.

Franceschet, Susan. 2001. 'Women in Politics in Post-Transitional Democracies: The Chilean Case', *International Feminist Journal of Politics*, 3 (2), 207–236.

Franceschet, Susan and Jennifer Piscopo. 2014. 'Sustaining Gendered Practices? Power, Parties, and Elite Political Networks in Argentina', *Comparative Political Studies*, 47 (1), 85–110.

Freidenberg, Flavia and Steven Levitsky. 2006. 'Informal Institutions and Party Organization in Latin America'. In *Informal Institutions and Democracy*, eds. Gretchen Helmke and Steven Levitsky. Baltimore: The John Hopkins University Press, pp. 178–200.

Freidenvall, Lenita. 2006. *Vägen Till Varannan Damernas. Om Kvinnorepresentation, Kvotering Och Kandidaturval i Svensk Politik 1970–2002*. Stockholm: Department of Political Science, Stockholm University.

Gallagher, Michael and Michael Marsh. eds. 1988. *Candidate Selection in Comparative Perspective: The Secret Garden of Politics*. London: Sage.

Hanmer, Jalma. 1990. 'Men, Power and the Exploitation of Women'. In *Men, Masculinities and Social Theory*, eds. Jeff Hearns and David Hopcraft John Morgan. London and New York: Unwin & Hyman and Routledge.

Hawkesworth, Mary. 2005. 'Engendering Political Science: An Immodest Proposal', *Politics & Gender*, 1 (1), 141–156.

Helmke, Gretchen and Steven Levitsky. 2006. *Informal Institutions and Democracy: Lessons from Latin America*. Baltimore: John Hopkins University Press.

Hinojosa, Magda. 2012. *Selecting Women, Electing Women: Political Representation and Candidate Selection in Latin America*. Philadelphia: Temple University Press.

Holgersson, Charlotte. 2012. 'Recruiting Managing Directors: Doing Homosociality', *Gender, Work & Organization*, 20, 454–466.

Ibarra, Herminia. 1992. 'Homophily and Differential Returns: Sex Differences in Network Structure and Access in an Advertising Firm', *Administrative Science Quarterly*, 37, 422–447.

Ibarra, Herminia. 1997. 'Paving an Alternative Route: Gender Differences in Managerial Networks', *Social Psychology Quarterly*, 60, 91–102.

Kenny, Meryl. 2013. *Gender and Political Recruitment: Theorizing Institutional Change*. Basingstoke: Palgrave.

Kenny, Meryl. 2014a. 'Gender and Political Recruitment'. In *Deeds and Words: Gendering Politics after Joni Lovenduski*, eds. Rosie Campbell and Sarah Childs. Colchester: ECPR Press.

Kenny, Meryl. 2014b. 'A Feminist Institutionalist Approach', *Politics & Gender*, 10 (4), 679–684.

Kenny, Meryl and Tánia Verge. eds. 2015. 'Critical Perspectives on Gender and Political Recruitment', *Politics & Gender*, 11 (4).

Kenny, Meryl and Tánia Verge. eds. 2016. 'Candidate Selection: Parties and Legislatures in a New Era', *Government & Opposition*, 51 (3).

Kenny, Meryl and Vivien Lowndes. 2011. 'Rule-Making and Rule-Breaking: Understanding the Gendered Dynamics of Institutional Reform', Paper presented at the UK PSA Annual Conference, 19–21 April.

Kittilson, Miki Caul. 2006. *Challenging Parties, Changing Parliaments: Women and Elected Office in Contemporary Western Europe*. Columbus, OH: Ohio University Press.

Kittilson, Miki Caul. 2013. 'Political Parties'. In *The Oxford Handbook of Gender and Politics*, eds. Georgina Waylen, Karen Celis, Johanna Kantola and Laurel S. Weldon. Oxford: Oxford University Press.

Krook, Mona Lena. 2009. *Quotas for Women in Politics: Gender and Candidate Selection Worldwide*. Oxford: Oxford University Press.

Krook, Mona Lena. 2010a. 'Why Are Fewer Women Than Men Elected? Gender and the Dynamics of Candidate Selection', *Political Studies Review*, 8, 155–168.

Krook, Mona Lena. 2010b. 'Beyond Supply and Demand: A Feminist-Institutionalist Theory of Candidate Selection', *Political Research Quarterly*, 63 (4), 707–720.

Lawless, Jennifer and Richard L. Fox. 2005. *It Takes a Candidate: Why Women Don't Run for Office*. New York: Cambridge University Press.

Lovenduski, Joni. 1993. 'Introduction: The Dynamics of Gender and Party'. In *Gender and Party Politics*, eds. Joni Lovenduski and Pippa Norris. London: Sage, pp. 1–15.

Lovenduski, Joni. 2005. *Feminising Politics*. Cambridge: Polity Press.

Lovenduski, Joni. 2009. 'Thoughts on Feminist Institutionalism So Far', Roundtable presentation at the European Conference on Politics and Gender, Belfast.

Lovenduski, Joni. 2011. 'Foreword'. In *Gender, Politics and Institutions: Towards a Feminist Institutionalism*, eds. Mona Lena Krook and Fiona Mackay. Basingstoke: Palgrave, pp. vii–xi.

Lovenduski, Joni and Pippa Norris. eds. 1993. *Gender and Party Politics*. London: Sage.

Lowndes, Vivien. 2014. 'How Are Things Done around Here? Uncovering Institutional Rules and Their Gendered Effects', *Politics & Gender*, 10 (4), 685–691.

Mackay, Fiona. 2011. 'Conclusions: Towards a Feminist Institutionalism?' In *Gender, Politics and Institutions: Towards a Feminist Institutionalism*, eds. Mona Lena Krook and Fiona Mackay. Basingstoke: Palgrave, pp. 181–196.

Mackay, Fiona. 2014. Nested Newness, Institutional Innovation, and the Gendered Limits of Change', *Politics & Gender*, 10 (4), 549–571.

Mackay, Fiona, Meryl Kenny and Louise Chappell. 2010. 'New Institutionalism through a Gender Lens: Towards a Feminist Institutionalism?' *International Political Science Review*, 31 (5), 573–588.

Murray, Rainbow. 2010. *Parties, Gender Quotas and Candidate Selection in France*. Basingstoke: Palgrave.

Murray, Rainbow. 2014. 'Quotas for Men: Reframing Gender Quotas as a Means of Improving Representation for All', *American Political Science Review*, 108(3), 520–532.

Niven, David. 1998. 'Party Elites and Women Candidates: The Shape of Bias', *Women and Politics*, 19 (2), 57–80.

Niven, David. 2006. 'Throwing Your Hat Out of the Ring: Negative Recruitment and the Gender Imbalance in State Legislative Candidacy', *Politics & Gender*, 2 (4), 473–489.

Norris, Pippa. 1993. 'Conclusions: Comparing Legislative Recruitment'. In *Gender and Party Politics*, eds. Joni Lovenduski and Pippa Norris. London: Sage, pp. 309–330.

Norris, Pippa. ed. 1997. *Passages to Power: Legislative Recruitment in Advanced Democracies*. Cambridge: Cambridge University Press.

Norris, Pippa and Joni Lovenduski. 1993. 'If Only More Candidates Came Forward: Supply-Side Explanations of Candidate Selection in Britain', *British Journal of Political Science*, 23 (3), 373–408.

Norris, Pippa and Joni Lovenduski. 1995. *Political Recruitment: Gender, Race and Class in the British Parliament*. Cambridge: Cambridge University Press.

Ostrom, Elinor. 1999. 'Institutional Rational Choice: An Assessment of the Institutional Analysis and Development Framework'. In *Theories of the Policy Process*, ed. Paul Sabatier. Boulder, CO: Westview, pp. 35–72.

Pierson, Paul. 2004. *Politics in Time: History, Institutions and Social Analysis*. Princeton, NJ: Princeton University Press.

Sanbonmatsu, Kira. 2006. *Where Women Run: Gender and Party in the American States*. Ann Arbor, MI: University of Michigan Press.

Scott, Joan W. 1986. 'Gender: A Useful Category of Historical Analysis', *American Historical Review*, 91 (5), 1053–1075.

Shepherd-Robinson, Laura and Joni Lovenduski. 2002. *Women and Candidate Selection in British Political Parties*. London: Fawcett.

Siavelis, Peter and Scott Morgenstern. 2008. *Pathways to Power: Political Recruitment and Candidate Selection in Latin America.* University Park, PA: The Pennsylvania State University Press.

Tremblay, Manon and Réjean Pelletier. 2001. 'More Women Constituency Party Presidents a Strategy for Increasing the Number of Women Candidates in Canada?' *Party Politics,* 7(2), 157–190.

Verge, Tánia. 2015. 'The Gender Regime of Political Parties: Feedback Effects between "Supply" and "Demand"', *Politics & Gender,* 11 (4), 754–759.

Verge, Tánia and Maria de la Fuente. 2014. 'Playing with Different Cards: Party Politics, Gender Quotas and Women's Empowerment', *International Political Science Review,* 35 (1), 65–79.

Conclusions

Georgina Waylen

This book has aimed to both improve our understanding of informal institutions and contribute to the development of a feminist institutionalism. It has interrogated how informal institutions are gendered, how they interact with formal institutions and the roles they can play – both positive and negative – in efforts to promote gender equality. In doing this, the chapters and the book as a whole contend with and illuminate the key themes that are involved in the study of gender and informal institutions. Each of the chapters has contributed to answering some, or all, of the three core questions that were posed at the beginning of the book – questions that also concern all feminist institutionalists who want to improve our understanding of informal *and* formal institutions. These three core questions were: First, how should informal institutions be defined, identified and classified (including their relationships with formal institutions on the one hand as well as networks and informality on the other hand)? Second, how should informal institutions be researched? And finally what are the implications for gender-equality strategies? As we have seen, for each question, the chapters demonstrated both how far we have come in our understanding and how much more research there is still to be done in this field.

In answer to the first question, a number of the chapters demonstrated how we can identify various informal institutions in a range of different contexts. Leah Culhane, for example, showed how the rules and norms of 'localism' have acted to exclude women from selection as candidates by political parties in the Republic of Ireland. In their study of the construction industry in Australia, Louise Chappell and Natalie Galea identified homosocial loyalty, presentism and total availability as key informal rules that prevent women professionals from achieving promotion on the same terms as men. But it is clear that there is scope for much more systematic identification of the multiplicity of informal institutions and rules and of how these act in gendered ways that is still to be undertaken by feminist institutionalist scholars.

The chapters also explored some of the key mechanisms through which informal institutions can operate. Chappell and Galea, for example, focused on enforcement, reinforcing the importance of recognising that not only sanctions, but also rewards, are highly gendered in the ways in which they operate, highlighting that this has been relatively neglected so far. Many of the authors (such as Waylen, Chappell and Mackay) agreed that informal rules do not necessarily have to be recognised by participants in order to operate as informal institutions, but Susan Franceschet argued, following Lowndes, that they do need to be. The chapters also showed that there is much more research yet to be done by feminist scholars before we can fully understand the range of mechanisms through which informal institutions operate.

Many of the authors looked at the role of networks as one important way in which informal institutions interact with actors. As we have seen, the chapters varied somewhat in how they conceptualised networks – whether as bearers of institutions for a number of contributors like Verge and Claveria, or intermediaries between formal and informal institutions, or as actors in their own right like Piscopo. And although the chapters differed in whether they looked at predominantly male networks that can act to undermine women actors (like Culhane) or female networks that act to promote gender equality policies (like Piscopo and Nazneen) or Verge and Claveria who discuss both male and female networks, they all agreed that this is an important area where more research needs to be done to explore exactly how networks interact with and relate to informal institutions as well as impact on formal institutions.

A number of the chapters examined the relationship of formal and informal institutions, bolstering our knowledge of the variation in the nature and outcomes of this interaction that were outlined in the first two chapters (Waylen, Chappell and Mackay) in the volume. Hinojosa, for example, charts the emergence of a reactive, endogenous and accommodating informal practice to undermine a new gender-friendly formal rule, while Verge and Claveria demonstrate the complementarity that can exist between the formal and informal, charting how the informal can bolster, complete and reinforce the formal. And while most authors assumed that formal and informal institutions are relatively distinct entities, Verge and Claveria argued that they exist on a continuum. Again, while the chapters make important strides in increasing our knowledge, they also demonstrate that we still need to know more about this complex interaction and the different ways in which it can reinforce or undermine institutions.

In answering to the second question, we saw a variety of methods employed by the authors in their research. As perhaps might have been expected, the majority of chapters used in-depth qualitative case study work, primarily relying on interviews together with observation in a number of cases (Culhane, Franceschet, Piscopo, Nazneen, Hinojosa). But one chapter (Chappell and Galea) used an innovative technique – rapid ethnography – which has rarely been used by feminist institutionalists or political scientists until now. They argue forcefully that it has many advantages over interviews and should be adopted more widely for research of this type. However, Nazneen and Chappell and Galea recognise that the positionality of the researcher can impact on the data that is collected using in-depth qualitative methods, and as in Nazneen's case can impact on what it is possible to do with the data. At the other end of the methodological spectrum, Verge and Claveria used large N quantitative data and a qualitative meta-analysis to undertake their analysis, reinforcing the contentions of scholars such as Weldon that these methods also have their uses in the study of informal institutions.

Third, translating research findings into practice is probably the area where there is still most work to be done, but it is, of course, a top priority for both feminist scholars and activists. The findings reported in a number of the chapters do have implications for the strategies of actors attempting to increase gender equality. Identifying informal institutions and their impact, such as how the primacy of localism when selecting candidates privileges men in Ireland (Culhane), is an important part of being able to reveal and then challenge those informal rules and practices that undermine efforts to increase gender equality. Other chapters (such as Piscopo, Nazneen) demonstrated the informal strategies that have been effectively used by actors attempting to get gender equality measures adopted or strengthened. But they also highlighted their limitations. So, for example, the clientelist state that facilitated a female network's success in securing the passage of a domestic violence law in Bangladesh also mitigated against its successful implementation.

Overall, the chapters in this book share many key themes, but they also range widely in their subject matter. First it is worth considering the spread of the empirical cases. Three chapters focused on Latin America, one on South Asia, and one of the first world cases (Ireland) can also be construed as a postcolonial state. How far is this coincidental? And if it is not, is it significant that a preponderance of the research done by gender scholars on themes relevant to informal institutions has been undertaken outside the long-established democracies? It may do no more than remind us that there is a need for more work on gender and informal institutions in the long-established democracies. Second, reflecting an important pattern in FPS scholarship overall, many of the chapters looked at some form of political recruitment – both within political parties and increasingly within the executive too. And several also looked at the introduction of quotas into the legislative arena, considering whether and how they are subverted or how they can be defended and strengthened. Both are areas of considerable importance to gender and politics scholarship. But it would be beneficial for FI scholars to use the knowledge gained in these fields to broaden their research agenda to examine other areas such as processes of policy making and implementation at different levels of bureaucracies. More research is needed on the themes examined here – such as networks, enforcement and the interaction of the formal and informal – but extended into different arenas. And as Bjarnegård and Kenny argue in their chapter, it is also important to undertake more comparative work in the future. It may be that quantitative work will prove invaluable here, as there are well-known limits to the utility of in-depth single case study research.

Therefore, while focusing on informal institutions, the book as a whole makes a contribution to FI and feminist political science. It has demonstrated the importance of both the informal more generally, and informal institutions in particular, to FI. It has increased our understanding of how to analyse informal institutions, and shown some ways in which the informal – whether in the form of networks or rules and norms – can act in ways that both promote and also undermine greater gender equality.

Index

Note: Page references for figures, tables and boxes are italicised.

Author Biographies

Elin Bjarnegård (Sweden) is Senior Lecturer and Associate Professor at the Department of Government at Uppsala University. Her research interests are within the field of comparative politics with a particular focus on gender, masculinities, conflict, political parties and informal institutions. Her publications have appeared in journals such as *Comparative Politics, Government & Opposition* and *International Interactions*. Her book *Gender, Informal Institutions and Political Recruitment: Explaining Male Dominance in Parliamentary Representation* was published in 2013.

Louise Chappell is Professor in the School of Social Sciences, Faculty of Arts and Social Sciences, at UNSW. Her research explores questions of the nature of gendered institutions and their effect on political, legal and corporate practices and outcomes. Chappell has published widely in this area, and her most recent book *The Politics of Gender Justice at the International Criminal Court: Legacies and Legitimacy* (2016) considers the gendered legacies of international law and their influence on the implementation of the International Criminal Court's gender justice mandate in its formative years. She is currently completing a project with a team of UNSW researchers applying a feminist institutionalist approach to understand the attraction, retention and promotion of women in the Australian Construction sector. Chappell is a codirector of the Feminism and Institutionalism International Network, based at the University of Edinburgh.

Sílvia Claveria is Postdoctoral Researcher in the Department of Social Sciences at Universidad Carlos III (Madrid, Spain). Her research focuses on women's representation in executive office, as well as gender differences in ministerial careers. Her research has been published in international journals such as *West European Politics* and *European Journal of Political Research*.

Leah Culhane is currently a PhD student in political science at the University of Manchester. Her research is part of a broader ERC funded project entitled 'Understanding Institutional Change: A Gender Perspective'. She holds a master's degree in equality studies from the School of Social Justice, University College Dublin and a BA in communication studies from Dublin City University. Her research interests lie in the area of social change, gender and social policy.

Susan Franceschet is Professor of Political Science at the University of Calgary (Canada). She has researched and published extensively on gender, politics and policy in Latin America, and gender quotas and women's political representation in comparative perspective. She is the author of *Women and Politics in Chile* and the coeditor of *The Impact of Gender Quotas* (with Mona Lena Krook and Jennifer M. Piscopo), and *Comparative Public Policy in Latin America* (with Jordi Díez). Her current research, funded by an Insight Grant from the Social Sciences and Humanities Research Council of Canada, explores the gendered dimensions of the cabinet appointment process. Together with Claire Annesley and Karen Beckwith, she is completing a book manuscript called *Cabinets, Ministers, and Gender*, a comparative study of gender and cabinet appointments in seven parliamentary and presidential democracies.

Natalie Galea is Research Associate and a PhD candidate in the Faculty of Built Environment at UNSW, Australia. She is the lead researcher on an Australian Research Council Industry Linkage project focused on gender equity and diversity in the Australian construction sector. Galea's research in the construction sector draws her back to her earlier working life as a construction professional and through this experience she was able to be an 'insider' in the ethnographic research conducted on construction sites, which is discussed in her chapter. Her PhD research draws on feminist institutionalism to highlight the role masculine privilege plays as a barrier to women's recruitment, progression and retention in the construction sector.

Magda Hinojosa is Associate Professor of Political Science in the School of Politics and Global Studies at Arizona State University (United States). She is the author of *Selecting Women, Electing Women: Political Representation and Candidate Selection in Latin America* (2012). She has also published articles in journals such as *Politics & Gender*, *Political Research Quarterly* and *Latin American Politics & Society*. Her work has been funded by the Ford Foundation, Fulbright Scholar Program and the United States Agency for International Development.

Meryl Kenny is Lecturer in Gender and Politics at the University of Edinburgh and codirector of the Feminism and Institutionalism International Network (FIIN). She is an elected trustee of the UK Political Studies Association (PSA), and co-convenor of the PSA's Women and Politics Specialist Group. Her current research focuses on two main areas: gender and political recruitment, and feminist institutional theory. She is the author of *Gender and Political Recruitment* (2013), as well as articles published in the *European Journal of Political Research, Government & Opposition, Politics & Gender, Publius: the Journal of Federalism,* and *Parliamentary Affairs,* among others.

Fiona Mackay is Dean of the School of Social and Political Science at the University of Edinburgh, and Professor of Politics. Her research interests include gender and politics at local and international levels, women's political representation, feminist institutionalism and gendered institutions. She is currently working on gendered institutional change in the UN system, and on the gendered dimensions of political settlements in post-conflict countries. She is founder and codirector of the Feminism and Institutionalism International Network (FIIN; see www.femfiin.com), an international collaboration that seeks to develop a distinctive approach to the study of gender and politics. Fiona's most recent book is *Gender, Politics and Institutions: Towards a Feminist Institutionalism* (2011 and 2015), coedited with Mona Lena Krook. Fiona is a Fellow of the Academy of Social Sciences (FAcSS).

Sohela Nazneen is Research Fellow based at the Gender and Sexuality Research Cluster, at the Institute of Development Studies (IDS), University of Sussex, UK. Her research largely focuses on gender and governance, rural livelihoods, social and women's movements in South Asia and sub-Saharan Africa. Before joining IDS, she taught at the Department of International Relations, University of Dhaka, and served as an adjunct fellow at the BRAC Institute of Governance and Development (BIGD), BRAC University, Bangladesh. Sohela has worked as a consultant on gender and development issues for UNDP, FAO, Academy of Education Development (AED), the Bill and Melinda Gates Foundation and other international agencies. She is the coeditor of *Voicing Demands: Feminist Activism in Transitional Contexts* (2014). She holds a PhD in development studies from IDS, University of Sussex.

Jennifer M. Piscopo is Assistant Professor of Politics at Occidental College. Her research on representation, gender quotas and legislative institutions in Latin America has appeared in eleven peer-reviewed journals, including *Comparative Political Studies*, *The Latin American Research Review*, *Latin American Politics and Society* and *Politics & Gender*. With Susan Franceschet and Mona Lena Krook, she is coeditor of *The Impact of Gender Quotas* (2012). She has contributed to several edited volumes and won research awards from the American Political Science Association, the International Political Science Association and the Latin American Studies Association. Previously, she was a visiting research fellow at the David Rockefeller Center for Latin American Studies at Harvard University. She completed her PhD in political science at the University of California, San Diego. A Gates Cambridge scholar, she received her MPhil in Latin American Studies with distinction from the University of Cambridge.

Tània Verge is Associate Professor in the Department of Political and Social Sciences at Universitat Pompeu Fabra (Barcelona, Spain). Her primary research interests lie in the intersection of gender with political representation and political parties. Her research has been published in international journals such as *Party Politics*, *Politics & Gender*, *Journal of Women, Politics and Policy*, *West European Politics* and *European Journal of Political Research*.

Georgina Waylen is Professor of Politics at the University of Manchester, UK. She is a codirector of the Feminism and Institutionalism International Network (FIIN). From 2012 to 2017, she was PI on a European Research Council Advanced Grant 'Understanding Institutional Change: A Gender Perspective'. She has published on gender and politics in journals such as *World Politics*, *Comparative Political Studies*, *New Political Economy* and *Public Administration*. Her book *Engendering Transitions* (2007) was awarded the 2008 APSA Victoria Schuck prize for the best book published on women and politics published in 2007.

Printed in Poland
by Amazon Fulfillment
Poland Sp. z o.o., Wrocław

83535777R00148